God & BASEBALL

My Spiritual & Sporting Quests

Michael N. Marcus

———

SILVER SANDS BOOKS

Milford CT, USA ◈ 203.878.8383
SilverSandsBooks123@gmail.com

Version 2.68/12.18.19
ISBN: 978-0-9988835-9-5
Library of Congress Control Number: 2019950071
Printed in the USA

Big Thanks To:

Rabbi Alan Alpert
Meryl Marcus Alpert
Steven R. Bruck
Rabbi Tully Bryks
Pastor Mike Bulkley
Michelle Cafarelli
Ken Crouch
Reverend Adam Eckhart
Joel Friedlander
Jewish Virtual Library

Fanchon Kessner
Jerome Kowalski, Esq.
Rector Matthew J. Lindeman
Julie Jacquess Liniger
Hunter J. Marcus
Dawn Montemarano
My Jewish Learning
Religion News Service
Wikipedia
Rabbi Schneur Wilhelm

"I am a Jew. Hath not a Jew eyes? Hath not a Jew hands, organs, dimensions, senses, affections, passions? Hath not a Jew chicken soup?"

—William Shakespeare, in *The Merchant of Venice,*
    with help from Buddy Marcus, the author's funny father

Author's Notes:

- This is a **BIG BOOK.** Unlike a novel, it is *not* sequential—and does *not* have to be read from beginning to end. I recommend that you read the first few chapters and then poke around and read what interests you when and if you choose to.

- In the summer of 2016 I had a pleasant, stimulating conversation with a Catholic priest outside a medical building on Washington Avenue in Hamden, Connecticut. I wanted to resume the conversation and wrote down the priest's name and phone number. Alas, I lost the note. Father: if you read this, please contact me.

- Despite my religious skepticism, I have long enjoyed speaking to clergy people. I have found most to be smart, knowledgeable and friendly.

- Please use the email address on the title page for corrections, questions and comments.

- This is an early version with some uncorrected errors.

- Some items appear in several chapters, as appropriate. Please don't complain about duplication.

- Portions of this book were previously published by the author online and in other books.

- Some material comes from Wikipedia and other sources. I thank them. Material from Wikipedia can be re-shared.

- Lengthy quotations from media are usually set in a distinctive typeface, like this sentence. Some quotations have been slightly edited to save space. Some quotations are provided with permission of the copyright-holders; others are provided as "fair use."

- If you own any copyrighted material in this book and want it removed, please contact the publisher.

- I am a human being and am not free of unintentional biases. I am an American and a Jew and a liberal and a skeptic; and the book may contain Jewish, American, liberal and skeptical biases.

- If I seem irreverent and cynical, it's because I am. You can blame my father, and his father.

- Where I say "Supreme Court," "President" and "Congress" I mean the United States' Supreme Court, President and Congress unless I say otherwise.

- I assume that gentile readers are familiar with basic Jewish terms such as "synagogue" and "kosher." I also assume that all readers are familiar with such Christian terms as "confession," "communion" and "Eucharist."

- *Bar mitzvah* is Hebrew for "son of commandment." When a Jewish boy turns 13, he has all the rights and obligations of a Jewish adult. *Bat* (or *"bas"*) *mitzvah* is Hebrew for "daughter of commandment." When a Jewish girl turns 13 (or perhaps 12), she has all the rights and obligations of a Jewish adult. The coming-of-age status is often celebrated with a ceremony in a synagogue and a party. The bar/bat/bas mitzvah status is automatic, whether or not a ceremony or celebration is held. A young man *becomes* a bar mitzvah and *has* a bar mitzvah (in contemporary English). Some dogs, including my Hunter J. Marcus, have *bark mitzvahs*. I hoped that my FIAT 124 Spider would have a *car mitzvah*, but it didn't last long enough.

- I do not italicize *The* in the names of most media, except for short names such as *The Hill* and *The Atlantic*.
- I try to put non-English words in *italics* the first time they appear (but am not consistent).
- I use "Hasidim" and "Haredim," not "Chasidim" and "Charedim"—but I prefer "Chanukah" to "Hanukkah." Transliteration of non-English terms is inconsistent.
- I use "antisemitism," not "anti-Semitism." I try to avoid hyphenated words, especially if they include uppercase letters. Please don't complain that this is demeaning to my fellow Semites.
- I do not capitalize "he," "his," or "him" when referring to Jesus. I am not a Christian.
- I use "Gramma" and "Grampa" out of love, not because of sloppiness.
- I do not capitalize "heaven" or "hell." I do not believe that either exists (at least not when I started writing this book).
- I am willing, however, to capitalize "God" and "Divine" even though I am not a believer (at least not when I started writing this book).
- To form the possessive of "Jesus," I use an apostrophe plus an "s." I do the same thing for my last name (Marcus's). I do not understand why some people say or write "in Jesus' name" without an added "'s."
- This book is *not* an exhaustive exploration of religions.
- I use the less-Christian (and more neutral and more academic) *BCE* and *CE*, instead of *BC* and *AD*. There's a chapter about this.
- To save time, space and money, this book does not have "headers" or an index.
- Some of the photos look dull. To make them look great would have required expensive paper, greatly increasing the price of the book. The ebook has many nice color photos.
- Some pages have apparently irrelevant "fillers." The price to print a book page does not vary with the number of words on it. You did not pay extra for jokes. Laugh and be happy.
- The tentative title of the book was: ***I Didn't Understand Baseball Until I Was 55. Can I Figure Out God Before I'm 70?***
- Just as actors and musicians are motivated by applause, and chefs may be inspired to cook even better if you shake their hands after great meals, authors need the reinforcement of compliments from readers. Good reviews also help sell more books, and most authors need money. If you find a book useful and/or entertaining, please tell others and please leave a nice review on booksellers' and readers' websites such as Goodreads.com.

Contents

"The Government of the United States—which gives to bigotry no sanction, to persecution no assistance—requires only that they who live under its protection should demean themselves as good citizens, in giving it on all occasions, their effectual support."
—**George Washington**, first president of the USA

"God is the force that transforms the acorn into the oak tree, a bad baseball player into a good one, and an immoral person into a moral one."
—**Rabbi Elliot Dorff**, professor of philosophy, American Jewish University

"Ninety percent of baseball is mental, and the other half is physical."
—**Yogi Berra** (baseball catcher, manager, coach, raconteur)

Introduction

In the beginning, according to the Bible, God created heaven and earth. In the beginning of my life as a book publisher, I created a memoir. A memoir is often written near the end of a life. I didn't know when I'd die, so I wrote my memoir when I was 62, back in 2008.

Now I'm 73. I'm still alive—and I still don't know when I'll die. Maybe I won't finish writing this book, or this page.

I've lived my adult life as a Jew and a non-believer, but I'm open to well-thought-out disagreement. I don't expect to have a deathbed conversion, but who knows? If it happens, you may read about it in the end of this book.

MNM

Chapter 1
The Mick & Me

I was born in the Bronx, New York in 1946 (at the beginning of the postwar baby boom), and spent the first six years of my life in a very nice apartment house just a few miles north of Yankee Stadium. The house was just a little bit farther from the Polo Grounds in upper Manhattan where the baseball Giants played before moving to San Francisco in 1958. The Dodgers were a bit farther away, in Brooklyn, but still accessible with a 20-cent round-trip subway ride.

Many entire <u>states</u> did not have major league baseball teams, but my New York <u>City</u> had *three* teams.

Despite this proximity, I never became a baseball fan like most American boys—probably because I never received a proper explanation of the sport, nor parental encouragement. Maybe my father should be blamed for this book, and other things. (When I was a teenager I fought a lot with my parents and was sent to a psychiatrist. At one point the 'shrink' wanted to speak to my parents, but my father said, "I'm not going to pay to be told it's MY fault that you're messed up.")

Brooklyn-born Pop was a low-key Dodgers fan, and he apparently never made the trek to Brooklyn's Ebbets field after marrying my Bronx-born-and-bred mother and moving to her home borough, where I was born in the *Royal* Hospital. (Yes, I am "of Royal birth." You can bow down now.)

Pop was busy in the retail business, and also taught college at night. We had limited leisure time together and he never took me to a ball game, but sometimes we took long rides. We went deep-sea fishing off Montauk on the far eastern end of Long Island and swimming at Peach Lake, about an hour north of our apartment.

I remember seeing Great Grampa Joe in Brooklyn, wearing long johns with an ass flap, and wondering if he could open-up fast enough to defecate neatly. I remember a trip to Quakertown, Pennsylvania to see an elaborate electric train setup.

My father loved to explore but Mom was less enthusiastic. She preferred to spend Sundays horizontal on her bed with a book. Often Pop would suggest a car ride and she'd respond, "*You* want to go for a ride? *You* go for a ride." (Years later Mom shared driving duties with my father when we traveled cross-country, and she drove me from New Haven to Pittsburgh for a college interview without complaint.)

I have strong memories of Pop teaching me to identify tropical fish and pushing me around the Bronx in my huge, heavy baby carriage—but absolutely *no* memories of us throwing a ball back and forth (playing "catch").

That was fine for *Father Knows Best* and *Leave it to Beaver* on television, but was not reality for Pop and me.

Little League® Baseball and Softball was founded in Pennsylvania in 1939. The program has had millions of players aged 4 through 16, including many future major leaguers—but not me. I don't know if there was a Little League presence in the Bronx when I was a kid. If there was, it bypassed me (perhaps its players were mostly in the suburbs and rural areas).

I *do* remember some kids wearing badges promoting the **Police Athletic League**. The League's website says: "In 1914, Police Commissioner Arthur Woods began a social movement that would eventually be known as the Police Athletic League. He was concerned for the poor children who lived in congested tenements and organized a city-wide search for vacant lots to be converted into playgrounds. He also set aside city blocks where traffic was prohibited. A goal of the program was to reduce tensions between police officers and youth. When Commis-

sioner Woods inspected play streets, mothers rushed to thank him and children cheered his efforts."

I have a persistent memory that there were two types of PAL badges, available in two different colors, probably blue and green. The badges were sold in neighborhood stores (for a quarter, I think) and the money apparently helped finance the PAL programs. One color badge allegedly had higher status than the other and I had the low-status badge. The badges were shaped like police "shields," and perhaps the kids who wore them thought of themselves as junior cops. The first-graders I knew were much too young to drive, so their PAL memberships would not help to beat parking tickets like the insignias on politicians' cars.

I don't think I ever had a ball and a glove as a kid. My huge house contains a huge collection of assorted stuff, but my sole relics of life in the Bronx are a Nazi holster given to me by a neighbor who was a soldier in Europe in the Second World War, and a cloth book with a zipper and buttons that was designed to teach me how to get dressed.

As a child I didn't care about baseball and could not understand why other kids (and adults) did. When boys in the schoolyard at Public School #8 in the Bronx where I attended first grade asked me who my favorite player was, I'd quickly answer "Mickey Mantle." It was an easy answer because "The Mick" and I shared initials and nobody would dispute my answer. I was lucky that none of the boys asked me about The Mick's batting statistics.

My mother's parents, who lived near us in the Bronx, were big baseball fans (Giants fans, specifically), and wanted to convert me to fandom. They surprised me when I was five with a trip to Yankee Stadium for a double-header. It was a *double-dose of torture*, the longest day of my young life.

It seemed like the *ten* longest days of my life, with hour after interminable hour spent staring at white marks on a green field and listening to old men belch into their beers, while I kept asking Gramma and Grampy, "can we go home yet?" They meant well, but this was child abuse!

Below—Other kids liked the sport more than I did. (Apparently the paper was twisted in the typewriter and Mick's signature faded over the years. I obscured the fan's name and address.)

New York Yankees

BUSINESS AND TICKET OFFICES
YANKEE STADIUM, BRONX 51, N.Y.

CYPRESS 3-4300 • CYPRESS 3-6000

September 9, 1961

Dear Matthew:

I'm delighted to hear that you are one of my most avid rooters.

Your mother informs me that you are very unhappy because the pitchers walk me and not Roger Maris. You shouldn't feel badly about it, because I don't. You see Matthew, our ultimate motive is to win the ball game and eventually the pennant. Surely, it would be grand if one of us compiles a record-breaking performance. But you must remember that I have received over 115 walks this season. That means most of the times I am in a good position to score with fellows like Yogi, Elston Howard, Johnny Blanchard and Moose Skowron following me with base hits.

As you grow a bit older and participate in sports, you will learn, through experience, that a team that works together will always win from a team of individualists. That applies, not only in sports, but in every endeavor and particularly among nations. History will show that a democratic country, united in its effort towards peace, will win over a country ruled by a dictator.

Your interest in myself and the N.Y. Yankees is duly appreciated.

Sincerely yours,

MM:wa

Mickey Mantle

I moved from the Bronx to New Haven, Connecticut in April of first grade. The entire state of Connecticut didn't have any major-league baseball teams, so most folks were focused north on the Boston Red Sox, still within New England.

In my first days in New Haven I actually got beaten up *twice* because it was assumed that any kid from the Bronx *had to be* a Yankees fan. The Red Sox fans thought they could beat me into submission, to change my assumed allegiance to match my new New England address.

In reality, I had no interest in baseball and didn't care who won a single game, or the World Series, or if neither team ever played another game. But not caring about baseball was un-American and un-masculine. I might have gotten a worse beating if my new neighbors knew I didn't love baseball, than if I merely didn't love the Boston Red Sox. In around fourth grade I won a baseball bat in a contest at our dry cleaner. I doubt that I ever used it.

In later years I did not come to like baseball any more than I did as a child. In mandatory ball games in high school gym class my favorite position was to be "left out."

In college I went through a strange metamorphosis. There was an intramural softball program and a bunch of hippies and assorted misfits thought it would be fun to form a team with the intention of losing (like the Broadway show "Springtime for Hitler" in *The Producers*, that was intended to lose money).

We thought it would be cool to play stoned on weed (we called it "grass" back then). We'd work on our tans and get free T-shirts. It seemed like a good plan.

What I did *not* plan on, however, was that I turned out to be a "power hitter," a "home run king," just like The Mick back in the Bronx.

I found no joy in running around the bases or fielding balls hit by others, but I sure *loved* whacking the balls as far as I could. My teammates thought I was a traitor to the cause and the team fell apart when a few other players got serious about the game.

It was many years before I saw another ball game.

In around 2001 a nephew and nieces begged me to take them to a game at Yankee Stadium—the site of my ancient but never-forgotten day of abuse.

I liked the kids and agreed to go. I packed a radio with a headset and plenty of reading material and resolved to endure the afternoon as pleasantly as possible. At least, the weather was nice.

When we arrived at the stadium, the butch-bitch rent-a-cop at the entrance searched my bag. I assume she was looking for weapons, but she strangely seized my plastic bottle of Diet Pepsi. I doubt that she thought I'd hit anyone with it, but she probably wanted to insure that if I got thirsty I'd have to pay eight bucks for a refreshing drink from her co-conspirators upstairs.

She would not let me drink it before entering the stadium, take it outside to drink, or leave it with her to reclaim after the game. She slowly and sadistically poured the beverage into a trash barrel while I glared at her and contemplated appropriate torture methods. I watched helplessly as my money and refreshment slowly dribbled away. This was, I thought, not a good omen for the afternoon ahead.

When we got settled in our seats I took my radio from my bag, plugged in my headset and set the radio to WCBS, allegedly an all-*news* station. I was shocked and disappointed to encounter a play-by-play analysis of the baseball game being played

in front of me. Apparently WCBS was the "official radio station" of the Yanks.

For some unknown reason I did not immediately select another station; and soon, *for the first time in my life*, I began to understand "the great American pastime."

In baseball, it had always seemed to me, that it was the *hitters* who were the *heroes*. People like Babe Ruth, Ted Williams, Mickey Mantle (and even me) hit the balls that became runs and drove up the scores that won games and the World Series.

But what I learned from listening to the radio that afternoon was that it was the *pitchers and catchers*, not the hitters, who were really in control.

Balls—not bats—made the big difference.

Throwing was more important than hitting, and it was the silent, stealthy, sneaky catchers squatting in the dirt behind home plate who signaled secret instructions to pitchers who caused those hero hitters to strike out.

Because of those good pitchers, even *really good hitters* seldom got good hits. And, if they did, the balls were usually caught by *really good fielders*, and the good hits did *not* become home runs.

I actually *enjoyed* baseball that day.

If someone had properly explained baseball to me in around 1950 my life might have turned out very differently. I might have become a home run king for the Yanks, or even the Giants or Dodgers or my high school or college teams.

As Marlon Brando said in *On The Waterfront* in 1954, shortly after I left the Bronx, "I coulda been a contender. I coulda been somebody."

My closest physical contact with the major leagues was receiving a ball autographed by Jimmy Pearsall (1929-2017). He played center field for five teams over 17 years and suffered from bipolar disorder. Apparently Pearsall was a friend of someone who wanted to sell something to my father and assumed that I would be thrilled to own the ball. I was not.

Chapter 2
God & Me

The premise of this book is that my impression of God parallels my impression of baseball, based on inadequate information, and childhood images of an old guy with a long beard up on a cloud.

I had no religious education when I was a kid in the Bronx. I suppose I knew that I was Jewish (whatever that meant) and that some people were not Jewish. I was aware of some Jewish holidays, foods, words and rituals. My parents sometimes spoke Yiddish (the common language of Jews from Eastern Europe) when they did not want my younger sister or me to understand what they were saying.

I don't remember my parents ever attending synagogue services when we lived in the Bronx. I sometimes visited my paternal grandparents in Brooklyn and once went to an Orthodox synagogue with Grampa Walter. It was a strange, alien environment—as strange as the Tatooine cantina scene in the original *Star Wars* movie. I saw old men with prayer shawls over their heads rocking back and forth, chanting in a language I did not recognize or understand.

I had heard snippets about God in popular culture ("God bless you," "God damn you," "God-awful," "God-fearing," "God willing," "God forgive me," "God forbid," "for God's sake," "from your mouth to God's ears," "God will get you"). But all I knew was that if I did something bad, God might punish me.

One winter when I was around four or five years old I was sledding down a hill, lost control, and crashed into a tree.

I was not injured. My sled was not damaged. But I thought I was in *big* trouble for hurting Mother Nature, who was *God's wife*. I started chanting "I love God, I like God, I love God, I like God, I like God, I love God." Apparently my penance was effective because the tree did not fall on me, my sled did not go into a flaming abyss, I was not struck by lightning, and I am still alive to tell the tale. In retrospect, my ad-libbed chant may have been like the "say 10 Hail Marys" often prescribed by Catholic priests to sinners.

Our family moved to New Haven in 1952, when I was six years old. My parents joined a Conservative synagogue (B'nai Jacob) and I probably started attending Sunday School when I was in second grade and "Hebrew School" after regular school twice a week, likely in fourth grade.

I was mostly unimpressed and uninspired by my education. We kids were presented with a mixture of Jewish history, culture, religion and the Hebrew language. A few teachers were superb, but some lessons were dispensed by teachers of inadequate quality, with inadequate thought and inadequate explanation. I remember being taught that during the Holocaust, Nazi doctors sterilized some Jewish people. I thought this meant that the victims were dumped into vats of boiling water, as opposed to enduring involuntary surgery to prevent reproduction.

א	ב	ג	ד	ה	ו	ז	ח	ט	י
Alef	Bet	Gimel	Dalet	He	Vav	Zayin	Chet	Tet	Yod
(silent)	(B/V)	(G)	(D)	(H)	(V)	(Z)	(Ch)	(T)	(Y)

כ	ך	ל	מ	ם	נ	ן	ס	ע
Kaf	Khaf	Lamed	Mem	Mem	Nun	Nun	Samech	Ayin
(K/Kh)	(Kh)	(L)	(M)	(M)	(N)	(N)	(S)	(silent)

פ	ף	צ	ץ	ק	ר	ש	ת
Peh	Feh	Tsadeh	Tsadeh	Qof	Resh	Shin	Tav
(P/F)	(F)	(Ts)	(Ts)	(Q)	(R)	(Sh/S)	(T)

In our first year of Hebrew language instruction, we were expected to learn and remember the meanings of indecipherable strings of alien symbols. We were not taught what the individual symbols (*graphemes*) represented. We were not prepared to recognize those symbols so we could determine that a string would be pronounced to produce the Hebrew words for "boy" or "pen." It was like being expected to recognize the English words "cat," "him" and "bicycle" without knowing the sounds that the letters represent. Our class of apparently normal kids was as dysfunctional as a class of dyslexics.

The religious instruction was limited to learning how to read several dozen Hebrew prayers that were used in synagogue services on the Sabbath and other holidays. I remember that my father was shocked to learn that one of the first prayers we learned was the "Mourner's Kaddish," the prayer said by mourners at funerals and regular services. Perhaps Pop thought that the school was premature in preparing young children for the demise of their relatives. Maybe he just did not want to confront his own mortality.

London* Sopotskin*

Paris*

Rome*

Athens*

As a young child in 1906, Pop's pop, **Grampa Walter Marcus**, immigrated from Sopotskin, a village in what was then Poland and is now in Belarus. I saw him three or four times each year and he rewarded me with a quarter for each prayer that I mastered. I also earned a quarter for each new bicycle trick I could perform. I preferred learning tricks to prayers.

The only religious activity I recall demonstrated by my America-born paternal grandmother, **Gramma "Gee"**

(Genevieve), was the cooking of mostly sticky and sweet kosher food. I hated it. My father loved it. My mother tolerated it. Like many Jewish families of that era (and even now), the Marcuses of Brooklyn were *selectively kosher*. There was no *treyf* (non-kosher food) in their apartment on Ocean Parkway, yet when outside their home, they enjoyed vast varieties of food in restaurants, hotels and the non-kosher homes of relatives and friends.

Mom's parents (the Jacobses, both born in the USA in the late 1800s) were not even remotely kosher like Pop's parents. Like many Germanic Jews of that era, they were unobservant, secular, cynical, assimilated and borderline antisemitic. They were not the only ones. Actress Kyra Sedgwick described her mother, Patricia Rosenwald Sedgewick, as an "antisemitic Jew."

A large Jewish Community Center/synagogue was conveniently located across the street from my maternal grandparents' apartment on Valentine Avenue in the Bronx, but they were not members and apparently never went there. (The building is now "El Mundo," a Latino-focused department store offering everything "From toothpaste to high-end furniture.")

If a Jewish "high holy day" of *Rosh Hashanah* or *Yom Kippur* was on a Wednesday, when neighbors were likely to be in Bronx synagogues, my maternal grandparents were likely to be in Manhattan at a Broadway matinee.

Gramma "Del" (Adele) Jacobs was particularly hostile to recent immigrants who "speak with a heavy handwriting." When she was single she refused to date any Jewish man with an accent. After she became a widow, she had a long romance with a heavily accented man from Ireland. He

23

wanted to marry her, but she preferred to just live with him—first in the Bronx and later in Florida.

Gramma was a Yankee of sorts, born in Manhattan's "Hell's Kitchen" neighborhood west of Times Square (now gentrified as "Clinton"). She viewed herself as an inheritor of high-class Viennese culture, and initially dismissed my father-to-be as a "Polish peasant." Pop did some historical research and determined that her forbears were just as Polish as his were.

Grampy Jay did not trust Orthodox Jews in business. He warned, "the bigger the beard, the bigger the lie." Despite their cynicism, however, Gramma and Grampy were very proud of their grandchildren's achievements in religious school and glad to attend bat and bar mitzvahs. Grampy recommended religious school for his grandchildren so they'd gain the knowledge to make up their own minds about religion.

My mother felt deprived because of her lack of Jewish education and in-home observation. On Friday afternoons, when her Jewish schoolgirl friends were rushing home, eagerly anticipating the approaching Sabbath rituals and meals, Mom had nothing special to look forward to.

The family had no Chanukah candles or special Passover meals but Gramma did make a slight effort for some Jewish holidays. She had matzos on the table for Passover, but there was no praying.

As an adult, my mother was active in Jewish organizations, studied Hebrew, became a bat mitzvah when she was 60-plus, and fought antisemitism. I remember going with her to a mobile home park in around 1960 that had been accused of turning away potential Jewish residents. She posed as a customer and asked the salesman about nearby synagogues. Ironically, this was in Milford, Connecticut, where I've lived since 2001, and there are very few synagogues.

I "outgrew" religion when I was 12 years old (before my bar mitzvah) and could not get a good explanation for why the mighty Supreme Being who smote the enemies of the ancient Jewish people did not stop the Spanish Inquisition, Attila the Hun, the Black Plague, the Holocaust and the KKK.

An Orthodox rabbi explained the un-blocked mayhem by telling me that Jews did not pray enough to be worthy of rescue by God.

That seemed like baloney in 1970, and does so now. If God really did exist in the old days, then she, he or it must have been protective even *before* people decided to pray.

Apparently God can be loving or vicious.

Another horrid justification for the Holocaust is that it was God's punishment for assimilation and Zionism. Did a Jewish infant in Europe deserve to be grabbed by the legs by a Nazi soldier and have its head smashed into a brick wall?

I think not.

From the *Modern Jewish Library*: "The Holocaust also impelled many theologians to reconsider the Jewish conception of God. According to biblical theology, evil and suffering afflict the Jewish people as a result of their sins. However, the extensive horrors of the Holocaust made this theological explanation unacceptable to many thinkers. Richard Rubenstein has articulated the most radical theological response to the Nazi atrocities. According to Rubenstein, God is dead. One cannot viably assert traditional Judaism or a belief in the Jewish God in light of the Holocaust."

I wondered if the allegedly omniscient, omnipresent, omnipotent King of the Universe was absent, distracted, no longer cared, or *never actually existed*. Maybe God was a mythological creature—created in man's image rather than the other way around.

Other people probably wonder this, too. The nonreligious population is estimated to be 16% worldwide, 76% in Japan, 21% in the USA and 1% in Iran and Uganda. Nonreligion is growing in most American states, even in the conservative South. According to the Pew polling people, the percentage for Mississippi grew from 6% to 14% between 2007 and 2014.

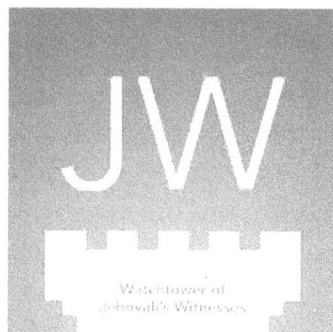

JW

Watchtower of
Jehovah's Witnesses

Jehovah's Witnesses and some other Christian groups admire our extremely complex world and point out that it must be the result of "intelligent design," not violent collisions of electrons and random mutations. I've come to admire the Witnesses for, among other things, rejecting fundamentalist Christian ideology that the earth is just a few thousand years old and was created in six 24-hour days. (This is a common belief among Ultra-Orthodox Jews, too.) However, Witnesses *do* believe the story of Noah and his ark. I do not. Witnesses will *not* accept blood transfusions. I would.

the BIG BANG THEORY

©CBS

I can accept the notion of a creative force (which I label "The Prime Catalyst") but I *cannot* make a transition from a **Big Bang** to a **Supreme Being** that should be feared and prayed to.

I called myself an agnostic ("I don't know if God exists") from around age 12 to 40, and then I started using the atheist label ("I assume that God does not exist").

I was initially reluctant to "come out" as a heathen for fear of being attacked verbally, economically or physically.

Also, I felt it was egomaniacal to assume that I knew everything, so I avoided the atheist label until I was well into adulthood. Since I was living with the assumption that there is no God, I saw no reason to avoid the atheist label anymore. After a while I encountered so many other "out" nonbelievers that I felt that there is safety in numbers and was no longer worried about my personal security. I recognized that I don't know everything, but the possibility of there being an omniscient, omnipresent, omnipotent super-being is so remote that I was willing to live my life as if *it does not exist*.

When I was a young teenager I told my father that I thought I was a hypocrite for attending family *seders* (Passover meals with prayer) since I was a nonbeliever and not actually praying. Pop's wise response was that if I thought that Judaism was worth preserving, I should continue to participate. I did and I *do*.

I have never conducted a seder in any of my own homes, but I do light Chanukah candles and chant the appropriate prayers. I am not actually praying *to* anything or anyone, but I enjoy the sounds of Jewish prayer. (I sing favorites in the shower.) The words and melodies *feel good*, help connect me to the tribe, and take me back to my innocent, uncynical

childhood; and I have an opportunity to keep my Hebrew language skills active.

Similarly, I attend synagogue *yahrtzeit* services on the anniversaries of my parents' deaths. The services help me to connect with my parents as well as my tribe, I enjoy the sounds, and I have an excellent opportunity to refresh my Hebrew.

I even light yahrzeit memorial candles at home to remember my parents. It helps me to think of them and other departed members of my tribe. It's sad—but feels good.

In the preceding paragraphs I referred to the Jewish "tribe." I suppose this is a good place to quickly discuss just what Judaism is (millions of words have been written about the topic by others, and I will not compete with those possessing more knowledge and wisdom than me.)

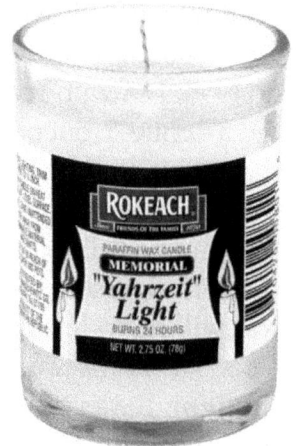

Judaism is a *religion*, probably the first monotheistic religion, going back thousands of years, with perhaps 15 million adherents worldwide. About 6 million Jews were murdered by Nazis during the Holocaust of the 1930s and '40s.

The number of Jews is hard to pin down because of varying definitions of what makes someone a Jew. Traditionally you were a Jew if either (a) your mother is Jewish or (b) you convert. A growing number of people recognize patrilineal determinacy of Judaism, or accept anyone as a Jew who says she or he is one.

As with many aspects of Judaism, conversion is subject to debate and dispute. In general, Orthodox Jews do not recognize conversions performed by 'too liberal' Reconstructionist, Reform or Conservative rabbis; and Israel may not grant citizenship to Jews converted outside Israel, particularly if converted by non-Orthodox rabbis.

Like other religions, Judaism has laws (613, actually) that may or may not be observed. They cover every imaginable aspect of life, but some are not applicable in the 21st century. We no longer have slaves or sacrifice animals. Some of the laws make perfect sense, and some are bizarre. Some have logical explanations, and some are said to exist just to keep Jews different from non-Jews.

> ## Two women are at a buffet restaurant.
>
> First Woman: "I love this kind of eating. I can take what I like and ignore what I don't like."
>
> Second Woman: "Yes, it's just like reading the Bible!"

Within Judaism there are three main divisions (also called "denominations," "movements," "streams" or "branches"): **Orthodox**, **Conservative** and **Reform** (not Reform**ed**)—with different rules and customs.

The labels can be confusing. Conservative (with uppercase "C") Jews are *less* conservative (lowercase "c") than Orthodox Jews, and likely to be *politically liberal.*

In some countries, "**Liberal**" is the equivalent of the American "Reform." In Israel, most Jews are either Orthodox or secular. Reform Judaism includes such label variations as "Mainstream," "Classical," and "Progressive" Reform.

"**Conservadox**" is a largely American hybrid blend of Conservative and Orthodox practices. A "**Jewnitarian**" is a Jewish member of the Unitarian Universalist Church.

There are varieties within the main groups, particularly within Orthodoxy, such as "**Modern Orthodox**" and various shades of "**Ultra-Orthodox**" (*Haredim*), as well as

smaller groups such as **Reconstructionists** and **Buddhist Jews** ("Bu Jews" and "Jew Bus"). "So many Jews are also Buddhists it's almost a cliché," wrote Matthew Rozsa in *Slate*.

Kabbalists are followers of Jewish mysticism. There have been famous *gentile* Kabbalists including Madonna, Lindsay Lohan and Marla Maples (the second Mrs. Donald Trump).

Some of the most pious Jews are called *Hasidim* ("im" is a common plural suffix for Hebrew words, even words used by Christians, such as "*cherubim*" and "*seraphim*").

The term **Hasidim** comes from the Hebrew *hasid*, which means someone who is pious, and often wise and learned. Hasidim may be considered to be a subset of **Haredim** (but some will argue). That word comes from the Biblical *hared*, (two syllables), translated as one who trembles at the word of God, similar to Christian Quakers. Haredim strive to follow Jewish laws and customs by segregating themselves from modern society in such places as Brooklyn and Jerusalem. **Yeshivish** Haredim tend to be more worldly than other Haredim (particularly in the USA), and more likely to be employed or be in business, rather than just studying. **Frum** is a Yiddish word for someone who is very observant. The term may be positive or negative.

Within Hasidim there are geographical groups carried from Europe to other continents. The **Bobovers** originated in Bobowa, Poland. **Boyan** is named after the town of Boiany, now in Ukraine. The **Satmars** started in Szatmárnémeti, Hungary (now Satu Mare, Romania). **Skverer** Hasidism began in Skvyra, in present-day Ukraine.

These groups are *dynasties*, led by rabbis (often called *rebbes*, pronounced "rebb'-uhz") who descended from other rebbes. Some of the Hasidic groups were nearly destroyed during the Holocaust—but have been repopulated by high birth rates. It's common for *Haredi* (an adjective/noun form) Jews to have huge families, often with 10 or 12 children.

The greatest growth has come from the **Chabad-Lubavitch** movement. Its last head was Rebbe Menachem Mendel Schneerson (1902-1994), who turned insular Chabad into a growing institution of actual Hasidim plus supporters.

Schneerson built Chabad into an influential movement in Jewry, with a huge international network of religious, educational and social facilities. His teachings fill many volumes, and Schneerson is noted for contributions to Jewish religious thought as well as Torah scholarship. In 1994, he was posthumously awarded the Congressional Gold Medal for his "outstanding and lasting contributions toward improvements in world education, morality, and acts of charity."

In Manhattan, Chabad men often use vans ("mitzvah tanks") for outreach to unaffiliated Jews who are invited in to say prayers. Some people regard Chabad as a cult. I do not.

Chabad *shuls* (shul is a Yiddish term for synagogue, based on the word for "school") are usually headed by a rabbi and wife, and exist in large and small communities including places with tiny Jewish populations. They provide outreach, support and meals to local people and travelers—even in Nepal near Mount Everest. *Chabadniks* welcome all Jews, regardless of their degree of observance or commitment. You need not even be human. (Ahead) My dog, Hunter J. Marcus, celebrated his "bark mitzvah" at a Chabad shul in Connecticut in 2014.

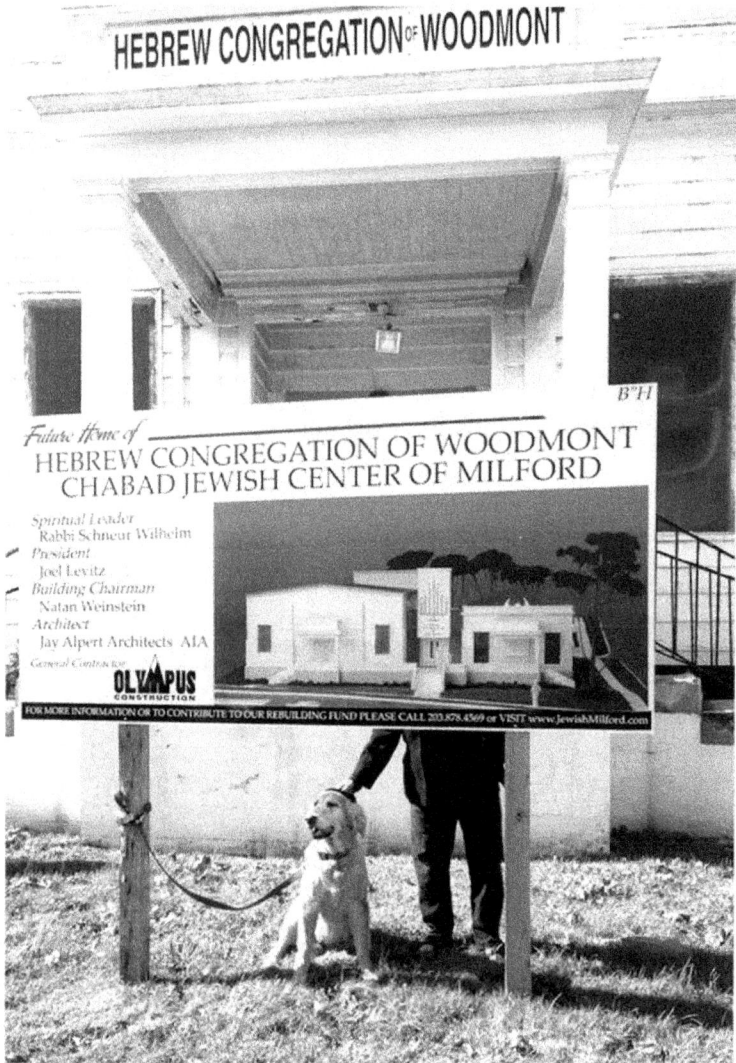

There are even **atheist Jews**, and, yes, there are atheist synagogues, many affiliated with the **Society of Humanistic Judaism**. Jewish nonbelievers use such terms as "secular Jew," "ethnic Jew," "non-theist Jew," "social Jew" and even "pagan Jew."

Some Jewish pagans are Wiccans ("Jewitches") and there's at least one **lesbian Jewish Wiccan**, called "Sapphire." That's a good Jewish name, based on the Hebrew *sapir.* The family names Safer, Safire and Shapiro are related.

The human-centered **Ethical Culture Society** in the USA was founded by the son of a rabbi and has many Jewish members. Albert Einstein was a supporter. Two cousins of my Gramma Del were members. **Unitarian Universalist** Congregations have Jewish members, including Jewish atheists.

The longstanding idea of Jewish denominations has been contested by some Jewish people and organizations, which consider themselves to be "**trans-**" or "**post-denominational.**" A number of new organizations have appeared that lack denomination affiliations, including schools and rabbinical seminaries. Israel's "BINA" secular yeshivas (academies) want government funding like the Orthodox yeshivas receive.

Judaism is a *culture*, including literature, art, music, food, clothing, rituals, etc. As Jews wandered around the world, they adopted and modified aspects of the cultures they encountered. An *Ashkenazic* Jew from Ukraine has a very different lifestyle (and daily language) from a *Sephardic* Jew born in Portugal or a *Mizrahi* Jew from Yemen.

Jews are *argumentative* and we often *interrupt.* I like to say that Jews may not excel at archery or the high jump, but we are hard to beat in verbal jousting—our best sport. If you need a law firm or want to form a debate team, select some Jewish people.

In an article published in *The Jewish News of Northern California,* linguist Deborah Tannen explained that what some people see as interrupting is not rude, and is actually "high-involvement cooperative overlapping."

"Cooperative overlapping—talking as another person continues to speak—is typical of Jewish conversational style and can be a way of showing interest and appreciation," Tannen said.

She is a professor of linguistics at Georgetown and an author of scholarly and popular books, including *You Just Don't Understand: Women and Men in Conversation.*

"Jewish conversational style is not a precise term. Not all Jews exhibit its characteristic features and not all people who exhibit them are Jewish," according to Tannen. "But the pattern of conversation found among many Jews from New York and its environs, especially those of Eastern European origin, differs in significant ways from that of most non-Jewish Americans from the South, Midwest and West."

Along with cooperative overlap, she said Jewish-style conversational patterns include a "fast rate of speech, the avoidance of inter-turn pauses and faster turn-taking among speakers."

In a conversation among Jews, participants find the simultaneous talk and quick turn-taking unremarkable; they interpret silences and pauses as evidence of lack of rapport and/or interest.

But those not accustomed to that style, according to Tannen, may see such active listening behaviors as rudeness, verbal hogging and lack of interest in the speaker. *The very characteristics that promote good conversation among the in-group can create discomfort or hostility among mixed groups.*

Beyond that, people make judgments about the personality of individuals based on conversational style. According to Tannen, negative stereotypes of New York Jews as pushy may be the result of clashing linguistic patterns rather than character flaws.

"Jewish argument is convoluted," according to Steven R. Bruck in *Back to Basics: God's Word vs. Religion*. He said: "A Jewish person won't tell you what something is, they'll tell you everything it isn't. In *Romans*, Shaul talks about the Torah in a way that, without understanding the ethnic and historical context, as well as how Jews argue, sounds like a polemic against Torah. In fact, he is making an apologetic for it. This is one of many misunderstandings about the New Covenant that need to be corrected."

Another speech characteristic of many Jewish people is **LOUDNESS**. Allegedly God does not have a religion, but in *History of the World: Part I*, when Mel Brooks, as Moses, was on Mount Sinai receiving God's commandments, Moses complained that God was too loud.

Senator Bernie Sanders is a prime example of a loud Jew. Some reactions from Twitter:

- All this talk about Bernie yelling really drives it home that most Americans don't know any Jews!! This is just the way we TALK when we've got something IMPORTANT to say, ALRIGHT?
- I'm no Bernie supporter. But all of you people complaining about him yelling about everything clearly did not grow up with New York Jews. To me, listening to

him is like hearing a sweet lullaby that takes me right back to my childhood.

- People asking "why does Bernie always have to yell" have clearly never been to a Jewish family thanksgiving.

J ews are *generous, united* and *supportive*. Despite strong differences, if a Jew is in trouble anywhere in the world, help will usually be on the way from other Jews. (Sadly, Europe in the 1400s and 1940s were notable exceptions.)

Charity boxes (called *pushkas* in Yiddish) are used in many Jewish homes and businesses for collecting coins. Some are simple, some are ornate. They're distributed by charities and synagogues, given as gifts and sold by Amazon.

Facebook has several groups that enable Jews to help other Jews worldwide.

When Jews arrived in the United States from Europe, they quickly formed burial societies and no-interest loan funds to aid each other.

TIME OUT: The Hebrew word for charity is *tzedakah* and it's on the pushka above. Charity is considered mandatory even for Jewish people with limited means. In *Fiddler on the Roof*, Nahum the beggar asked Lazar Wolfe, the village butcher, for a handout. Lazar offered one kopek. Nahum was disappointed and responded, "One kopek? Last week you gave me two kopeks." Lazar then told him, "I had a bad week." Nahum asked, "So, if you had a bad week, why should *I* suffer?"

ALSO: The last name of singer **Neil Sedaka** is a transliteration of "tzedakah." Yes, Neil is Jewish, but he has recorded Christmas songs. Many popular Christmas songs, including "White Christmas," "Let It Snow" and "Rudolph the Red-Nosed Reindeer" were written by Jews.

HIAS (Hebrew Immigrant Aid Society) was founded in a storefront on Manhattan's Lower East Side in 1881 to assist Jews fleeing pogroms in Russia and Eastern Europe.

This was not new. "The Jews would be the first people in the ancient world to establish a welfare system that was the admiration of their pagan neighbors," Karen Armstrong wrote. HIAS now aids refugees worldwide, and most of those aided are not Jewish. Mark Hetfield, HIAS president and CEO, said: "We used to take refugees because they were Jewish. Now we take them because *we're* Jewish."

IsraAID is the Israel Forum for International Humanitarian Aid, an Israel-based organization that responds to emergencies *all over the world*. It provides disaster relief including search and rescue, rebuilding, aid packages, medical assistance, micro-financing and post-psycho-trauma care.

Formed in 2001, IsraAID has also been involved in an increasing number of international development projects concentrating on agriculture, medicine and mental health. The Christian Broadcasting Network offers a video about IsraAID.

To be fair, I should mention that non-Jews have admirable relief operations, too. Catholic Relief Services provides aid in over 90 countries and territories. Catholic Charities USA helps Americans in need, regardless of religion, and has a building about one mile from where I'm typing this. Lutheran World Relief is an international organization that focuses on sustainable development projects and disaster relief and recovery. The Salvation Army is a Christian religion (based on Methodism) and an international charitable organization. United Sikhs provide humanitarian aid in many countries. Some religious charities are local, such as San Francisco's Episcopal Charities.

Many churches, such as my nearby Kingdom Life and United Church of Christ, have food pantries and distribute clothing and household items to the needy. Despite its Hebrew name that means "House of God," the local Beth-El Center is sponsored by 20 *churches* and provides beds, meals and clothing. Not to be outdone by its believer brethren, the Foundation Beyond Belief is a *humanist* charity that promotes secular volunteering and charitable giving

Jews are *divisive.* This old joke does a good job of demonstrating it: After a ship sank (or maybe after a plane crashed—see, I'm being divisive right now), a religious Jew was stranded on an island and gathered branches and leaves to build two primitive synagogues. After surviving alone for a decade, he was asked by a rescuer, "with your limited resources, why did you build *two* synagogues?" The Jew answered, "One is for me to pray in. The other one I wouldn't be caught *dead* in!"

Judaism has been called a *nation,* especially since the reestablishment of a national home in Israel in 1948. Interestingly, there have been several other less-known, and unsuccessful, attempts to create a Jewish homeland (without the connection to ancient Jewish history that Israel has).

- In 1820, Mordecai Manuel Noah tried to found a Jewish homeland at Grand Island, New York, in the **Niagara River**, to be called "Ararat" (after Mount Ararat, the traditional resting place of Noah's Ark). He erected a monument at the island which read "Ararat, a City of Refuge for the Jews, founded by Mordecai M. Noah in the Month of Tishri, 5586 (September, 1825) and in the Fiftieth Year of American Independence." In his *Discourse on the Restoration of the Jews* Noah proclaimed his faith that the Jews would return and rebuild their ancient homeland. Noah called on America to take the lead in this endeavor. Some have speculated that Noah's utopian ideas may have influenced **Joseph Smith**, who founded the Latter Day Saint (Mormon) movement in Upstate New York a few years later.

- The British **Uganda** Program was a plan to give 5,000 square miles of the Mau Plateau in what is now Kenya to the Jewish people as a homeland. The idea was brought to the World Zionist Organization in 1903 in Basel and a fierce debate ensued. The African land was described as an "ante-chamber to the Holy Land," but other groups felt that accepting the offer would make it more difficult to eventually establish a Jewish state in Palestine. Before the vote on the issue, the Russian delegation stormed out in opposition. In the end, the motion to consider the plan passed by 295 to 177 votes. The next year, a three-man delegation was sent to inspect the plateau. Its high elevation gave it a temperate climate, suitable for Euro-pean settlement. However, the observers found a dan-gerous land *filled with lions and other predators*. Addi-tionally, it was populated by a large number of Maasai who did not seem amenable to an influx of Europeans. After receiving this report, the Congress decided in 1905 to politely decline the British offer. Some Jews, who viewed this as a mistake, formed the Jewish Territorialist Organization with the aim of establishing a Jewish state elsewhere.

- In 1928, the Presidium of the General Executive Com-mittee of the **USSR** passed a decree "On the attaching for Komzet of free territory near the Amur River in the Far East for settlement of the working Jews." According to Stalin's national policy, each of the national groups that formed the Soviet Union would receive a territory in which to pursue cultural autonomy in a socialist framework. The idea was to create a new "Soviet Zion" in Birobidzhan where a proletarian Jewish culture could be developed. Yiddish, rather than Hebrew or Russian, would be the national language, and new socialist literature and arts would replace religion as the primary expression of culture. The geography and climate of Birobidzhan were harsh: the landscape was largely swampland. Some have claimed that Stalin was motivated by antisemitism in selecting Birobidzhan—that he wanted to keep the Jews far away from the centers of power. By the 1930s, a massive propaganda campaign was underway to induce more Jewish settlers to move there—even leaflets promoting Birobidzhan dropped from an airplane over a Jewish neighborhood in Belarus and a government-produced Yiddish film that told the story of a Jewish family that fled the Depression in the United States to make a new life in Birobidzhan. The Birobidzhan experiment ground to a halt in the mid-1930s, during Stalin's first purges. Jewish leaders were executed and Yiddish schools were shut. Shortly after this, World War II abruptly ended the efforts to move Jews east. There was a slight revival in the Birobidzhan idea after the war as a potential home for Jewish refugees. During that time, the Jewish population of the region peaked at almost one-third of the total. But efforts to form the homeland ended with the establishment of Israel as a Jewish state, and Stalin's second wave of purges. Again the Jewish leadership was arrested and efforts were made to stamp out Yiddish culture—even the Judaica collection in the local library was burned. In the ensuing years, the idea of an autonomous Jewish region in the Soviet Union was all but forgotten. With the dissolution of the Soviet Union and new liberal emigration policies, most of the remaining Jewish population left for Germany and Israel and the remaining Jews now constituted less than 2% of the local population. Nevertheless, Yiddish is again taught in schools, a Yiddish radio station is in operation, and a local newspaper has a section in Yiddish.

- Despite the little evidence to suggest that the **Japanese** had ever contemplated a Jewish state or a Jewish autonomous region, Rabbi Marvin Tokayer and Mary Swartz published a book called *The Fugu Plan* in 1979. In this partly fictionalized book, Tokayer and Swartz gave the name "Fugu Plan" to memoranda written in the 1930s' Imperial Japan proposing settling Jewish refugees escaping Nazi-occupied Europe in Japanese territories. Tokayer and Swartz claim that the plan, which was viewed by its proponents as risky but was potentially rewarding for Japan. It was named after the Japanese puffer fish, a delicacy which can be fatally poisonous if incorrectly prepared. Tokayer and Swartz based their claim on statements made by Captain Koreshige Inuzuka. They alleged that such a plan was first discussed in 1934 and then solidified in 1938, supported by notables such as Inuzuka, Ishiguro Shiro and Norihiro Yasue. However, the signing of the Tripartite Pact with Germany and Italy in 1941 and other events prevented its full implementation. The memoranda were not called The Fugu Plan. Ben-Ami Shillony, a professor at the Hebrew University of Jerusalem, confirms that the statements upon which Tokayer and Swartz based their claim were taken out of context, and that the translation with which they worked was flawed. Shillony's view is further supported by Kiyoko Inuzuka. In *The Jews and the Japanese: The Successful Outsiders*, he questioned whether the Japanese ever contemplated establishing a Jewish state or a Jewish autonomous region.

- The **Madagascar** plan was a suggested policy of the government of Nazi Germany to forcibly relocate the Jewish population of Europe to the island of Madagascar off the east coast of Africa. This was not a new concept. Henry Hamilton Beamish, Arnold Leese, Lord Moyne, German scholar Paul de Lagarde and the British, French, and Polish governments had previously contemplated the idea. Nazi Germany seized upon it, and in May of 1940, in his *Reflections on the Treatment of Peoples of Alien Races in the East*, Heinrich Himmler declared, that "I hope that the concept of Jews will be completely extinguished through the possibility of a large emigration of all Jews to Africa or some other colony." Although some discussion of this plan had been brought forward from 1938 by other well-known Nazi ideologues, it was not until June, 1940 that the plan was actually set in motion. As victory in France was imminent, it was clear that all French colonies would soon come under German control, and the Madagascar Plan could be realized. It was also felt that a potential peace treaty with Great Britain would put the British navy at Germany's disposal for use in the evacuation. With Hitler's approval, Adolf Eichmann released a memorandum on August 15, 1940 calling for the resettlement of a million Jews per year for four years, with the island governed as a police state under the SS. The plan was postponed after the Germans failed to defeat the British in the Battle of Britain later in 1940. In 1942, the so-called "Territorial Solution to the Jewish question" was abandoned in favor of the "Final Solution to the Jewish Question" (i.e. extermination).

- In March of 1940 the idea of a Jewish Homeland was suggested for **British Guiana** (now Guyana) in South America. But the British Government decided that "the problem is at present too problematical to admit of the adoption of a definite policy and must be left for the decision of some future Government in years to come."

- The Italian government during the Fascist period proposed offering to resolve the "Jewish problem" in Europe and in Palestine by resettling Jews into a Jewish self-governing territory within the northwest territory of **Italian East Africa** that would place them among the Beta Israel Jewish community already living there. Jews from Europe and Palestine would be resettled in the northwest Ethiopian districts of Gojjam and Begemder, along with the Beta Israel community. The proposed Jewish self-governing territory was to be within the Italian Empire. The Fascist regime at the time showed racist attitudes towards the Beta Israel Jews of Ethiopia since they are racially black, and the Fascist regime deemed whites to be superior to blacks. Racial laws enacted in Italy also applied to the Beta Israel Jews in Italian East Africa that forbid intimate relationships between blacks and whites. Mussolini's plan was never implemented.

- In 1941 a wealthy gentile Australian named Critchley Parker Jr. proposed a Jewish settlement at Port Davey, in barren and isolated southwest **Australia**. Parker surveyed the area, but his death while exploring on foot in 1942 put an end to the idea. He wrote that "To die in the service of so noble a cause is to me a great satisfaction; if, as I hope, the settlement brings happiness to many refugees and in so doing serves the state of Tasmania, I die happy."

Judaism is a *people*, that includes individuals and families from all over the world, who may look, act, pray, speak and even eat very differently. Despite the diversity, if a Jew from Brazil entered a synagogue in Japan on the Sabbath or during a holiday celebration she would probably be able to figure out what is going on—and would be warmly welcomed.

Some people consider Jews to be an *ethnic group*, or even a *race*. I don't. Antisemites, particularly Nazis, declare that Jews are a non-white race, even if they look as white as Norwegians.

In 2017, a white nationalist calling himself "The Nordic Nation," proclaimed, "You can say #WhiteGenocide now, Trump has brought it into the mainstream—white genocide being the risible notion that the increasing power of Jews, African Americans, Latinos, and other minorities, not to mention the mingling of racial blood, constitutes a planned threat to the Caucasian **race**."

Neo-Nazi Andrew Anglin, in the same year, proclaimed that "The Jews are a vicious, diseased **race** of evil monsters, and it is they who deserve to be banned as a terrorist group. Their entire existence, going back all through their recorded history, has been a series of terrorist incidents."

In 1998 Louis R. Andrews, a professor of psychology at California State University, said that Jews have "biological drives and behavioral patterns which come into direct conflict with the goals and values of the White **race**."

Long before that, in 1654, nearly two dozen Portuguese Jews from Brazil (then a Portuguese colony that had attracted Inquisition refugees) arrived in what was then New Amsterdam and would later become New York City (the world's largest 'Jewish City'). Antisemitic Dutch colonial governor **Peter Stuyvesant** wanted them to *stay out*. In a letter to the directors of the Dutch West Indies Company that financed the colony, he stated, "We have, for the benefit of this weak and newly developing place and the land in general, deemed it useful to require them in a friendly way to depart, praying also most seriously in this connection, for ourselves as also for the general community of your worships, that the deceitful **race**—such hateful enemies and blasphemers of the name of Christ—be not allowed."

I like to think of Judaism as a *tribe*, a group of millions of people who may live anywhere in the world, observe or shun specific beliefs and practices, but feel a *very strong connection* to each other.

Jews sometimes refer to other Jews as "**MOTs**" (Members **O**f the Tribe). Certain core traits seem common to all MOTs: generosity, righteousness, devotion to family, business acumen and reverence for education.

This cluster of traits applies to other groups, including Chinese, and Sikh Indians. A Sikh man once told me that Sikhs are sometimes referred to as "the Jews of India," but Sikhs are *not* Jewish and there are actual Jews in India.

There is an undeniable affinity between Indians and Jews. In the summer of 2019 Israel's Prime Minister Netanyahu wrote to India's Prime Minister Modi: "The deep connection between Israel and India is rooted in the strong friendships between Israelis and Indians. We cooperate in so many areas. I know our ties will only strengthen in the future!" At the United Nations, because of alphabetical order, the delegates from India, Ireland and Israel sit near each other. That helps build cooperation.

A wise rabbi once told me that if you are not politically liberal, you are a bad Jew. But there are many politically conservative Jews, particularly among the Orthodox in the USA and Israel. Some right-wing Jews (such as David Horowitz, Michael Savage, Dennis Prager and Mark Levin) have significant media presence and fervid online fans. They think liberal Jews are bad Jews, even "self-hating" Jews. I've been accused of being one. I don't hate myself—or Judaism. I am extremely unlikely to seek foreskin replacement surgery, burn my *ketubah* (Jewish marriage certificate), or dispose of my *menorah* (Chanukah candle holder) or *mezuzah* (prayer on a piece of parchment in a decorative wall-mounted housing—shown at right).

The multiple meanings, aspects and implications of Judaism are part of what makes it *special*. Judaism may be the only religion that permits *non-believers* to remain. You can't be an atheist Catholic and probably not a Buddhist Presbyterian, but you *can* be an atheist Jew (or, less-assertively, a "secular" or "humanist" Jew).

According to the all-knowing Wikipedia, some secular Jews include: Sigmund Freud, David Ben-Gurion (an important founder of Israel), Emma Goldman, Bernie Sanders, Noam Chomsky, Karl Marx, Leon Trotsky, Gustav Mahler, Albert Einstein, Billy Joel, Marc Chagall, Alan Dershowitz, Heinrich Heine, Theodor Herzl, Louis Brandeis, Hayim Bialik, Jerry Seinfeld, Larry David, Boris Pasternak, Stan Lee, Stephen Fry, Marilyn Monroe, J. Robert Oppenheimer, Baruch Spinoza and Ayn Rand.

In researching this book I hope to arrive at an "adult" understanding of God. However, according to Karen Armstrong: "The Rabbis pointed out that he was utterly incomprehensible. Not even Moses had been able to penetrate the mystery of God: after lengthy research, King David had admitted that it was futile to try to understand him, because he was too much for the human mind.

Jews were even forbidden to pronounce his name, a powerful reminder that any attempt to express him was bound to be inadequate. The whole point of the idea of God was to encourage a sense of the mystery and wonder of life, not find neat solutions.

The Rabbis even warned the Israelites against praising God too frequently in their prayers, because their words were bound to be defective. How did this transcendent and incomprehensible being relate to the world? The Rabbis expressed their sense of this in a paradox: "God is the place of the world, but the world is not his place:" God enveloped and encircled the world, as it were, but he did not live in it as mere creatures did. In another of their favorite images, they used to say that God filled the world as the soul fills the body: it informs but transcends it. Again, they said that God was like the rider of a horse: while he is on the horse, the rider depends upon the animal, but he is superior to it and has control of the reins. These were only images and, inevitably, inadequate: they were imaginative depictions of a huge and indefinable "something" in which we live and move and have our being. When they spoke of God's presence on earth, they were as careful as the biblical writers to distinguish those traces of God that he allows us to see from the greater Divine mystery which is inaccessible. They liked the images of the "glory" (kavod) of YHWH and of the Holy Spirit, which were constant reminders that the God that we experience does not correspond to the essence of the Divine reality."

My late understanding of baseball made me appreciate the sport, but it *came too late* to make me a fan. Similarly, **I had my first coffee on my 70th birthday**. I liked it, but never became a fan.

Will a better understanding of God make me a believer? Maybe even a fan? Perhaps. The answer is ahead. This book is a spiritual and sporting journey. Enjoy the ride.

Sampling Synagogues

From about 1965 to 2005 I made informal visits to various synagogues in several American cities. I attended ordinary Saturday services and a few special celebrations. I was not

looking to become a member. I was curious to see how the religious services *felt*. I wondered if I would get zapped by a holy spark. But, nothing exciting happened. Mostly I felt the same boredom that had repulsed me as a child and teenager.

As Sarah Hurwitz wrote about her own childhood, "we squirmed through the endless droning melodies, halfheartedly recited the prayers that alternated between incomprehensible Hebrew and stilted English translations, and obeyed the seemingly random calls to stand up and sit down."

In addition to Sarah's accurate objections, I always felt that the services were *simply too long*. (My father was infamous for falling asleep in the synagogue, and my mother had to wake him if his snoring got too loud or if it was time to stand up.)

Saturday services were usually 90 minutes long, or even longer. On the "high holy days" of Rosh Hashanah and Yom Kippur, the services seemed to be *endless*.

Jewish weddings and funerals, however, are usually just 20 to 30 minutes long. If Sabbath services could be that length, I am confident that attendance—and maybe even synagogue membership—would increase greatly!

My Heavenly Name

"Michael" is the name of an archangel (very important angel) in Judaism, Christianity and Islam. For many Christians my namesake is "Saint Michael" (shown above as feminine looking, slaying Satan in a 1636 painting by Guido Reni). Michael is worthy of multiple paintings, statues, feasts and church names. Strangely, there has never been a Pope Michael. I feel neglected, but I probably could not be a pope.

Angelic Michael was considered to be a defender of Torah-era Jews. Later, in the New Testament, Michael led God's armies against Satan's armies in the Book of Revelation, and defeated Satan.

I like my full name. Please DO NOT call me "Mike" or "Mickey." Shown here in Hebrew, my name means "who is like God." It's actually a question, but when I was younger I wondered if it was *describing* me. Did my parents pick my name because they thought I was Godlike, prenatally?

It's customary in most Jewish families to name a baby after a deceased relative. The new kid usually gets a similar name or sometimes just a name with the same initial. There are very few Jewish juniors, seconds or thirds.

I was named after two relatives. My first name was adapted from Meyer Polaner, my maternal grandmother's uncle, who was not connected to the Polaner jelly company. (The name just means "someone from Poland," and *lots* of people came from Poland.) My lack of connection to the jelly people doesn't bother me because I *hate* jelly and I don't want freebies or discounts.

Meyer Polaner's children, Helen and Nat, lived together as adults. I assumed they were husband and wife and I didn't learn that they were siblings until I was a teenager. (That's not so bad. According to *Time* magazine, half of American high school seniors think **Sodom and Gomorrah** were married.)

I find it amusing that the former president of the Soviet Union, (atheist) Mikhail Gorbachev was given an ancient Biblical name. I wonder if he knows it. The Russian pronunciation, by the way, is much closer to the Hebrew than the way most Westerners mispronounce it.

My Other Biblical Connection

Many centuries ago, in Old Testament times, **Mizpah** was a village in ancient Canaan.

The name means a "watchtower" or a "lookout."

The Bible tells a tale of intra-familial deceit and intrigue that ends at Mizpah. It's an eerie precursor of what happened between two aunts of my wife that began at the American Mizpah—thousands of years later and thousands of miles away.

Genesis relates the rivalry between Jacob and Esau, the twin sons of Isaac and Rebecca, and grandsons of Abraham. Esau decided to kill Jacob. When Rebecca found out, she sent Jacob to live with her brother, Laban.

Jacob stayed with Uncle Laban for 20 years and worked as a shepherd. Jacob wanted to marry Laban's younger daughter, his cousin Rachel. Laban pulled a wedding night switcheroo, substituting older Leah for Rachel. When Jacob protested, they negotiated a package deal for him to marry *both* Leah and Rachel.

Through some slick wheeling and dealing, Jacob ended up with most of Laban's animals and other valuables. Apparently fearing a revenge attack by his cousins and uncle, Jacob headed back to Canaan with his family, animals and household goods while Laban was away, shearing sheep.

Laban caught up with him at Mizpah, where he planned to attack Jacob

and take back his daughters, grandchildren and sheep. Laban changed his mind after a dream in which God warned him not to hurt Jacob.

The final parting of Laban and Jacob was peaceful, and they erected a stone monument to serve as a physical reminder of Laban's final blessing for his daughters: "**God will watch over us when we are apart**."

Other Mizpah-like monuments were erected elsewhere to symbolize an emotional bond between people separated by distance or even by death. The word "Mizpah" and the blessing from Genesis appear on gravestones and charms.

Louise and Tina, two aunts of my wife, inherited a piece of Mizpah, in the "Pine Barrens" of southern New Jersey. Unlike its namesake in the Holy Land, it came with *no* blessing and *no* emotional bond.

Despite its apparent barrenness, the Pine Barrens have supported human endeavors since prehistoric times. The Lenape tribe of Native Americans passed through during their annual migrations from their inland home territory to the Atlantic Ocean, and they hunted as they traveled. Colonists from Europe built farms, ironworks and sawmills to make use of the natural resources.

After less-expensive sources of iron were developed farther west in Pennsylvania, new industries such as papermaking, glassmaking and berry farming started up.

Despite its closeness to Philadelphia and New York City and the major highways that run through it, the Pine Barrens are still mostly rural and barren. Villages were formed near local industries, and when factories failed or moved, homes were often abandoned and land was reclaimed by the forest. There are few people, often called "Pineys." Wikipedia says that "Mizpah was established as a Jewish colony ... and was planned out by a New York firm of cloak makers. It originally had a factory, 30 houses, and about 100 settlers."

Development in the area is under the control of a joint State/Federal commission. Some areas are off-limits to construction and attract hunters and hikers—not builders.

A real estate company had a web page for Mizpah in 1991. There were about a dozen categories of homes for sale, but *not even one* home was listed in any category. Clicks for community or school information revealed *nothing*.

Mizpah is now like a ghost town with little more than a name. If you were to parachute into a random part of Mizpah, you are much more likely to startle a bird, a deer or a skunk than to be greeted by another human being. When you walk around, what you see will be pretty much what has been seen for thousands of years—or never seen before.

Despite this depressing environment, the abundant land attracted the attention of a real estate developer at the beginning of the 20th century.

This huckster divided hundreds of cheaply bought acres into small house-sized lots on streets with fanciful names like Broadway, Main Street and Paradise Avenue.

Some roads are named for distant and more glamorous municipalities. Mizpah has a New Orleans Avenue and Los Angeles Avenue and Riviera Street and, strangely, even a Brooklyn Avenue. Both Boston Avenue and Venice Avenue dead-end into the trees. Mizpah has a Zip Code and a part-time post office not much bigger than an outhouse, but no school or movie theater.

The real estate mogul peddled his vision of a rural Utopia to recent immigrants who were sweating in the squalor of New York City's South Bronx (where Yankee Stadium opened in 1923). The easy payment plan and attractive promotional brochures attracted the attention and nickels of many, including Giuseppe, the father of three girls (Tina, Louise and Michele) and Joseph—father of my wife.

Giuseppe never moved to Mizpah nor built a home there. He never saw his rural real estate in the 10 years he owned it. He died in 1913, at the age of 36. He left behind a wife, four young children and a deed to a small part of the USA.

He had little life insurance, and young widow Mary had no way of supporting her kids. She knew that education would be the family's salvation, put the children into a Catholic home for indigent children, and studied nursing.

When she graduated and got a job, she went to reclaim her family. Tina, Louise and Joseph returned home. Michele, the youngest girl, had died—while in an institution that was supposed to care for children whose parents could not care for them. Mary said Michele was a happy, healthy, pink-cheeked girl when she was left in the care of the nuns. She died of an unspecified cause (apparently neglect), and Mary did not receive a death certificate.

Mary was still young and pretty and had a source of income. She soon attracted a new husband, Theodore, who became the father of a boy, my wife's Uncle Teddy. Unfortunately, Mary was soon a widow again, and again had four young children to support.

Mary quickly attracted husband number-three, Angelo. Unlike the first two marriages, this union produced no offspring, but it was like those marriages in another unfortunate way: Mary outlived the husband. Mary outlived *three* husbands and a child, and even a grandchild.

For over 70 years, through most of the 20th century, Mary paid the annual real estate tax bills for the Mizpah property, which gradually escalated from $12 to $29 per year. It was not much money to keep her first love's dream alive.

When she died in 1984 at the age of 96, the deed was passed to the two surviving children of Giuseppe—the warring, seldom-communicating Tina and Louise. Both sisters realized that, with their mother gone, there was probably little point in continuing to pay the real estate tax to keep the property, although it made little real impact on their bank account balances.

Neither sister was willing to surrender her half to the other. But since they were in their 80s, they had the uncommon common sense to realize that if they did not reach a settlement, after they both died there could be a dozen or more heirs of Giuseppe and Mary who would have to agree on a solution.

Louise, a well-off and clever investor, decided that the best solution was to sell her share to her even wealthier sister, Tina. The heirs of their deceased brother, Joseph (my father-in-law whom I never met), just wanted the land to go away as simply as possible.

Naturally, Louise wanted to extract as much money as possible from her sibling—partly to get back at her for years of teasing and criticizing. Tina wanted to pay as little as possible, preferably nothing.

Somehow, *I* was recruited to perform the role of impartial investigator and real estate appraiser, to help the two old crones make a deal.

Armed with the ancient deed and a real estate developer's map and a crappy rented Ford Pinto paid for by Louise, wife Marilyn and I ventured south on a nice day in 1991.

Our first stop was at the Mays Landing Town Hall. We hoped we'd have an easy way out and find some "comparative values" for recent sales of similar property. Alas, there were *no* recent sales and almost no ancient sales.

Our next stop was at a local real estate agent's office. He reinforced the impression we got from the government. He also advised that, in the foreseeable *centuries*, there was little chance that there would be a market for the land we hoped not to inherit. He said that, unless we knew we would use it, our best option was to stop paying taxes and surrender the land to the town.

That sounded like a good option, but curious and duty-bound, we resolved to see and set foot on Giuseppe's ancient dream. We might be his only relatives ever to do so, and maybe the only human beings to be there since the Lenape tribe last hunted there.

There was no Global Positioning System for civilian use in 1991, but I've always been good with maps and I have an accurate internal compass. With some basic directions from the real estate agent, we headed toward the wilderness.

The main road into and through Mizpah is Route 40, the dreary "Harding Highway." It's named to honor the horrid 29th American president, Warren G. Harding. (I wrote several term papers about him when I was in school.)

We saw some homes and businesses on the road, and there were clusters of development both to the north and south of it. We had been directed to turn right and travel north. In a few minutes we were beyond any indication of recent economic activity, and clearly in the Pine Barrens.

The overwhelming impression was failure, and our overwhelming emotion was sadness. We discovered exactly two businesses—a garage and a dilapidated grocery store—and very few cars or people. Mizpah seemed to have been trapped in a state of suspended animation.

We saw dozens of foundations for homes that were never built on them, and the remains of homes that were completed, perhaps inhabited, but burned down and never replaced. The scenario was like a post-apocalyptic sci-fi movie about a pleasant suburb after a nuclear war when vegetation was replacing humanity.

There were some street signs in the forest—some recent, most ancient—and many wounded by shotgun pellets. With intensive mental navigation, I was able to surmise where Giuseppe and Mary's Promised Land should be. I hiked beyond the road and paced-off what seemed to be an appropriate distance, walking on a soft carpet of fallen pine needles, decorated with pinecones and broken branches. I saw one skunk, two deer and too many squirrels to count.

When I reached the center of what could have been a good spot for a house, I carved a shallow "X" on a tree, along with the year to indicate to anyone who might follow me, that at least one person had been there before.

After hiking back to the road, we drove some more. We saw more unfinished and burned-down homes, office furniture, mattresses, tires and abandoned cars. We finally saw a man in a driveway at a nice house on "our street" at a point just before it dead-ended at a wall of pine trees.

He told us that he had moved there about 20 years earlier, and his house was the newest in the neighborhood.

I later called Louise and gave her an accurate report. She wanted me to type up a *phony* report to present to Tina.

I was asked to inflate the value far upwards of zero, glamorize the neighborhood and suggest that the Atlantic City building boom would soon make the land even more valuable. In reality, the boom reached just one block west of the boardwalk casinos, not 25 miles into the forest primeval that was Mizpah. And if, for some weird reason, someone *did* want to live in Mizpah, there were hundreds of other building lots available—much closer to civilization.

Because I would not lie for her, Louise eventually told the truth to Tina. They finally agreed to abandon the property which their father had bought for them 89 years earlier.

Chapter 3
God & The Jews

The photo shows **Mel Brooks as Moses** in *History of the World: Part I* with the **original 15 Commandments** on three tablets. In the movie, Moses dropped one tablet, so we have just 10 Commandments. (There are 613 actually, for Jews, but some can be ignored now.)

Traditionally, in 1275 BCE the Torah was received by an estimated 1.2 million Jewish people at Mount Sinai after they left Egypt. Between 1275 BCE and 200 CE, the Torah, along with a large number of oral laws, was passed to generations of Jews who taught, studied and obeyed or ignored them for many years.

Between 200 and 500 CE, after the Jewish nation was exiled from Israel, Rabbi "Judah the Prince" realized that much of the Oral Torah could be forgotten or accidentally altered. Working with other scholars, he collected and compiled the oral tradition into 63 volumes that became known as the **Mishna** (Aramaic for "learning by repetition").

The lengthy Mishna was followed by a far more elaborate **Talmud**. In 1563 CE the combined laws of Torah, Mishna and Talmud were organized by Rabbi Yosef Caro in a Code of Jewish Law called **Shulchan Aruch**. Divided into four sections, Shulchan Aruch is a complete guide to Jewish life. It includes instructions on personal conduct, kosher food, relationships, reproduction, finance, law and more.

Rabbinic Judaism (the few centuries following the destruction of the Temple in 70 CE), as well as earlier Biblical Judaism, has a concept of belief, but not necessarily an assertion that God exists.

According to Daniel Septimus in *My Jewish Learning*, "scholar Menachem Kellner, for one, points out that the biblical word *emunah*, 'belief' or 'faith,' connotes trust, belief in, as opposed to the affirmation of propositions. Of course, one might argue that trusting in something implies that that something exists, but the distinction between belief *in* and belief *that* helps in understanding the priorities and emphases of the rabbinic worldview."

This approach to belief changed in the Middle Ages, when Jewish philosophers began proposing *official* doctrines of Judaism. Moses ben Maimon (also known as Maimonides and Rambam) was a Jewish Sephardic philosopher, rabbi, Torah scholar, astronomer and physician. He was born in Córdoba (currently Spain) in 1135. He worked in Morocco and Egypt and died in Egypt in 1204, and was buried in Tiberias (in what is now Israel).

His **13 principles of faith** have dogmas about God including the assertion that God exists. The actual principles articulated by Maimonides were not revolutionary. What *was* revolutionary was Maimonides' claim that belief in these principles was *essential* to one's Jewish identity. He might not consider me Jewish.

1. **The existence of God.** [I'm not ready for this.]
2. **God's unity and indivisibility into elements.** [There goes the Trinity.]
3. **God's spirituality and incorporeality**. [There goes the "Supreme *Being*."]
4. **God's eternity.** [This makes sense.]
5. **God alone should be the object of worship.** [No saints or statues!]
6. **Revelation through God's prophets.** [What is revelation?]
7. **The preeminence of Moses among the prophets.** [OK with me.]

8. **That the entire Torah (both the written and oral law) are of Divine origin and were dictated to Moses by God on Mount Sinai.** [I have big trouble with this one.]
9. **The Torah given by Moses is permanent and will not be replaced or changed.** [There probably were changes, but not recently.]
10. **God's awareness of all human actions and thoughts.** [More powerful than Amazon's Alexa!]
11. **Reward of good and punishment of evil.** [Like Santa Claus, courts and parents?]
12. **The coming of the Jewish Messiah.** [Not Jesus.]
13. **The resurrection of the dead.** [Spooky.]

Maimonides compiled the principles from various Talmudic sources. They were controversial when first proposed, and were ignored by much of the Jewish community for the next few centuries. However, the principles later became widely held by observant Jews and are considered to be the *cardinal principals of faith* for Orthodox Jews. Two poetic restatements of these principles (*Ani Ma'amin* and *Yigdal*) eventually became canonized in many editions of the Jewish prayer book (*Siddur*) and are sung during services.

In *Judaism Without God? Judaism as Culture and Bible as Literature,* Professor Yaakov Malkin wrote: Secular Jews believe in the freedom to choose one's own path in Judaism and in freedom from religious authority, from the obligation to observe religious precepts, and from exclusively religious interpretations of the Bible, holidays, tradition, and all of the works of Jewish literature created within all streams of Judaism. Prevailing beliefs among secular humanistic Jews support the perception of Judaism as a culture rather than a religion:

- Belief that Jewish national identity is determined by membership in the Jewish People, regardless of a person's religion. Jews are members of the Jewish nation, whether by birth or choice. Their Jewishness is expressed in their awareness of their national identity—just as Englishmen or Frenchmen, for example, are aware of their respective national identities—as members of a people and participants in its culture.
- Belief that joining the Jewish People does not require religious conversion.
- Belief in humanistic values in keeping with Hillel's principle: "that which is hateful to you, do not unto others".
- Belief in humanistic values and humanization as a supreme value.
- Belief in "Judaism as culture" that includes religion but is not equivalent to it.
- Belief in God as a literary figure is common to many Jews, who believe that Yahweh, like the gods of all peoples, was created and fashioned by men and women.
- There is no equivalence between Jewishness and Jewish religiosity, and most Jews today are "non-religious" as the term is understood in the Jewish religion: they do not observe precepts and prayers, do not belong to a synagogue, do not send their children to religious schools, do not obey the rulings of rabbis, and do not vote for religious parties.
- Belief that the Jewish religion exerts only a marginal influence on the culture and lives of most Jews today.

Daniel Septimus asks: How important is belief in God? Can one be a "good Jew" without believing in God? These questions—articulated in this way—are relatively modern ones. However, while normative Judaism has always been God-centered, some thinkers—both ancient and modern—have conceptualized Judaism in ways that make beliefs about God less central.

The common quip that "there were no atheists in antiquity" is more or less true. The existence of God (or gods) was taken for granted in the ancient and medieval world. Even the medieval philosophers—Jewish, Christian, and Muslim—who tried to prove God's existence were concerned more with displaying the rationality of religion than demonstrating the existence of a deity.

Atheism and agnosticism only emerged as real options in the modern era, as consequences of secularization, the separation of church and state, and above all, the reliance on science for explanations of natural phenomena.

Nevertheless, on an official level, most Jews are uncomfortable with the idea of a Judaism without God. This is true for the liberal movements as much as it is for more traditional Jews. In 1994, the UAHC (the synagogue council of the Reform movement) rejected an application for membership from a synagogue that practiced "Judaism with a humanistic perspective" because the synagogue's principles deviated from "the historic God-orientation of Reform Judaism."

So, must a Jew believe in God? In a sense, it depends how you define four words: "must," "Jew," "believe," and, of course, "God." In short: probably. And probably not.

A Conservative rabbi told me that in Jewish tradition God is not a Supreme *Being*, as Christians believe. "God is living," he said, "and is the creator and a higher power, in control, larger than nature *but has no form.* Christians have it easier than we do, because churches are filled with statues and Christian homes have pictures of Jesus. They know who they are praying to. We have to be reminded. It's a much more difficult thing because we don't believe that God has a shape or any of that. There is a higher power and something has to be in control. It's not just nature; it's something larger. Some rabbis don't talk about it because it's a difficult subject."

"When bad things happen to good people, Christians say it's God's plan. The whole thing lacks substance in my view," he continued. "Some Jews believe it. I don't."

"Rabbis make decisions with imperfect science," this rabbi told me. "Why couldn't they evolve with what was found out later? Rashi, our greatest commentator, died 1,000 years ago, but wouldn't things change since then? Why can't rabbis today have more of an understanding about science? Why can't a chicken be regarded like a fish? **Why can't chicken parmigiana be considered kosher?**"

"Minutiae keep some Jewish people alive but *drive me nuts*," he concluded. "It's more important to stay alive than to follow every letter of the law."

In *The Nine Questions People Ask About Judaism*, Dennis Prager and Rabbi Joseph Telushkin tell us that: "According to Judaism, one can be a good Jew while doubting God's existence, so long as one acts in accordance with Jewish law. But the converse is not true, for a Jew who believes in God but acts contrary to Jewish law, cannot be considered a good Jew."

A few Jews' Views:

- Rabbi Joseph Telushkin wrote in 1986: "The purpose of Jewish existence is ... to **fight evil and to reduce suffering in the world**."
- Cantor Herbert Feder (later Rabbi Avraham Feder) told me in around 1963 that the essence of Judaism is **social justice**.
- Since the earliest days of CE (the *Common Era*), Jews have embraced the objective of *tikun olam*, meaning "**repair of the world**." Jews bear responsibility for the welfare of society through activities that may include acts of personal kindness, political activism, public service and charity. I like that. I'm a repairman.

Chapter 4
Catholicism & Me

The relationship between Judaism and Catholicism (and between Jews and Catholics) can be confusing, contradictory and troublesome:

The crucifix found in every Catholic church displays the letters "**INRI**" above the head of Jesus (a Jew, of course). INRI stands for Latin *Iesus Nazarenus Rex*

Iudaeorum, meaning "Jesus of Nazareth, King of the Jews."

This confused me because I knew that Jews did not consider Jesus to be king, until I asked a priest about it at a funeral in New Jersey in around 2015. He explained that it was the *mocking* notice Pontius Pilate had nailed over Jesus when Jesus was on the cross. Pilate was a Roman official ("prefect") in charge of Judea who presided at the trial of Jesus and reluctantly approved Jesus's crucifixion, according to Christian tradition.

For many years, Catholics (and other Christians) insisted that Jews killed Jesus. I was called a "Christ killer" in 1960 by a girl in junior high school.

In 1965, too late to help me, the Second Vatican Council absolved the Jews of the death of Jesus. The United States Conference of Catholic Bishops stated: The message of the council's statement is clear. Recalling in moving terms the "spiritual bond that ties the people of the New Covenant to Abraham's stock," the Fathers of the council remind us of the special place Jews hold in the Christian perspective, for "now as before, God holds them as most dear for the sake of the patriarchs; he has not withdrawn his gifts or calling." Jews, therefore, the Fathers caution, are not "to be presented as rejected or accursed by God, as if this followed from Holy Scripture." The Passion of Jesus, moreover, "cannot be attributed without distinction to all Jews then alive, nor can it be attributed to the Jews of today." The Church, the statement declares, "decries hatred, persecutions, displays of antisemitism directed against the Jews at any time and by anyone."

During the 1300s and 1400s, many thousands of Jews were tortured, murdered and forced to convert or go into exile during the Spanish Inquisition. Historians believe at least 200,000 Jews lived in Spain before the Inquisition. Many who refused to convert or leave were burnt at the stake. Spain now says the policy, instituted by monarchs Isabella and Ferdinand and "Grand Inquisitor" Tomás de Torquemada, was a "historical mistake."

In South America and the American west some Catholic descendants of "conversos" and "crypto Jews" still carry out Jewish rituals such as lighting Sabbath candles—but may not know why they do it.

According to Ana Veciana-Suarez in the *Miami Herald*, "Growing up in Brazil, Jonatas Da Silva knew there was something different about his family. The women went to the river to cleanse after their periods, relatives were buried within a day and no one celebrated Christmas or ate pork. But it wasn't until he was living in South Florida that the graduate student came to terms with a lost identity. Like thousands in Latin America, which has long been predominantly Catholic, he and his family are descendants of Jews who either converted to Catholicism under the threat of the Inquisition or practiced their faith in secret while pretending to be good Christians. After a series of encounters, Da Silva, now 33, eventually went on to search for his roots, taking Hebrew classes, submitting to a DNA test (he's Sephardic), and visiting various synagogues, before settling into a Miami Chabad. *Slowly the whole family became more culturally Jewish,* he said. *It was an awakening.*"

Spain recently began offering citizenship to Sephardic Jews who were descendants of Jews expelled during the Inquisition, and Jewish museums, synagogues and cemeteries are being renovated and opened to visitors. Several cities have revived "Jewish quarters." Most of the ancient synagogues that survived, survived because they were converted to churches, but Jewish traces can be detected.

For centuries, Christians hid their families' ancient Jewish origins. Now, those Semitic connections may be an advantage—particularly for attracting Jewish votes. After being accused of antisemitism, New York Catholic Congresswoman Alexandria Ocasio-Cortez revealed her Jewish roots in 2019.

There are many similarities in the religious practices. Catholic church services have adopted an important Jewish prayer. Here is one version of it: "The Lord bless you and keep you; The Lord make his face to shine upon you and be gracious to you; The Lord lift up his countenance upon you and give you peace."

- Catholic priests, cardinals and popes wear skullcaps like Jewish men.
- The "stole," a long, narrow strip of cloth worn by clergy when celebrating Mass, mimics the prayer shawl (*tallit* or *tallis*) used in Judaism. Then-candidate Donald Trump was given a tallit as a gift when he visited a church in Detroit in 2016.
- The first reading in the "Liturgy of the Word" is almost always from the Jewish Torah ("Old Testament").
- The Last Supper is traditionally believed to have been a seder meal. The Passover seder is a meal-and-prayer service held in Jewish homes in the evenings before the first two days of Passover.
- Some of the vocabulary used in Catholic churches has Jewish/Hebrew origin. *Amen* means "so be it." *Alleluia* (often *halleluiah*) means "praise the Lord." *Hosanna* means "save," "rescue" and "savior."

- "Hallelujah" is a song written by Canadian Jewish singer Leonard Cohen and first released in 1984. It is very popular, was recorded hundreds of times, and I've heard it performed in a Catholic church and in a synagogue.
- For millennia, Jews have prayed over bread: "Blessed are you, Lord our God, king of the universe, who brings forth bread from the earth." As he prepares the Mass, a Catholic priest says: "Blessed are you, Lord, God of all creation. Through your goodness we have this bread to offer, which earth has given and human hands have made. It will become for us the bread of life."
- Jews and Catholic priests pray over wine in a similar way.
- Priests wash their hands during mass, continuing a Jewish tradition common after visiting a cemetery.
- Catholic churches have "tabernacles" (sort of cabinets) storing the Eucharist wafers and wine used in communion. In synagogues, tabernacles ("arks") hold Torah scrolls.
- Many Jews and Catholics intermarry (even some in my family).
- In the summer between sixth and seventh grades I had a romance with a Catholic girl at day camp. In September, she was supposed to go to a convent to begin preparation to become a nun. I no longer remember her name, but I do remember that she was a great kisser.
- Mark Oppenheimer hosts the podcast "Unorthodox," a weekly, irreverent look at Jewish news and culture. He has a Ph.D. from Yale. He wrote: "In the United States, most Jews and Catholics trace their ancestry to working-class Europeans who arrived in the late 19th or early 20th centuries, seeking economic opportunity above all. Jews and many Catholics, like the Irish and Italians, were not considered truly white, until one day we all were, more or less; they can have testy, passive-aggressive relationships with clerical authority; and they

are both petrified that the whole shop is about to go out of business."

The following is from the United States Conference of Catholic Bishops. I thank them.

- Bishops of England and Wales appealed to Rome to change the Good Friday prayer for Jews. The prayer reads: "Let us also pray for the Jews: that our God and Lord may illuminate their hearts, that they acknowledge Jesus Christ is the Saviour of all men." The prayer was revised by Benedict XVI in 2008 after he permitted wider celebration of Mass in the older form with his apostolic letter Summorum Pontificum. Previously the prayer had included references to the "blindness" of Jewish people and their "immersion in darkness."
- But the prayer remains different from the Novus Ordo version introduced after the Second Vatican Council, which reads: "Let us pray for the Jewish people, the first to hear the word of God, that they may continue to grow in the love of his name and in faithfulness to his covenant."
- Archbishop Kevin McDonald, chairman of the bishops' Committee for Catholic-Jewish Relations, said the difference had caused "great confusion and upset in the Jewish community."
- He said: "The 1970 prayer which is now used throughout the Church is basically a prayer that the Jewish people would continue to grow in the love of God's name and in faithfulness of his Covenant, a Covenant which—as St. John Paul II made clear in 1980—has not been revoked. By contrast the prayer produced in 2008 for use in the Extraordinary Form of the liturgy reverted to being a prayer for the conversion of Jews to Christianity."

- He said the English and Welsh bishops had "added their voice" to that of the German bishops, who had already asked for the prayer to be amended.
- Archbishop McDonald said: "Such a change would be important both for giving clarity and consistency to Catholic teaching and for helping to progress Catholic-Jewish dialogue."
- Joseph Shaw, president of the Latin Mass Society, said: "It is surprising that the bishops are unhappy with a prayer composed by Pope Benedict as recently as 2008, which, like the prayer it replaced, though in more measured language, reflects the theology and imagery of 2 Corinthians 3:13-16."
- Blogger Fr. John Hunwicke said he hoped the bishops would clarify "what exactly it is in the prayer which contradicts which precise affirmations of [Vatican II document] Nostra Aetate."
- Jesus was a Jew. A devout, practicing Jew. He went to temple, observed the Sabbath and holy days, prayed the psalms, observed the dietary laws, and was a respected Jewish leader. But we Catholics believe that Jesus was also the Son of God, the Messiah that the Old Testament prophets had predicted would come one day to save us from our sins. Jews are still waiting for the Messiah to come. They do not believe that Jesus was the Messiah, though Jews recognize Jesus as a very holy Jew, a great Jewish prophet, but they reject the idea that Jesus was the Messiah. They are still waiting for the Messiah to come.
- But with the Jews, Catholics are waiting for the Messiah to come back. Catholics believe that the Messiah will return at the end of time to judge the world... So in a way, both Jews and Catholics are still waiting for the Messiah together. The Jews are waiting for the first coming of the

Messiah, while Catholics are waiting for the Second Coming....

- So in a world that seems to be increasingly divided and disunited, while we wait for the Messiah to come and straighten it all out, we should **focus on what unites us all**.... and then when the Messiah gets here, He might actually recognize those who have been waiting for Him...

- The United States Conference of Catholic Bishops in its Declaration on the Relationship of the Church to Non-Christian Religions of 1965, the Second Vatican Council issued an historic statement on the Jews and summoned all Catholics to reappraise their attitude toward and relationship with the Jewish people. The statement was, in effect, a culminating point of initiatives and pronouncements of recent pontiffs and of numerous endeavors **concerned with Catholic-Jewish harmony.**

- The call of the council to a dialogical encounter with Jews may be seen as one of the more important fruits of the spirit of renewal generated by the council in its deliberations and decrees. The council's call is an acknowledgement of the conflicts and tensions that have separated Christians and Jews through the centuries and of the Church's determination, as far as possible, to eliminate them. It serves both in word and action as a recognition of the manifold sufferings and injustices inflicted upon the Jewish people by Christians in our own times as well as in the past. It speaks from the highest level of the Church's authority to serve notice that injustices directed against the Jews at any time from any source can never receive Catholic sanction or support.

My first exposure to Catholicism was *extremely unpleasant.* I was scheduled for a return visit to Royal Hospital—my place of birth—to have my tonsils removed in 1952. Royal was overbooked, and I was instead sent farther west to Mother Cabrini Hospital. (She's at the right.)

Not only was it not Royal, but it provided my first exposure to nuns. I had never seen nuns before, and these were not like Singing Nun Debbie Reynolds or Flying Nun Sally Field. They had scary black clothing—like *witches*—and stern demeanors, and they poked needles in my ass.

I endured the horror and pain however, by focusing on my future sweet reward.

I was less than happy about the prospect of being cut open to have part of my body removed. But Dr. Casson, our family physician, had assured me that the surgery wouldn't hurt, and that when it was over, I could have any flavor ice cream that I wanted.

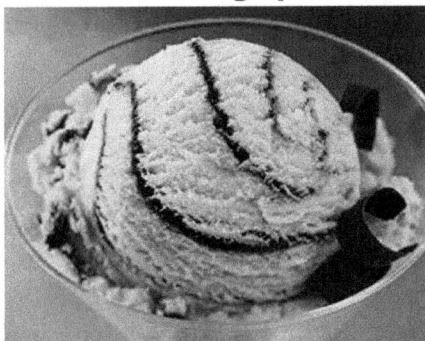

That was a deal I could live with, and Dr. Casson wrote in his notebook that I was to get *fudge ripple*, my favorite.

Had I known when I was led to my hospital bed that his promised prescription applied to Royal Hospital but *not* to Cabrini, I probably would have tied bed sheets together, gone out a window and hitchhiked home.

In blissful ignorance, I kept my eyes on the prize. I endured the anesthesia and surgery and awoke in the recovery room happily anticipating a pint of fudge ripple.

Then scary Sister Evil appeared, carrying a stainless-steel bowl. She reminded me of the wicked witch who stirred the boiling cauldron in *Snow White and the Seven Dwarfs*. That scene had scared me a few months earlier and I made my grandmother take me out of the movie theater.

The nun-witch put a bowl of disgusting reddish glop in front of me.

I thought she was showing me the *bloody tonsils* that the surgeon had cut out of me. Timidly, I asked what the stuff was. She said that it was my *strawberry ice cream.*

With a very hoarse voice, but as forcefully as a frightened six-year-old who had just endured surgery could be, I tried to explain that there must be a mistake. "Please lady. Dr. Casson said I could have fudge ripple," I pleaded.

With much more force, Sister Evil then replied, "You get what you get or you don't get any!"

I've remembered her exact words for *nearly 70 years,* and in all those years I have *never* eaten strawberry ice cream.

However, I might have ended up married to a Catholic woman, and I'm pretty sure she liked strawberry ice cream.

When I was in fifth grade, our synagogue distributed a survey with questions about parental attitudes on interfaith dating.

At the age of 11 I had little chance of being a traitor to the "Chosen People" and dating a pretty blonde gentile girl (a *shiksa*). But my politically liberal mother—probably with little thought about future consequences—indicated on the survey form that she and my father would allow me to date a girl who was not Jewish.

Fast-forward from age 11 to age 17.

In my senior year of high school, I was working part-time in my father's clothing store. So was Maria (name changed). She was not a blonde, but a dark-haired Italian-American who was a senior at Mary Immaculate Academy— unknown territory to someone like me who had studied religion at B'nai Jacob.

It was easy to be attracted to Maria. She was smart, gorgeous, played the guitar and seemed to like me.

We engaged in some mild flirting. I made frequent visits to her cash register to get change for big bills. Once, I even asked her to give me "three threes for a nine." She laughed. It was a good sign. The flirting was a little awkward at first, partly because I was the boss's son. If this happened today, I could be accused of sexual harassment.

Red Skelton (at right), a popular TV comedian at the time, had done an episode about an alien landing on Earth and needing change for the parking meter near his flying saucer. Red played the saucer pilot who asked a friendly Earthling something like, "**May I have three hizzins for a hern?**" I printed up a piece of hern currency in the store's sign shop and I asked Maria for change. She laughed at that, too.

My attraction to her was pretty obvious, and some employees encouraged me.

Mickey, who was the buyer for teenage girls' clothing, even revealed Maria's impressive bra size and urged me to ask her out. Eddie, an Italian-American who worked with me in the men's department, cautioned me to stay away. He said, "**Don't shit where you eat.**" I wondered if he was trying to give me useful advice or just wanted to protect a member of *his* ethnic tribe from an alien marauder.

Eventually, the hormone pressure was impossible to resist. After years of dating girls with last names like Cohen, Kaplan and Berkowitz, it was time to try a girl with a name that ended with a vowel.

In 2019, the notion seems quaint; but, in 1963, I asked my parents. I don't remember the dialog other than that there was a negative reaction. But, when I reminded Mom about the form she filled out years earlier, she gave me the keys to her Plymouth.

We dated on and off, even after I went away to college. It was a time of transition for both of us. I let my hair grow longer, grew a beard and discovered sex (but not with Maria). She dated some older Yalies. We hung out at the "Exit" coffee house and drove to Greenwich Village.

Our families tolerated the relationship. Her mother was a great cook, and I loved Italian food. I was terribly disappointed to learn that Italian mothers never cooked lasagna in the summer because it made the kitchens too hot.

Maria also crossed over the ethnic food line and liked to eat Jewish kosher deli foods. She even introduced me to Peking duck and Chinese rice chips.

Late one night, when we were a year or two under 21, we were in a car in a country club parking lot, drinking beer and eating corned beef sandwiches.

Suddenly, we saw the revolving light of a police car approaching. When the cop got out of his car and aimed his flashlight into our car, Maria was frantically stashing our Heinekens under the front seat.

He caught her with her hands under the seat, but he couldn't see the beer bottles. He asked what she was doing, and she quickly said, "Oh, I'm just looking for some salt for the corned beef." Fortunately the officer of the law didn't know enough about kosher cold cuts to realize that no one puts salt on corned beef; and Maria and I were not arrested for underage drinking. I assume that, after 50-plus years, this confession can't get us in trouble.

Although I liked her a lot (and maybe I loved her—whatever love is for a teenager) and thought about marrying her, I called Maria, "Maria" only one time. It just sounded *too Catholic* to me. Every other time, I used her nickname, "Marty." I also was not prepared to have a crucifix or a Jesus picture on the wall of my home.

Religion ruins a lot of good things.

So does bad communication. In 2009 I learned that Maria considered me to be her boyfriend back in 1963 and '64. It made me feel good, even though she was now a grandmother. Back then, we both dated others and I didn't realize I was that significant to her.

Revisionist History: in 2009 I also learned that Maria had become disenchanted with Catholicism back in high school. Had I known in 1964 what I learned 45 years later, I might *not* have thought our relationship was doomed and I could have tried harder to keep her as my girlfriend and maybe even make her my wife (but not at age 18).

What Catholics Believe:

"Our profession of faith begins with *God,* for God is the First and the Last, the beginning and the end of everything. The Credo begins with God the *Father,* for the Father is the first Divine person of the Most Holy Trinity; our Creed begins with the creation of heaven and earth, for creation is the beginning and the foundation of all God's works."
—the *Catechism of the Catholic Church,* no. 198

Catholic belief is succinctly expressed in the profession of faith or *credo* called the *Nicene Creed*:

I believe in one God,
the Father almighty,
maker of heaven and earth,
of all things visible and invisible.
I believe in one Lord Jesus Christ,
the Only Begotten Son of God,
born of the Father before all ages.
God from God, Light from Light,
true God from true God,
begotten, not made, consubstantial with the Father;
through him all things were made.
For us men and for our salvation
he came down from heaven,
and by the Holy Spirit was incarnate of the Virgin Mary,
and became man.
For our sake he was crucified under Pontius Pilate,
he suffered death and was buried,
and rose again on the third day
in accordance with the Scriptures.
He ascended into heaven
and is seated at the right hand of the Father.
He will come again in glory
to judge the living and the dead
and his kingdom will have no end.
I believe in the Holy Spirit, the Lord, the giver of life,
who proceeds from the Father and the Son,
who with the Father and the Son is adored and glorified,
who has spoken through the prophets.
I believe in one, holy, catholic and apostolic Church.
I confess one Baptism for the forgiveness of sins

and I look forward to the resurrection of the dead
and the life of the world to come. Amen.

Sadly, the Catholic Church, going back to the days of Torquemada in the Spanish Inquisition, has never been a paragon of tolerance.

Timothy Egan wrote in the *New York Times*: "In Indiana this summer, Archbishop Charles C. Thompson stripped a Jesuit prep school of its Catholic identity for refusing to fire a gay, married teacher. The same threat loomed over another Indianapolis school, until it ousted a beloved teacher with 13 years of service. He was fired for getting married to another man—a legal, civil action.

The archbishop claimed he was upholding Catholic teaching, an example of the kind of selective moral policing that infuriates good people of faith.

Catholic teaching also frowns on divorce. But when a divorced teacher, at the same school where the gay teacher was fired, remarried without a church-sanctioned annulment and posted her status on Facebook as a dare, the archbishop did nothing. For this is a road that leads to thrice-married, politically connected Catholics like Newt Gingrich, whose wife Callista (with whom Gingrich carried on an adulterous affair before getting married) is now Donald Trump's ambassador to the Vatican.

Archbishop Thompson says he tries to be 'Christ-centered' in his decisions. If so, he should cite words from Christ condemning homosexuality, any words; there are none. That may be one reason a healthy majority of Catholics are in favor of same-sex marriage, despite what their spiritual sentries tell them."

Why Knights of <u>Columbus</u>?

The **Knights of Columbus** (often "K of C") is the world's largest Catholic fraternal service organization. It was founded in 1882 in New Haven, Connecticut, a few miles from where I am typing this and where I lived as a kid. New Haven has long had a substantial Catholic Italian American population. The group was named in honor of Catholic Italian explorer Christopher Columbus. He was financed by Spain's Catholic Queen Isabella and King Ferdinand, who also backed the anti-Jewish "Spanish Inquisition."

The group was formed as a mutual benefit society for blue-collar Catholics (including recent immigrants), to provide financial aid to sick, disabled and needy members and their families. Aid is also provided to non-members, including victims of Hurricane Dorian as I write this. Social and intellectual fellowship is promoted among members and their families through educational, charitable, religious and other programs.

The Knights of Columbus has grown from one "council" with a handful of members to 15,900 councils and 1.9 million members in the United States and other countries.

Charitable activities include partnerships with Special Olympics, the Global Wheelchair Mission and Habitat for Humanity, plus local charities and the Knights' own Food for Families and Coats for Kids projects. Recent annual giving has exceeded $185 million.

The Knights support the Catholic Church's generally conservative positions on public policy issues, such as "marriage's fundamental nature is a life-long, indissoluble union between a man and a woman" and "marriage ... is an indispensable institution established by the Creator with its own essential properties, purpose, and nature, and that civil laws are unable to alter."

Membership is limited to practicing Catholic men aged 18 or older. The order consists of four different "degrees," each exemplifying a different principle of the order. The Knights have a junior organization, the Columbian Squires, and the Columbiettes for women.

The Knights of Columbus provide economic security and stability through life insurance, annuity and long-term care programs. The Knights have issued over two million insurance contracts. More than $100 billion worth of life insurance is in force, recently backed by $21 billion in assets.

The Knights were sued for $100 million in damages by a company called "List Interactive," alleging that Knights' executives breached an agreement in 2016 after realizing that a computer system List Interactive was developing for the Knights would expose alleged membership fraud.

List Interactive also sought to challenge the Knights' tax-exempt status, citing, among other things, high salaries paid to top executives, and accused the organization of racketeering—a charge dismissed by the court. The Knights vehemently disputed the fraud allegations, and in 2019 a jury ordered the Knights to pay List Interactive $500,000 for breach of contract, much less than $100 million requested.

(left) The distinctive K of C headquarters, built in 1969, is a New Haven landmark.

News to me: the Knights Templar still Exist

If you remember the crusades, perhaps from watching *Robin Hood* on TV, you may remember the **Knights Templar,** also called the **Poor Knights of Christ and the Temple of Solomon,** the **Order of Solomon's Temple,** or simply the **Templars.** It was a devout Catholic military order that combined the roles of knight and monk, founded in 1119 CE.

After Europeans captured Jerusalem in the First Crusade (1095–1099) many Christians made pilgrimages to the Holy Land. Although the city of Jerusalem was relatively secure, the rest of the "Crusader States" were not. Marauders slaughtered pilgrims as they attempted to travel from the port of Jaffa on the Mediterranean Sea to the Holy Land's interior.

The Templars originated in the Kingdom of Jerusalem when nine knights, mainly French, vowed to protect pilgrims. The knights gained support of King Baldwin II of Jerusalem who granted part of his palace for a headquarters in a section of the Temple Mount, called "Solomon's Temple."

By the 1170s, there were about 300 knights based in the Kingdom itself and more in other areas; and by the 1180s there were at least 600 knights in Jerusalem alone. The Order eventually attracted many thousands of knights and became increasingly powerful. By the late 13th century it may have had as many as 870 castles, preceptories and subsidiary houses across Christendom. During the 12th and 13th centuries the properties became a network of support, providing men, horses, money and supplies for Templars in the East.

Templars became bankers to nobles, kings, popes and pilgrims because they could offer credit, and exchange currency, through their holdings in both east and west.

The Order was active until 1312 when it was supposedly perpetually shut down by Pope Clement V.

That was apparently *not* the end, however. As this book was nearing completion, a website popped up, inviting me (notably a non-Catholic) to become "**Sir Knight of the Order**" for a mere $895.

That payment would get me **a** "FULL authentic Knightly/Dame ceremonial regalia, hand finished in Scotland by our Rosslyn Priory Brethren, including our famed white mantle/robe with red cross, Breast Jewel, Medal, Neck jewel with collarette, service beret with our original Skull of Sidon 'Soldier of God' cap badge, Embroidered white gloves with red cross and official pin badge."

I'd be invited to be enrolled in the sacred oath ceremony before my peers where I would be knighted with full military honors in an ancient and holy ceremony dating back 1,000 years. I will be responsible for travel costs but the local priory usually provides a free banquet and free tour for new Knights and Dames.

I was briefly tempted, but I decided not to convert to Catholicism and become a Knight Templar—or a Knight of Columbus. Can I be a Jewish knight? (On Passover I could ask, "Why is this knight different from all other knights?)

Chapter 5
Congregationalists, Yale & Me

Living in Milford, Connecticut—like living in many other cities, towns and villages in New England and New York—is like living in a history museum. It's hard to avoid structures that are centuries old, going back to colonial times, but are still used daily by 21st-century citizens. In some cases the ancient structures have been radically modified or even replaced, but the institutions remain and often flourish.

The First Church of Christ in Milford, now the First United Church of Christ (Congregational), was organized in nearby New Haven by The Reverend Peter Prudden and a group of 15 Puritan families.

The 'new' building now used by the church was built in 1823-'24 and replaces earlier structures (above) that date back to 1639, *long before the USA existed.*

The Puritans had arrived in Boston in 1637 from England. A year later they sailed to what is now New Haven and held their first religious service under a tree in 1638, with the founders of New Haven.

Desiring a church and a colony of their own, Puritans purchased land from Wepawaug Native Americans in 1639, in what is now Milford. (Coincidently, I lived in New Haven from 1952 to 1964, and have been in Milford since 2001.)

Originally, the government of the town was a theocracy, independent of all outside authority. God was the only ruler and the Bible the only rule book. Only Church members were permitted to vote and hold office.

In the early 1660s, members of the church and town helped hide two English judges who had signed a writ for King Charles I to be beheaded. The English unsuccessfully looked for the regicide judges in New Haven and Milford, and as political punishment, England made New Haven Colony merge into Connecticut Colony in 1665. At that time a law was changed and ownership of property became the basis of citizenship in place of church membership.

The early pastors of the Milford church were well educated, some being graduates of Cambridge, Harvard, Yale, Princeton, Amherst, Dartmouth, and Oberlin.

In the early days some Congregationalist churches restricted black members to balcony seating and had witch trials. But despite its unenlightened and Puritan past, the church is undeniably progressive and modern now (sermons are available online). First Church is "Open and Affirming" according to Rev. Adam Eckhart. This means that the church makes "a public covenant of welcome into [its] full life and ministry, to persons of all sexual orientation, gender identities and gender expressions." He told me that the congregation is a long-time supporter of civil rights, LGBTQ rights and women's rights (women, including his wife, are ministers). In this way the denomination is similar to the Episcopalians, but "has less organization," he said.

In 1701 10 pastors founded the "Collegiate School" so Connecticut would have a college to train ministers and other leaders closer to home than Harvard was. It is the third-oldest institution of higher education in the United States (after Harvard, and the College of William and Mary in Virginia). The school was renamed **Yale College** in recognition of a gift from British East India Company governor Elihu Yale.

"Eli" became an important name in New Haven and at Yale. A local radio station is "**WELI**." A Yale athletic cheer includes "Boola Boola, **Eli** Yale." "**Eli's**" is the name for a chain of local restaurants. One has an 80-foot-long horseshoe-shaped bar with 25 varieties of draft beer.

Rev. Eckhart, the son of a minister, attended Yale as an undergrad in religious studies and later was ordained by the Yale Divinity School.

In the 1970s and 1980s the church helped found Milford's homeless shelter, "Beth El Center," and launched its own transitional apartment ministry, "Sojourners Haven."

First Church supports an outreach ministry that feeds food-insecure Milford schoolchildren every weekend during the school year. The church has a Food Closet to help people in emergencies and during holidays, and volunteers deliver food to families in need. The Emma Davis Medical Equipment Ministry is a clearinghouse that has offered service for several decades. Emma Davis was a member of the church who spent a lifetime reaching out to the needy. Since she died in 1968, members of First Church have gathered used wheelchairs, walkers, hospital beds, etc., repaired them and made them available free of charge statewide.

With its stately front columns and tall white steeple, Rev. Eckhart acknowledged in a newspaper interview that "This is kind of a 'postcard church,' in that, for some people, we kind of fade into the beautiful downtown landscape. Some folks assume that every member here has lineage to the Mayflower or our founding fathers. Some do, but our First Church actually has a most interesting socioeconomic diversity—a lively membership that is completely committed to God and to our community."

"Our doors are always open," Rev. Eckhart said. "People in Milford deal with the same stresses and brokenness as others do. I love that this is a distinctive faith community with compelling programs, and with a progressive spirit unlike any place else in Milford. We must continue working to give meaning and hope that God intends for us."

The very congenial minister says that the church has "no dress code" for religious services. This reminded me of how jealous I was as a Jewish kid on hot summer days when I saw gentiles dressed to be comfortable in church, while I was forced to wear a jacket, dress shirt and tie. Today, many synagogues are less formal. Perhaps I was born too soon.

Congregationalist theology is comfortable, too. According to Rev. Adam, the biblical six-day creation timetable is not taken literally, the Communion bread and wine are not believed to be parts of Jesus, and Baptism (a sprinkling, not a dunking) can be done for infants or older people.

Three Judges, a mountain, a restaurant and me

Edward Whalley, **William Goffe** and **John Dixwell** were three of the English judges who sentenced King Charles I to death in 1649, dissolving the monarchy and placing Oliver Cromwell into power. When Charles II, the son of the executed king, gained the throne in 1660, he decreed that each judge should be *hanged, drawn and quartered*. To avoid this horrid fate, Whalley, Goffe and Dixwell fled to North America.

Dixwell stayed in New Haven, and Whalley and Goffe went to Boston, but they feared being recognized by royal loyalists. A warrant was issued for their arrests and they joined Dixwell in New Haven, where Puritans helped them. Initially they were hidden in the home of Reverend John Davenport (a Yale college is named in his honor). When that didn't prove safe enough, Whalley and Goffe hid in a large rock formation starting in 1661, on what is now West Rock Ridge State Park, a local mountain.

When a panther made the judges realize the danger of living in the woods, they fled to Hadley, Massachusetts, where they stayed for the rest of their lives. In their honor the rock formation was named "Judges Cave" and the path leading to it is "Regicides Trail." Three important New Haven streets were named to honor the judges. There is also a "Three Judges Motor Lodge" and there was a "Three Judges Restaurant." I ate there many times and used to hike on West Rock near the cave. "Judges Cave Cigars" is one of the oldest cigar brands, produced with Connecticut tobacco since 1884.

The cave has a commemorative plaque which reads in part, "**Opposition to tyrants is obedience to God.**"

Chapter 6
Jews For Jesus Are Not For Me

I receive *lots* of reading material, both in the physical world and online. Some of the physical newspapers, magazines, catalogs and ads are devoured immediately. Some are piled into a bin on a spare chair in my kitchen. When the bin gets close to overflowing, I perform triage. A quick analysis decides what will get read sooner, or later, or goes out on the street in the big blue recycling tub.

I sometimes wonder if an unread magazine will get shredded, mulched, pulped, dried and eventually repurposed as another magazine for me to read—or to ignore. I don't think human beings can be reincarnated, but magazines, books and catalogs certainly can.

Somehow, for at least 15 years I've had a free subscription to a small newsletter called *Issues: A Messianic Jewish Perspective.* It's so irrelevant to me that I don't even know how often the publication arrives. I think it comes monthly, and I flip through maybe one or two issues per year.

Messianic Jews, also known as **Jewish Christians**, **Jews for Jesus** or **J4J**, have, at various times, mystified, confused, amused or annoyed me. Some are *especially* annoying on Facebook where they are certain that they have all of the answers, even if they have merely crackpot theories.

Jews for Jesus confuse me because I don't understand how a Jewish person can also be a Christian, and accept Jesus as the Messiah. I don't understand how there can be a "Messianic Synagogue," but there are many.

Messianic Jews belong to a 'new, American religion,' like Jehovah's Witnesses, Christian Scientists and Mormons. Although the group sometimes claims to date back several thousand years, the American Jews for Jesus movement was founded in San Francisco at the height of the hippie era (1970) by Moishe Rosen as "Hineni Ministries." It was renamed "Jews for Jesus" in 1973.

[The following is adapted from MyJewishLearning.]

Messianic Judaism is a religious group that tries to straddle the line between Judaism and Christianity. According to this group, Jesus, (*Yeshua* in Aramaic) was the Messiah, he died on behalf of the world's sins, and that Jews are the chosen people.

The origin of the group goes back to the "Hebrew Christian" missions to the Jews in the 19th and early 20th centuries. By the 1960s and '70s Messianic Judaism was gaining popularity, and members were called "the Jesus people," and "Jews for Jesus."

Major Jewish denominations *reject* Messianic Judaism as a form of Judaism. Within Christianity, Messianic Judaism is sometimes seen as an evangelical group, and sometimes as a separate sect. It is often presented as an ethnic church for Jews, like a Korean church. Experts estimate only about half of members were born Jews.

Non-Jews who join a Messianic congregation may undergo a kind of conversion, although many within the group believe that it's impossible to convert to Judaism. Messianic Jewish conversions are not considered valid by any Jewish denomination. Non-Jews who join Messianic congregations are sometimes called "**spiritual Jews**," "**completed Jews**," or "**Messianic gentiles**."

Messianic Jews include the New Testament in their canon and believe that there is prediction of Jesus in the Old Testament.

Believers in Messianic Judaism adhere to some of the laws given in the Torah, but do not follow rabbinic law and deny the authority of the Mishnah and Talmud.

A core component of Messianic Judaism is missionizing to traditional Jews. Christian leaders have criticized Messianic Jews for aggressive missionizing to Jews and for misrepresenting themselves as Jews.

According to the evangelical theology accepted by Messianic Jews, those who are not "saved" are destined for *eternal damnation*. [I'm in trouble!] Helping to bring someone to Yeshua and thus to salvation is a responsibility of all Messianic Jews, and many embrace that role, particularly for family members. This often causes animosity between Messianic and mainstream Jews.

The Jewish community objects to the term "Messianic Judaism," because the messianism practiced by Messianic Jews is Jesus-focused, and thus by definition *not Jewish*. The use of the phrase "Messianic Judaism" strikes many as a subversive way of attracting Jews who do not know enough about their faith to realize that they are learning about *Christianity*.

There are an estimated 400 Messianic Jewish congregations worldwide, with 10,000-15,000 Messianic Jews in Israel, and about 200,000 in the United States. Congregations (called synagogues) can be found across the country, mainly in communities with large existing Jewish communities.

JEWS F✡R JESUS®

Here's how Messianic Jews explain themselves, with some editing:

- "Many Jews and gentiles have only a partial understanding of Christianity. Most know that Christians believe Jesus died to atone for the sins of all who believe in him and that Christians say he rose from the dead. Many do not understand how one becomes a Christian or much else about becoming a Christian.
- How can a person be certain that Jews who believe in Jesus are no longer Jews when there is confusion over what it means to be a Jew and to be a Christian?
- Some say that being Jewish is merely a matter of religion. Since the religion of Judaism teaches that Jesus is not the Messiah, that would certainly mean that a person who accepts Jesus is *not a Jew*.
- However, it would also mean that the majority of people now known as Jews are not. The definition excludes atheistic Jews, agnostic Jews and all other nonobservant Jews.
- Would it surprise you to know that someone who goes to a church all his or her life nevertheless must be converted in order to be a Christian? Jews and gentiles are what they are because of how they were born, but people become Christians because of what they believe. One cannot be born a Christian since people aren't born believing in anything, except maybe the importance of a full stomach and a clean diaper.
- The first Christians were Jewish followers of Jesus, and they were not known as Christians. They described their belief in Jesus and his teachings as "the Way."
- Believing in Jesus is more than a religious idea; it is a personal relationship that affects how one lives.
- The first ones to be called "Christians" were probably mostly gentiles who lived in Antioch. It was not an appellation they

chose for themselves. They were called Christians (probably by gentiles) because they were always talking about and trying to be like Christ, which is simply the Greek translation for "Messiah."

- Christians were and are Jews and gentiles who, of their own free will, chose to trust in Jesus, the Jewish Messiah, as the one who offered himself as a sacrifice for the sins of the world.
- Everyone who chooses Jesus is a convert, whether gentile or Jew. To convert means to turn, not from being a Jew or gentile, not from history or heritage, but from sin.
- The reconciliation with God that Jesus offered can be conferred only by rebirth. Therefore, being born Jewish or gentile has no bearing on if one is a Christian.
- Many people assume our belief in Jesus constitutes a decision to disassociate from our history, our Jewish people and our God, because we like someone else's history, people and God better. The accusation of self-hatred stems from the idea that we want to identify with those who have persecuted us. It would be a mistake to evaluate Jesus on the basis of those who profess him as Savior but practice hatred in opposition to his teachings. Besides, why would a self-hating Jew accept Jesus and then insist on calling himself or herself a Jew?
- Others seem to think we chose Jesus to avoid persecution. Someone said, "If there would be another Hitler, don't think that you would escape the ovens just because you believe in Jesus." That's true! People who don't like Jews generally don't care if they believe in Jesus, and those of us who do believe in him know that firsthand.
- The assumption that we chose to believe in Jesus because we didn't want to be Jews is entirely wrong. We chose to be open to discover. When it happened, we admitted and committed based on the discovery that Jesus is the Jewish Messiah foretold in the Jewish Bible.

- Further, we value our Jewishness. It is exciting to be a part of the people whom God promised would bring blessing to the whole world!
- Some have publicly accused us of employing a false (Jewish) identity to lure people into believing in Jesus. That is an untrue, unfair and illogical accusation.
- People cannot be motivated to believe in Jesus on the basis of something they already possess: namely, Jewish identity. Second, in order to honestly consider Jesus, a person must be willing to stop thinking about who he or she is and concentrate on who Jesus is. And third, potential Jewish believers in Jesus ought to be warned that they will be regarded as traitors by many who don't understand.
- Jesus was and is always a threat to the status quo.
- Most Jews know that belief in Jesus would make them objects of disappointment, displeasure and perhaps disenfranchisement.
- The Book of Hebrews in the New Testament describes faith as the "substance" of things hoped for, the "evidence" of things not seen and then goes on to illustrate by pointing out great heroes of faith.
- Faith is based on perception and rooted in reality. There are many religions and many ideas, but in order to qualify as faith in the biblical sense, a person's belief about God must be true.
- People can't choose "a faith" any more than they can choose "a reality." If there is one God, there is one faith.
- Once we choose to open our minds and hearts, we may find ourselves "seeing" with eyes of faith something other than our own preference or choice.
- Truth is singular by nature. It is either perceived or misperceived because there are no personal versions of truth. [What about Kellyanne Conway's "alternate facts?"]
- We cannot motivate you to consider Yeshua on the basis that you will remain Jewish... because you will also be Jewish if you don't believe in him. But we hope that you might be motivated by a desire to know if Jesus is God's answer to your needs, as a

Jew, and even more, as a human being in need of knowing the Being who created you.

- We believe that God created man in His image; that because of the disobedience of our first parents in Eden they lost their innocence and both they and their descendants, separated from God, suffer physical and spiritual death and that all human beings, with the exception of Jesus the Messiah, are sinners by nature and practice.
- We believe that Jesus the Messiah died for our sins, as a representative and substitutionary sacrifice; that all who believe in Him are justified by His perfect righteousness and atoning blood and that there is no other name under heaven by which we must be saved.
- We believe that Israel exists as a covenant people through whom God continues to accomplish His purposes and that the Church is an elect people in accordance with the New Covenant, comprising both Jews and Gentiles who acknowledge Jesus as Messiah and Redeemer.
- We believe that Jesus the Messiah will return personally in order to consummate the prophesied purposes concerning His kingdom.
- We believe in the bodily resurrection of the just and the unjust, the everlasting blessedness of the saved and the everlasting conscious punishment of the lost.

I long ago rejected the notion that Jesus was or is the Messiah spoken of in the Torah simply because the planet is filled with *terrible* people. Evil is rampant. Our Planet Earth is a horrible place, and getting worse.

Maimonides said of the Messianic Era: "And at that time there will be no hunger or war, no jealousy or rivalry. For the good will be plentiful, and all delicacies available as dust. The entire occupation of the world will be only to know God... the people Israel will be of great wisdom; they will perceive the esoteric truths and comprehend their Creator's wisdom as is the capacity of man. As it is written, *for the earth shall be filled with the knowledge of God, as the waters cover the sea."*

In Christian theology, the Messianic Era is a time of universal peace and brotherhood on the earth, without crime, war and poverty and is already here. But according to "inaugurated eschatology," which *I do not understand at all,* it will be completed and brought to perfection by the second coming of Christ.

According to Jewish tradition, the Messianic Era will be one of global peace and harmony, an era free of strife and hardship, and one conducive to the furthering of the knowledge of God. If Jesus was the Messiah, *he did a terrible job.* If we are now living in the Messianic Era, I am *not* impressed.

The theme of the Messiah ushering in an era of global peace is in two famous passages from the Book of Isaiah:

1. "The wolf will live with the lamb, the leopard will lie down with the goat, the calf and the lion and the yearling together; and a little child will lead them. The cow will feed with the bear, their young will lie down together, and the lion will eat straw like the ox. The infant will play near the hole of the cobra, and the young child put his hand into the viper's nest. They will neither harm nor destroy on all my holy mountain, for the earth will be full of the knowledge of the Lord as the waters cover the sea."

2. "They shall beat their swords into plowshares and their spears into pruning hooks; nation will not lift up sword against nation, neither shall they learn war any more." [These inspiring words are on a wall in Ralph Bunche Park, a "peace park" opposite the United Nations headquarters in Manhattan, shown ahead.]

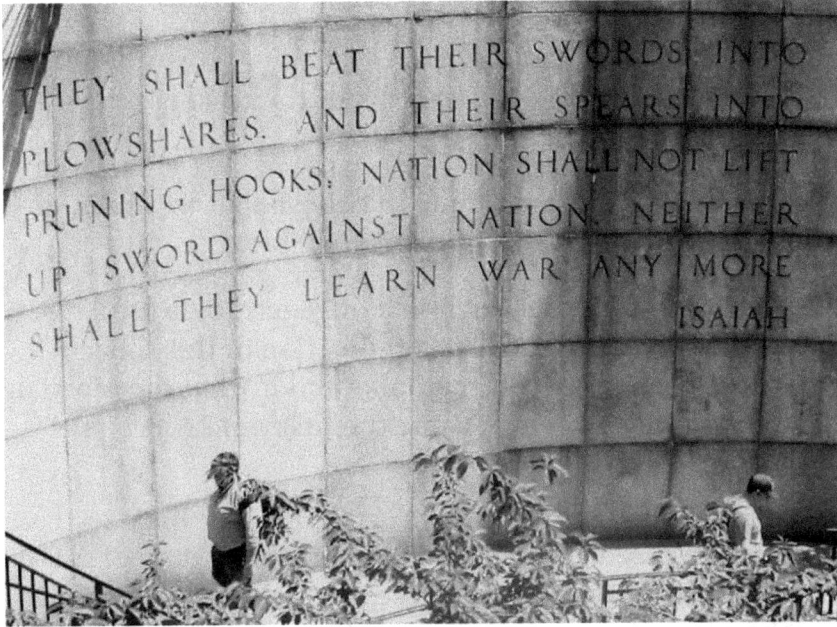

THEY SHALL BEAT THEIR SWORDS INTO PLOWSHARES. AND THEIR SPEARS INTO PRUNING HOOKS; NATION SHALL NOT LIFT UP SWORD AGAINST NATION. NEITHER SHALL THEY LEARN WAR ANY MORE

ISAIAH

My J4J Online Chat

▲ The upward arrow shows what the J4J person said.
▼ The downward arrow shows my words.

▲ Hi! My name is Reagan, how can I help you today?

▼ Should I care about Jesus? If so, why?

▲ Good question. If he is who he claimed to be then, yes. He is the whole fulfillment of Tenakh [sic] and what it pointed to. What type of Judaism do you practice?

▼ I was raised conservative, but now am secular/cynical.

▲ Understood. So what made you think about Jesus?

97

▼ He is hard to avoid.

▲ Very true. Have you ever read any of the reasons why we believe he is the Messiah?

▼ Probably not. It's hard for me to believe that we are in the Messianic Age, since the world is so terrible.

▲ I agree totally. We believe it will only get worse until he physically returns. Can I paste a prediction of the Tanach that was written in 700 BC that talks about what the Messiah would accomplish when he came the first time ?

▼ Sure, please paste

▲ He was despised and rejected by mankind, a man of suffering, and familiar with pain. Like one from whom people hide their faces he was despised, and we held him in low esteem. Surely he took up our pain and bore our suffering, yet we considered him punished by God, stricken by him, and afflicted. But he was pierced for our transgressions, he was crushed for our iniquities; the punishment that brought us peace was on him, and by his wounds we are healed. We all, like sheep, have gone astray, each of us has turned to our own way; and the Lord has laid on him the iniquity of us all. Isaiah 53

▼ I don't see how that is specifically about Jesus.

▲ It doesn't call him by name but Moses wasn't foretold by name to Abraham. But when he came on the scene he proved his calling was from G-d.

▼ How did Jesus prove he was predicted by Isaiah?

▲ He preformed [sic] many miracles. He rose the dead, calmed the sea, multiplied bread, healed lepers and the blind. Isaiah predicted that the Messiah would heal the blind and the deaf. Jesus did this. But then Jesus said he came to do more. He came to reverse the curse of sin that started in the beginning. Then he went to die as our blood atonement (remember the lambs at the temple?). He then rose from the dead.

▼ Maybe Isaiah was predicting someone else, not Jesus. How can we know? How can someone who is really dead, rise? Maybe Jesus was not really dead.

▲ Only God is in control of resurrecting. So it had to be God. WE know he died because the Romans were experts and they put the spear into his side/pericardium. All his Jewish followers claimed to have been with him after the resurrection and he was perfectly healthy, unlike someone who would have survived a crucifixion. They all went to their horrible execution deaths (except John) claiming his was risen. Have you ever read the book of Matthew?

▼ I read it many years ago.

▲ I can paste a link to it so you don't have to buy a New Testament. Would you be willing to read through it again? Have you ever asked G-d (assuming he is there) who Jesus is and to reveal the truth to you?

▼ OK, so the Romans killed him. How do we know he was resurrected? I have a full OT & NT. I have never asked God anything.

▲ Would you be willing to ask him to reveal the truth to you? You can ask him from right where you are. Just talk to him.

▼How do I talk to God? How can I tell if I am being heard? How do I get an answer?

▲He will always hear a sincere plea for the truth about him. Just talk out loud to him and say something like "God I want to know the truth about you and Jesus, please show me." He will find a way to show you in a way that you will understand. He is God. He knows you more than you know yourself! :) and he Loves you.

▼OK, I'll try it now. How long do I wait for a response? Do you speak to God?

▲I was an agnostic and prayed that prayer. He answered me about 8 months later but I was actively seeking truth in the meantime. Reading evidence for the resurrection like questions you are asking. I do speak to him daily now.

▼How can you tell you are getting a response from God, and not just imagining it?

▲Much of my reason for faith was based on evidence. Like studying the prophecies that Jesus fulfilled and the evidence of history. When I was satisfied that we have a reasonable faith with actual evidence I was able to trust him about other things. Now he usually answers me during my daily Bible reading. He has given me a peace I never had before. Do you have an email that staff can connect to? It is nice to have someone that you can bounce questions off of.

The following is from Israeli newspaper *HaAretz*: "The closest Messianic Jew to Trump is undeniably Jay Sekulow, one of the president's personal attorneys for more than two years and a familiar face on cable television vigorously defending the president."

Sekulow, who wrote a personal account of his spiritual path on the Jews for Jesus website in 2005 ("How a Jewish Lawyer From Brooklyn Came to Believe in Jesus"), came to Trump as a celebrity legal warrior for conservative Christian causes. The Messianic Jew is affiliated with Jews for Jesus and has served on its national board and as its general counsel. He argued and won a landmark case on behalf of the group before the Supreme Court in 1987. He is currently the chief counsel at the American Center for Law and Justice, a Christian activist organization founded by televangelist Pat Robertson.

Commenting on Sekulow's rise to prominence at Trump's side, conservative columnist Jonathan Tobin wrote in Haaretz, "though heresy is an outdated concept outside of the ultra-Orthodox world, Messianics are still considered beyond the pale and a threat, winning gullible converts with false advertising and misleading theology. Coming to terms with Sekulow means being willing to accept that pro-Israel Messianics and their evangelical allies are politically if not religiously kosher."

At a political rally in Michigan ahead of the midterm elections, and two days after the gunman declared all Jews should die and opened fire at the Tree of Life Congregation Synagogue—the worst attack on Jews in US history—Vice President Mike Pence invited a rabbi onstage to say a prayer for the victims. That rabbi turned out to be Loren Jacobs, a prominent figure in the Messianic Christian movement. At the event, he invoked "Jesus the Messiah." [Oy vey!]

Whether or not Jesus was the Messiah is not the most important question that divides Judaism and Christianity, according to Rabbi Joseph Telushkin and Dennis Prager.

"The major difference between Judaism and Christianity lies in the importance each religion attaches to faith and actions. In Judaism, God considers people's actions to be more important than their faith; acting in accordance with Biblical and rabbinic law is the Jews' central obligation. As Christianity developed, however, it did away with most of these laws, and faith became its central demand. Though faith became the essence of Christianity, Christian history reveals that this emphasis on faith over works was held by neither Jesus nor his followers. The New Testament often notes that Jesus and his early followers stressed and observed Jewish law: *Do not imagine that I have come to abolish the Law or the Prophets,* Jesus declared to his early disciples. *I tell you solemnly, till heaven and earth disappear, not one dot, not one little stroke will disappear from the Law until its purpose has been achieved.*"

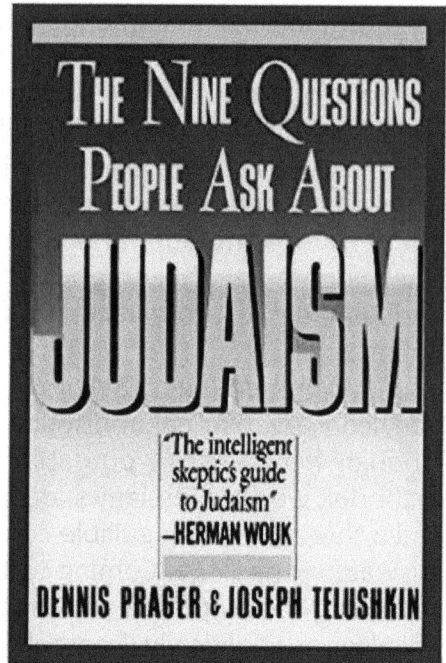

A Jewish Messiah?

Orthodox rabbi Menachem Mendel Schneerson, known to many as "the Lubavitcher Rebbe" or simply as "the Rebbe," was the last rebbe of the Lubavitcher Hasidic dynasty.

He is considered to be one of the most influential Jewish leaders of the 20th century. Many of Schneerson's ad-admirers believe that he is the Messiah. His gravesite attracts both Jews and gentiles for prayer. Despite being born in Eastern Europe to an old rabbinical family, he was modern and outreach-oriented.

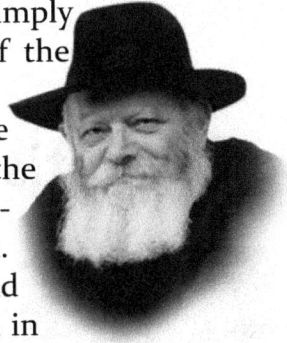

Although I do not consider the Rebbe to be the Messiah, I do like the following advice:

- "You cannot add more minutes to the day, but you can utilize each one to the fullest."
- "When you waste a moment, you have killed it in a sense, squandering an irreplaceable opportunity. But when you use the moment properly, filling it with purpose and productivity, it lives on forever."
- "This is the key to time management—to see the value of every moment."

What About George Burns?

Anybody who could turn Lot's wife into a pillar of salt, incinerate Sodom and Gomorrah and make it rain for forty days and forty nights has got to be a fun guy.

"Oh, God!"

A JERRY WEINTRAUB PRODUCTION
GEORGE BURNS · JOHN DENVER · "OH, GOD!"
TERI GARR
DONALD PLEASENCE · Based on the Novel by AVERY CORMAN
Screenplay by LARRY GELBART · Produced by JERRY WEINTRAUB
Directed by CARL REINER

Comedian, actor, writer, singer George Burns (1896–1996), lived over a century, has three stars on the Hollywood Walk of Fame, won an Oscar, was married to Gracie Allen, and played God in three movies.

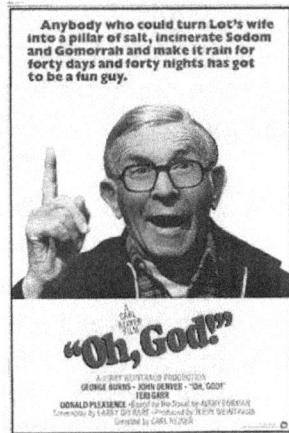

Chapter 7
Antisemitism & Me

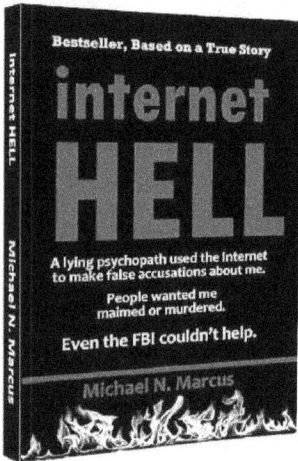

I was born after Hitler died. I was not denied admission to college or discouraged from buying houses because I was Jewish. I was beaten up twice in first grade because I did not prefer the Boston Red Sox to the New York Yankees (*not* because I denied the divinity of Jesus). In seventh grade a "hood" put out a cigarette on my head and poked holes in my bicycle tires —but the attacker was as Jewish as I was. In ninth grade I was stabbed in a country club swimming pool—but the attacker was as Jewish as I was. As a teenager I was allowed to join a club at the YMCA and the Y's membership form allowed me to indicate "Hebrew" as my religion.

I did not suffer from "ethnic cleansing" (AKA "genocide") as in Bosnia & Herzegovina, Georgia or Myanmar.

I did not suffer much for being a Jew, but—like most Jews—I was *not* isolated from antisemitism.

In junior high school a female classmate accused me of being a "Christ Killer." I laughed off the accusation and said that not only did I not kill Jesus, I never even met him.

Two other incidents could not be laughed off.

In around 2005 a Florida competitor of my telecommunications business launched a hate-filled, copyright-infringing website. It included stolen photographs I personally had taken and words that I had personally written.

The antisemitic pirate even altered a photograph of me to make me look 'more Jewish' by combining my face with the face of an Orthodox Jew who had a black hat, a longer beard and side locks (*payot* in Hebrew, *payoss* in Yiddish).

He altered a photo of a parts cabinet in the repair department of my business by labeling drawers "gold" and "diamonds." It took some work, but I was able to get the website shut down.

This was annoying and unpleasant, but not the worst attack I had to endure.

Early on a Saturday morning in the summer of 2010, I received an alarming call from an old friend. The friend said that she had received an email saying that I was a convicted child rapist, published child pornography, burned my wife, was in prison for four years, drove drunk, used the Internet to find children to have sex with, was part of an international pedophile ring, was a threat to my neighbors, and had even **RAPED MY DOG**.

As shocking as these false accusations were, things rapidly got worse.

The anonymous accuser sent similar emails to my friends, relatives and business associates and members of the media, wrote accusatory letters to newspapers, set up online petitions to have me put on a list of sex offenders, and established a libelous blog with a huge number of false accusations. He even published pictures of me and my house—and directions to get there.

The attacker created multiple false identities to join in the attack, formed a phony organization to add credibility, and tried to halt printing and sale of books I wrote. People called for my **imprisonment, castration and execution**.

From the very beginning, there was only one obvious suspect, but police and the FBI could not prove who the perpetrator was. I was able to get some lies removed from the web, but some are still there—and may remain there for as long as the Internet exists.

The likely attacker was diagnosed as a "paranoid psychopath" known to hate blacks, Latinos, Catholics and Jews—and had a child with the wife of a Jewish man. The presumed perpetrator attracted like-minded allies.

Here's some of what they posted online on a neo-Nazi website:

- **"We got your number and address. Its [sic] about time to get into action. Anyone who is close to this Jewboi [sic], get a gun and blow his head off. Its [sic] about time to blow up a Jewboi [sic] head and start moving to the second phase."**
- **"Is it possible you'll be catching bullets soon? More than probable i'd [sic] say, you repulsive shit kike! Rot with your filthy family of rats, bastard jew!"**
- **"I expect you'll get shot in your fat arse a few times, before you get your neck snapped. Rat faced kike!"**

My wife and I lived in fear for months and our house received stepped-up police patrols. When home or away we made sure our alarm system was active. We dreaded leaving our home, and in restaurants, stores or parking lots we were constantly scanning people who approached us.

I was reminded of a story my mother told. She lived in the Bronx until she married and moved to Washington D.C. Mom took the subway into Manhattan to attend

Hunter College's high school (for brainy girls) on the Upper East Side. According to the school, students accepted to Hunter represent the top one-quarter of 1% of students in New York City. Hunter has the highest average SAT score, the highest average ACT score and the highest percentage of National Merit Finalists of *any* high school in the United States, public or private.

Now, Hunter's student body is largely Asian. Back in the 1930s when my mother attended Hunter, a great many students were white and Jewish. The school was adjacent to Yorkville, the neighborhood that was the home of the "German American Bund," the most notorious American pro-Nazi group. When you couple possible academic jealousy with antisemitism, it is not surprising that girls walking from the subway station to the school were harassed.

Jewish girls were subjected to insults, groping, and book damage. However, word quickly spread within the Jewish community—and soon my mother and her classmates were escorted between the subway station and school by some large, tough Jewish men. The harassment halted.

In addition to my mother (who later graduated from Hunter College), graduates of Hunter College High School include:

Elena Kagan, Supreme Court Justice
Martina Arroyo, opera star
Ron Brown, Secretary of Commerce for President Clinton
Ruby Dee, actor and writer
Lin-Manuel Miranda, composer, lyricist, actor, singer
Bobby Lopez, Broadway musical composer
Mildred Spiewak Dresselhaus, Presidential Medal of Freedom recipient, professor of physics and electrical engineering at MIT, recipient of 28 honorary doctorates for work in physics, and advocacy for women in science.

In 1543 German religious reformer **Martin Luther** wrote: [slightly edited below] "What shall we Christians do with this rejected and condemned people, the Jews:

- First, set fire to their synagogues or schools ... in honor of our Lord and of Christendom ...
- Second, their houses also be razed and destroyed.
- Third, I advise that all their prayer books and Talmudic writings—in which such idolatry, lies, cursing, and blasphemy are taught—be taken from them.
- Fourth, I advise that their rabbis be forbidden to teach henceforth on pain of loss of life and limb ...
- Fifth, I advise that safe-conduct on the highways be abolished for they have no business in the countryside ...
- Sixth, all cash and silver and gold be taken from them ...
- Seventh, I recommend putting a flail, an ax, a hoe, a spade, a distaff, or a spindle into the hands of young, strong Jews and Jewesses and letting them earn their bread in the sweat of their brow ... But if we are afraid that they might harm us or our wives, children, servants, cattle, etc., ... then eject them forever ..."

Even now, in the presumed safety of 21st-century America, after being threatened by Nazis and with a president who acknowledged "fine" Nazis in Charlottesville's mayhem, it's

very hard for me to have a normal life. *For Jewish people anywhere in the world, antisemitism is never far away.* Most of us were born after the Holocaust, but we are definitely aware of recent anti-Jewish terrorism in the USA (Pittsburgh) and in other countries (France).

Russian Czar Nicholas II (at left) abdicated his throne in

1917 at the start of the Bolshevik (Communist) Revolution and was shot in 1918 along with his family and servants. The killing was ordered by Vladimir Lenin and Yakov Sverdlov. Yak was Jewish. Vlad had a Jewish grandfather.

Russian antisemites play down the Jewish origins of Communism. American antisemites play it *up*. Antisemites also complain about Jewish capitalists. Our tribe gets blamed for everything. Except for Jesus. It seems very strange that so many antisemites think God had a Jewish son, and pray to him. No Christian antisemite calls Jesus a "kike."

Some Jews who lived in England and France have recently fled to Israel, and others keep suitcases packed to be used if they feel threatened. While Jewish Americans have been subjected to a lot of prejudice (and scattered muggings and even arson and murder), there has been little of the large-scale violence that occurred in Paris or has been directed at African-Americans, Muslims and Hispanics in the USA. (I don't recall ever hearing of violence directed at Presbyterians or Congregationalists.)

The killing of 11 and wounding of 6 Jews at a Pittsburgh synagogue in 2018 has so far been a sad exception.

Still, the 2017 parade of torch-wielding Nazis in Charlottesville, chanting "**Jews will not replace us**" is discouraging. Many Jewish institutions now have armed guards—which would have been previously unthinkable. Some Jewish people who would proudly have worn necklaces with Jewish symbols in the past, now hide them inside their clothing. A 2019 survey by the American Jewish Committee found that

nearly one in three American Jews fears wearing something that might identify their religion. 84% of respondents said antisemitism has increased over the past five years.

The American Jewish community experienced very high levels of antisemitism in 2018, including a doubling of antisemitic assaults and the single deadliest attack against the Jewish community in American history, according to the Anti-Defamation League. Its annual Audit of Antisemitic Incidents recorded a total of 1,879 attacks against Jews and Jewish institutions in the USA in 2018, the third-highest year on record.

"We've worked hard to push back against antisemitism, and succeeded in improving hate crime laws, and yet we continue to experience an alarmingly high number of antisemitic acts," said Jonathan Greenblatt, head of the ADL.

"The Jews have been a persistent minority for thousands of years, living in exile, living in diasporas, and the Jews have been made convenient scapegoats for various purposes," said Greenblatt after Donald Trump's accusation of "disloyalty" in August, 2019. "That's why they often call antisemitism the oldest hatred."

As far back as the Middle Ages, Jews were tagged in their communities as inherently untrustworthy and suspect, incapable of being loyal to their ruler because of their ties to other Jews around the world. They were also viewed as a threat to the church because of their religious beliefs.

In 1894, a French/Jewish military captain, Alfred Dreyfus, was falsely accused of passing military secrets to the Germans and was convicted in a French military court. "People were willing to believe it, even though the evidence from the very outset was shaky, because it made sense to them," according to Deborah E. Lipstadt, a professor of modern Jewish history and Holocaust studies at Emory University.

"They had been so exposed to this stereotype, it had become so much the pivot point and the central element of anti-semitism that Jews have other loyalties, that it seemed like it must be true, and they were ready to believe the worst."

While there have been few 'major' terrorist attacks aimed at Jewish institutions in the USA, there have certainly been Jewish victims in such horrific massacres as Las Vegas (2017) and Sandy Hook (2012).

> **Published on 26 October 2014**
> This video is dedicated to Lenny Posner, the biggest pile of dogshit to ever walk the corridors of hell. When you smell him, run as fast as you can, preferably to a Church, no way he follows you there. When you emerge, grab your Bible and a chunk of the lectern and run him off, back home to Tel Aviv.

Lenny Pozner, whose 6-year-old son Noah was the youngest victim in the attack at the Sandy Hook elementary school in Connecticut, was often singled out by crackpot hoaxers because he is Jewish. Not only did a discredited book claim that Noah's death certificate had been faked and the child never existed, but a Florida woman was sentenced to five months in prison for sending Pozner death threats. Fearful for his safety, he has moved at least six times since Noah's death and has his mail sent to post office boxes.

Press TV, the official state media outlet of Iran, blamed "Israeli death squads" for the shooting.

According to the *Los Angeles Times*, photos of Noah Pozner with pornographic and antisemitic content have been distributed on websites. Lenny Pozner believes his family became a particular target because they were the most openly Jewish family that lost a child, and because his wife was speaking publicly about gun control.

There has been much discussion recently about whether being anti-Israel (or opposed to specific policies of the Israeli government) is the same as being antisemitic. Some people, such as neo-Nazis, are both, but others are not.

There are some even Jews, *including Jews who live in Israel,* who think the country should not exist. **Neturei Karta** (literally "Guardians of the City") is a group of Haredi Jews, created in Jerusalem during the British Mandate of Palestine in 1938. Neturei Karta opposes secular Zionism and calls for dismantling the State of Israel in the belief that Jews are forbidden to have their own state until the arrival of the Jewish Messiah. While the Neturei Karta consider themselves true Jews, the **Anti-Defamation League** has described them as "the farthest fringes of Judaism."

Neturei Karta states that no official count of members exists. The Jewish Virtual Library puts their numbers at 5,000, while the Anti-Defamation League estimates that fewer than 100 members take part in anti-Israel activism.

Neturei Karta asserts that the mass media deliberately downplays their viewpoint and makes them out to be few in number. Their protests in America are usually attended by, at most, a few dozen people. In Israel, the group's protests typically include several hundred people.

According to the ADL, members of Neturei Karta have a long history of extremist statements and support for notable anti-Zionists and Islamists.

Neturei Karta says: "The Jewish faith and Zionism are two very different philosophies. They are as opposite as day and night. The Jewish people have existed for thousands of years. In their two thousand years of Divinely decreed exile no Jew ever sought to end this exile and establish independent political sovereignty anywhere. The people's sole purpose was the study and fulfillment of the Divine commandments of the Torah."

Members stress that the Jewish people went into exile from Israel because of their sins. Additionally, members insist that any form of forceful recapture of the Israel is a violation of Divine will. They believe that the restoration of Israel to the Jews should happen only with the coming of the Messiah, not by self-determination.

Neturei Karta is not a Hasidic but a *Litvish* group; they are often mistaken for Hasidim because their style of dress is very similar to that of Hasidim. Most members of Neturei Karta are descendants of Hungarian and Lithuanian Jews who settled in Jerusalem in the early 19th century. They were vocal opponents of Zionism that was attempting to assert Jewish sovereignty in Ottoman-controlled Palestine. They resented the new arrivals, who were predominantly non-religious, while they asserted that Jewish redemption could be brought about only by the Jewish Messiah.

Other Orthodox Jewish movements, including some who oppose Zionism, have denounced Neturei Karta. According to *The Guardian*, "Neturei Karta are regarded as a wild fringe." Neturei Karta's website states that its members "frequently participate in public burning of the Israeli flag." In July 2013, the Shin Bet (Israel's Security Agency) arrested a member of Neturei Karta for allegedly attempting to spy on Israel for Iran.

The Chabad Lubavitch group is theologically conservative, but very much pro-Israel. According to Rabbi Schneuer Wilhelm, Chabad Rebbe Menachem Schneerson was a "big fan of Zionism," but warned that "Zionism is not a replacement for religion."

After two men associated with Neturei Karta participated in a 2004 prayer vigil for Yasser Arafat outside the hospital in Paris where he lay on his death bed, Neturei Karta was widely condemned by other Orthodox Jewish organizations, including other anti-Zionist organizations.

Neturei Karta leader Moshe Hirsch from Jerusalem and an "impressive contingent" of other members attended Arafat's funeral in Ramallah. In the USA, Neturei Karta is led by Moshe Ber Beck. He courted controversy by meeting with Louis Farrakhan, the Nation of Islam leader accused of inciting antisemitism and describing Judaism as a "gutter religion" (Farrakhan insists his words were misinterpreted).

BDS is the abbreviation for **Boycott, Divestment and Sanctions,** a Palestinian-led campaign promoting various forms of boycott (economic, arts, education) against Israel until it meets what the campaign describes as Israel's obligations under international law. This is defined as withdrawal from the occupied territories, removal of the separation barrier in the West Bank, full equality for Arab-Palestinian citizens of Israel, and "respecting, protecting, and promoting the rights of Palestinian refugees to return to their homes and properties."

The campaign is organized and coordinated by the Palestinian BDS National Committee and seeks support from municipal governments, student groups, politicians, performers and others. Several American politicians strongly *support* BDS. Some groups and public people have been vocal in their *opposition* to BDS.

Protests and conferences in support of the campaign have been held in several countries. There is at least one pro-BDS website and Facebook group, and pro-BDS protests have been common on American college campuses. BDS supporters compare BDS to the 20th-century anti-apartheid movement and view their actions similar to the boycotts of South Africa during its apartheid era.

Critics of BDS reject its charge that Israel is an apartheid state, asserting that in Israel (outside of the West Bank) "Jews and Arabs mix freely and increasingly live in the same neighborhoods... there is no imposed segregation." Critics have also argued that the BDS movement is antisemitic, drawing analogies to the Nazi boycott of Jewish businesses and accusing it of promoting the delegitimization of Israel.

Rabbi Jaymee Alpert told her Northern California congregation that "BDS might masquerade as an activist group, but in reality, it is a hate group that gives license to its followers to hate both Israel and Jews."

The **American Zionist Movement** "declares anti-semitism to be among the foremost challenges facing the American Jewish community today, and that the AZM will mobilize its constituent organizations to coalesce in an effort to educate Americans about antisemitism and to recognize, identify, call-out, and condemn antisemitism ..."

AZM says: "While democratic principles allow room for individuals to openly disagree with actions taken by a government, any attempt to delegitimize Israel's right to exist must be acknowledged as a form of antisemitism. This includes making inflammatory remarks or factually inaccurate claims accusing Israel of operating as an apartheid state or a perpetrator of genocide. Stories fabricated to falsely represent international Jewish or Zionist influence and control have become part of the national discourse—engendering dangerous antisemitic attitudes that now permeate aspects of the media, academia, and politics. Elected officials and candidates for office—including from major political parties—have adopted anti-Israel and antisemitic agendas, rhetoric, affiliations, and associations. Regardless of party affiliation, it is deeply concerning that there is a growing acceptance of such harmful ideologies."

Piotr Cywiński, director of the Auschwitz-Birkenau State Museum in Poland, told the *New York Times*: "If you are speaking with somebody who is defending some anti-Israeli ideologies, maybe not in the first minute, maybe not in the second minute, but in the third minute you will find that the same old story accusing Jews of every bad thing in the world. For me, that's very, very clear. I never saw any anti-Israeli theory that was not antisemitic. I can't see why people feel free to compare Israel to the Nazis. It's an insult to the victims and an insult to the survivors and an insult to a whole country, to a whole society."

A fictional pro-semite (from *The Chosen Image: Television's Portrayal of Jewish Themes and Characters,* by Jonathan Pearl & Judith Pearl)

The plight of Holocaust survivors seeking to enter British-ruled Palestine was recounted in uncommon detail in a 1985 episode of the popular detective series *Magnum, P.I.* This description presents an unusual picture of a British soldier in Palestine with feelings of sympathy and justice for the arriving Jewish refugees. An elderly Holocaust survivor, Rabbi Solomon, recounts to the series' hero Thomas Magnum the origins of his friendship with Magnum's British associate, Higgins, explaining that immediately after the war, the rabbi and some friends sought to enter Palestine, "then ruled by the British, and for Jews it was impossible to emigrate — they wouldn't allow it. Naturally it didn't stop us." Under the cover of night, they took a lifeboat from the ship they were on to reach the shore, but "when we got there, there was a British patrol standing there. *Got in himmel!* ... I was looking straight into that British soldier's face. I could see the struggle in his eyes. And all of a sudden he made a smart left turn as if he never saw us and walked away, leaving us free to scatter into the dark and to freedom."

Years later, Rabbi Solomon went on to explain, he spotted the soldier in London, embraced and thanked him and asked, "'How could a British soldier disobey a standing order?' And he answered very calmly, 'I was obeying a higher law that does not permit me to shoot unarmed refugees looking for a home.'"

I should note a coincidental Jewish connection: Jonathan Quayle Higgins III had a first name from the Torah.

Jonathan (*Y'honatan* in Hebrew) was the eldest son of Saul, the first king of Israel, and a close friend of David, who succeeded Saul as king.

Higgins was played by John Hillerman (1932-2017).

Chapter 8
Baptists, Anabaptists, Southern Baptists, Etc. Snakes, too

The photo shows the author (not Neptune) in Fort Lauderdale.

I love the water. I've often said that if God never got around to creating dry land, I would not complain. Water is a source of life, of fun, of food—and it's a means of travel and transportation. The human body is about half water (but beware of *water on the brain* and *water on the knee).*

When the Coast Guard issues a "Small Craft Warning," I hear "Surf's Up, Dude!" I can float for hours even in a choppy ocean, and I once nearly died when the tiny sailboat I was using almost got swept into the Atlantic Ocean during a horrible windstorm in Bermuda.

Although I love burgers, ribs and steaks, I prefer clams, scallops and lobsters. My father started taking me "deep sea fishing" when I was just three years old.

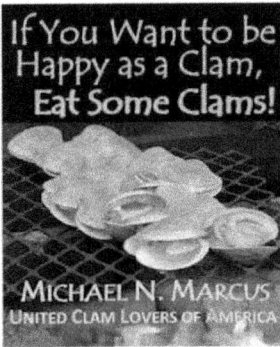

If You Want to be Happy as a Clam, Eat Some Clams!

MICHAEL N. MARCUS
UNITED CLAM LOVERS OF AMERICA

I used to be a SCUBA diver, and even dove under ice. In a high school swimming test I swam four laps of the pool *under water*. I still have my Red Cross "Water Safety Instructor" and "Senior Life Saver" patches earned over six decades ago. (Could I save myself now?)

I sometimes stay in the shower until the hot water runs out. The wet heat can be extremely invigorating—like a Finnish sauna or a Roman steam bath (*schvitz* in Yiddish). On the other hand I like my drinking water as cold as possible, even with slush forming in it.

Water is relaxing—and also stimulating. It soothes my aching body parts, and activates my brain. I've done some of my best creative work when wet: planning books and writing speeches. I sing wet, too.

My last name comes from Mars, the Roman god of war. It would be more appropriate for me to be not Michael Marcus, but **Michael Neptune**, named for the god of water.

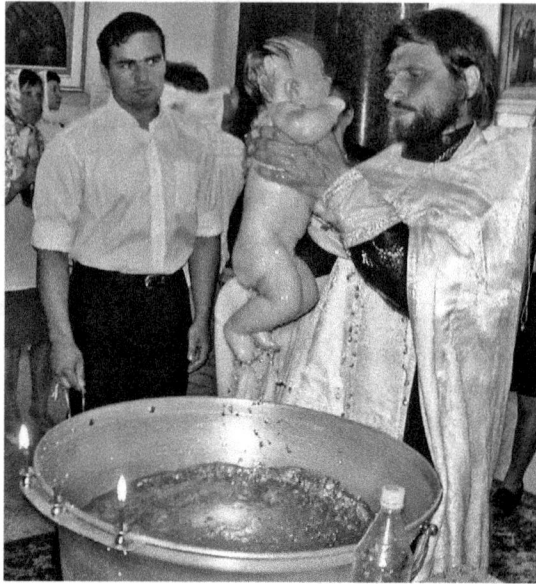

So, with this affinity for all things hydro, you might think that I gladly jumped into a baptismal font years ago. But no. I never got baptized (above)—nor have I dipped in a Jewish *mikveh* pool (below).

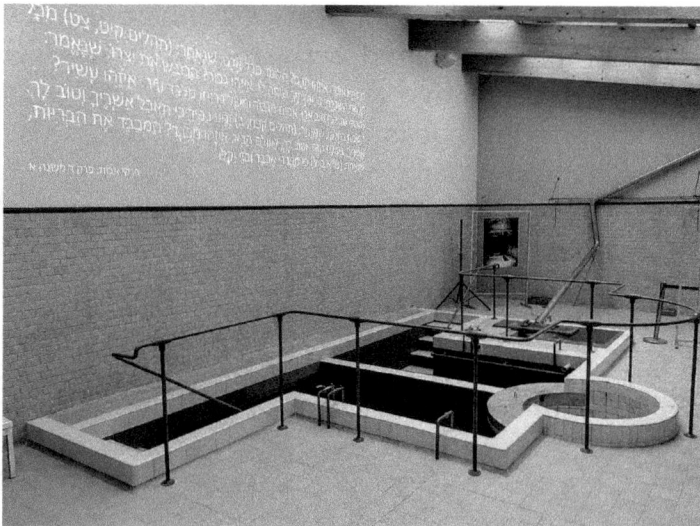

Baptism is a common (and varied) ritual in Christianity: the wetting of a baby, or a convert, child or adult who is committing to Christianity. Baptism is sometimes called **christening**, although that term is often reserved for the baptism of infants. The physical process and the amount of water vary among Christian groups. **Affusion** is baptism where water is poured on the head of the person being baptized. Other methods include **total submersion** baptism, **partial immersion** baptism, and **aspersion** (sprinkling).

Christian denominations which baptize by aspersion or affusion do not deny the legitimacy of baptizing by submersion or immersion; they simply consider the use of less water to be sufficient.

Affusion and aspersion tend to be practiced by Christian denominations that practice infant baptism. This may be due to the difficulty of totally submerging an infant—or reluctance by parents. Some Eastern Orthodox and Roman Catholics practice infant immersion. Amish, Old Order Mennonites and Conservative Mennonites practice baptism by affusion.

I know a Catholic woman who completely submerged her infant son in a pool for a moment—not for baptism but as a test of the Mammalian Diving Reflex. The boy survived the test just fine and later had no fear of the water.

Pastor Mike Bulkley of my nearby Kingdom Life Church traces his spiritual lineage to a renegade reverend who came to the USA from England in 1635—just a few years after the Pilgrims arrived.

Pastor Mike told me his church has performed baptisms in nearby Long Island Sound (which connects to the Atlantic Ocean), as well as in a large indoor tank. Baptisms are scheduled several times a year for participants who request it, not merely those who reach a certain age.

Pastor Mike's own daughter surprised him by requesting Baptism when she was seven years old—with no parental prompting.

Although many churches baptize infants, at Kingdom Life, children must be at least seven years old to participate. This is known as "believer's baptism" (as opposed to "infant baptism"). This makes sense to me. Infant baptism requires the approval of one parent who is already a member of the religious group, but no consent from the baby.

Saint John the Baptist is one of several Saint Johns. He was a Jewish traveling preacher in the early first century

CE and is said to have been a cousin of Jesus. John baptized many people, including Jesus in the Jordan River (earlier illustration).

According to John Piper (chancellor of Bethlehem College & Seminary) "My answer to the question of why Jesus insisted on being baptized is that this new people who were being gathered by John the Baptist on the basis of repentance and faith, not on the basis of Jewishness, would need to be justified. They would need to be counted righteous, because they weren't righteous. They would need to have a righteousness not their own. That righteousness included the fulfillment of all righteousness in life, the life of Jesus. All the righteousness that would be required of men before the court of God, Jesus performed. So he joined fallen humanity, for whom he was providing righteousness by sharing their baptism."

Most Christian denominations view the baptism of Jesus as a very important event and it's a basis for the rite of baptism. In Eastern Christianity, Jesus's baptism is commemorated on January 6, the Feast of **Epiphany** (an "ah-ha" moment). In the Roman Catholic Church, the Anglican Communion, the Lutheran churches and some other Western denominations, it is noted on the first Sunday following the Epiphany feast.

Baptism is one of the oldest Christian rituals, going back to the earliest days. It may be based on *tvilah*, a Jewish purification ritual of immersing in water, which is required for conversion to Judaism—and after menstruation, ejaculation and contact with an unclean animal carcass or human corpse. Tvilah is repeatable, but baptism is to be performed on a person just once in a lifetime. Some Jewish men and women frequently go to mikveh baths, but most never do.

The earliest Baptist churches in North America were founded in 1639 by Roger Williams and John Clarke in Rhode Island. **The Great Awakening** (a revitalization of religious piety in the 1730s in England and its American colonies) helped the Baptist religion to gain huge growth. Baptists became the largest Christian denomination in many southern states.

Roger Williams was a London-born Puritan minister, theologian and author who founded the Colony of Rhode Island and Providence Plantations. It later became the state of Rhode Island.

He was a staunch advocate for the abolition of slavery, for religious freedom, fair dealings with American Indians and separation of church and state.

Williams was expelled by the Puritan leaders from the Massachusetts Bay Colony for spreading "new and dangerous ideas," and he established the Providence Plantations in 1636 as a refuge offering what he called "liberty of conscience." He studied Indian languages and wrote the first book about the Narragansett Indian language, and he organized the first attempt to prohibit slavery in any of the colonies.

Many Baptist churches are affiliated with organizations such as the **Southern Baptist Convention**, formed in 1845. There also are many smaller groups, and Baptist churches that are independent of any organization. Most of the groups share basic beliefs about religion, but there are some disagreements such as the use of "speaking in tongues." There were also disagreements about national issues—notably slavery.

In the First Great Awakening, Methodist and Baptist preachers had opposed slavery and urged freeing of slaves, but over the decades they made an accommodation with slavery. They worked with slaveholders in the South to urge a paternalistic institution. Both denominations made direct appeals to slaves and free blacks for conversion. Baptists allowed blacks to have active roles in congregations. In the late 1700s some black Baptists began to organize separate churches, associations and mission efforts. After the Civil War, freed slaves formed churches and multi-church organizations

By the mid-19th century, northern Baptists tended to oppose slavery, but Southern Baptist Convention churches believed that the **Bible sanctions slavery** and that it was acceptable for Christians to own slaves. They believed that Baptist beliefs could make treatment of slaves less harsh. Many plantation owners were Baptists, and some prominent preachers owned slaves who worked on their plantations.

After the Civil War white preachers in Alabama expressed the view that God had given them a special mission to maintain "traditional" race relations. Slavery, they insisted, had *not* been sinful. Rather, emancipation was a historical tragedy and the end of Reconstruction was a clear sign of God's favor.

According to the usually authoritative Wikipedia, "Black preachers interpreted the Civil War, Emancipation and Reconstruction as: "God's gift of freedom." They long identified with Jews freed from slavery in the Book of Exodus. Freed blacks formed their own churches, associations and conventions to operate freely without white supervision. Black preachers said that God would protect black people.

The Southern Baptist Convention supported disenfranchising most blacks and many poor whites at the turn of the 20th century by raising barriers to voter registration, and passage of racial segregation laws. Its members largely resisted the civil rights movement in the South, which sought to enforce their Constitutional rights for public access and voting; and enforcement of midcentury federal civil rights laws."

In 1995, the Southern Baptist Convention adopted a resolution renouncing its racist roots and apologizing for its past defense of slavery. The resolution declared that delegates (called "messengers") would "unwaveringly denounce racism, in all its forms, as deplorable sin" and "lament and repudiate historic acts of evil such as slavery from which we continue to reap a bitter harvest." It offered an **apology to all African Americans** for "condoning and/or perpetuating individual and systemic racism in our lifetime" and repentance for "racism of which we have been guilty, whether consciously or unconsciously." Although Southern Baptists had condemned racism in the past, this was the first time the Convention, predominantly white since the Reconstruction era, had specifically addressed the issue of slavery.

In 2012 delegates at the SBC annual meeting elected New Orleans pastor Fred Luter by acclamation to lead the group—the first black head of the SBC.

> In the USA, Baptists are numerically most dominant in the Southeast. In 2007, the Pew Research Center's Religious Landscape Survey found that 45% of all African Americans identify with Baptist denominations.

Baptist theology and history can be confusing. So can labels. Some people confuse *anabaptism* with *antibaptism*, (I did) but they are very different. The name *Anabaptist* means someone who baptizes *again*. Their persecutors named them this, referring to the practice of baptizing people when they converted or declared their faith in Christ, even if they had been baptized as infants.

Anabaptists required that baptismal candidates be able to make a confession of faith that is freely chosen, and so rejected baptism of infants. The early members of this movement did not accept the name Anabaptist, claiming that infant baptism was not part of scripture and was therefore null and void. They said that baptizing self-confessed believers was their *first true baptism*.

There are about four million Anabaptists in the world. The most numerous include Mennonites, German Baptists, Amish and Hutterites. There are also some smaller Anabaptist groups.

There are large cultural differences between assimilated Anabaptists, who do not differ much from evangelicals or mainline Protestants, and traditional groups like the Amish, Old Colony Mennonites, Old Order Mennonites, Hutterites and Old German Baptist Brethren.

The early Anabaptists formulated their beliefs in Switzerland in 1527. Other Christian groups, such as Baptists with different roots, practice believer's baptism—but these groups are not considered to be Anabaptists.

Snake handling, and even **venom drinking**, are rare but conspicuous religious rites in some isolated, mostly rural, evangelical churches. The practice began in the early 20th century in Appalachia and practitioners believe serpent handling dates to antiquity and quote the Bible to support the activity:

- "And these signs shall follow them that believe: In my name shall they cast out devils; they shall speak with new tongues. They shall take up serpents; and if they drink any deadly thing, it shall not hurt them; they shall lay hands on the sick, and they shall recover."
- "Behold, I give unto you power to tread on serpents and scorpions, and over all the power of the enemy: and nothing shall by any means hurt you."
- "And when they were escaped, then they knew that the island was called Melita. And the barbarous people shewed us no little kindness: for they kindled a fire, and received us every one, because of the present rain, and because of the cold. And when Paul had gathered a bundle of sticks, and laid them on the fire, there came a viper out of the heat, and fastened on his hand. And when the barbarians saw the venomous beast hang on his hand, they said among themselves, No doubt this man is a murderer, whom, though he hath escaped the sea, yet vengeance suffereth not to live. And he shook off the beast into the fire, and felt no harm. Howbeit they looked when he should have swollen, or fallen down dead suddenly: but after they had looked a great while, and saw no harm come to him, they changed their minds, and said that he was a god."

The snake handlers do not worship snakes, but use them to show non-Christians that God protects them. In religious services, handlers reach into boxes, pick up venomous snakes and hold them up as they pray, sing and dance. Injured handlers often shun medical care. Those who die from snakebites are never criticized for lack of adequate faith; it is said that it was simply their time to die. Snake handling is illegal in several states.

To me, the Sun is as Vital as Water

Many ancient societies considered the sun to be a god. (The Egyptian sun god "Ra" is shown here.) The deification is not surprising, because the solar orb provides light and heat and helps crops to grow.

In our current effort to use non-fossil-fuel energy sources, an increasing number of homes and businesses have solar collectors on their roofs to produce electricity, and to heat water.

Solar-powered boats, cars and planes have been demonstrated, and the International Space Station has huge arrays of solar panels that generate electricity to charge batteries necessary for human habitation and science experiments. I own solar-powered calculators and a solar-powered radio. There are also solar-powered stoves, traffic lights and cell phone chargers.

I use the sun to charge my *internal* battery. It's as important and pleasing to me as my beloved water. On a lazy summer day, if my wife asks me what I want to do, I often reply with our private acronym: "**LITSLAOD.**" That means "**Lie In The Sun Like An Old Dog.**" The sun makes old dogs feel good, and old men too (if I don't get sunburn).

Chapter 9
Is The Episcopal Church Almost As Good As Catholic?

I'm a liberal Jew. I like the Episcopal Church for its liberal, enlightened attitudes on women's rights (women can be priests), LBGTQ rights and race relations. However, in early America, some Episcopalians—even priests—owned slaves, an issue now being addressed.

According to the Episcopal News Service, "Slavery is a thread stitched indelibly throughout the early history of the Episcopal Church in Maryland, where congregations to varying degrees enabled, benefited from or fought against the enslavement of Africans until slavery was outlawed. In Annapolis, St. Margaret's [Church] owned a plantation in the century where up to 100 enslaved laborers worked, and slaves likely built most of the congregation's early structures.

Over on the west end of the state, Emmanuel Church is well known today for once being a stop on the Underground Railroad, helping slaves escape north to freedom.

'Not everyone likes to deal with the history of slavery,' said Reba Bullock, who leads the diocese's Research and Pilgrimage Working Group. The group works with congregations to uncover such historical details, and it now is recruiting more churches to join the effort.

'Sometimes there is reluctance, but once they get on board they get excited because they find out things about the the church that they didn't know,' Bullock said.

In one congregation, Bullock said, a local professor discovered that slaves attended Sunday worship services in a balcony apart from the white members of the congregation, and some slaves had been buried in the church's graveyard.

The *Trail of Souls* website includes information on Emmanuel Church, which likely became a stop on the Underground Railroad after the arrival of the Rev. David Hillhouse Buel, who was active in the effort to free slaves. The congregation may not even have been aware at the time that the church was being used by the Underground Railroad, according to its Trail of Souls page.

'I would advise people to not be afraid,' Rev. Angela Shepherd said. "I think people are afraid of discovering the truth of the past, but I think the call to reconciliation is a call to be reconciled to our past.'"

The Episcopal Church is an American institution formed as part of the rebellion in the Revolutionary War against England, and has since expanded worldwide. It is an outgrowth of the ("Anglican") Church of England. It has no founder like Martin Luther or Joseph Smith.

Anglicanism emerged in the 16th and 17th centuries, combining Catholic doctrine taught by the established church in England and Protestant doctrines, notably Calvinism and Lutheranism, brought to England from abroad.

At the time of the English Reformation in the 16th century, the Church of England represented the Catholic Church in England. The Reformation did not disregard all previous doctrines. It kept core Catholic beliefs and some Catholic teachings which other Protestant groups rejected. Anglican doctrine is often said to tread a middle path between Roman Catholic and Protestant practices.

A distinctive English variety of Christianity was summarized in the **Thirty-Nine Articles of Religion** which were adopted by Parliament and the Church of England in 1571.

The Articles contain basic Reformed doctrines such as the sufficiency of the Holy Scriptures for salvation. Some of the articles oppose Roman Catholic doctrine, such as Article XXII which rejects Purgatory. Transubstantiation is rejected: i.e. the bread and wine remain bread and wine, but the presence of Christ in the Eucharist is believed.

Before the Reformation, Catholic worship was conducted in Latin, while the Articles required church services to use common speech (i.e., English).

Matt Lindemann is Rector of St. Peter's Church, a venerable 255-year-old neighbor of mine in Milford, Connecticut. Matt says he is the son

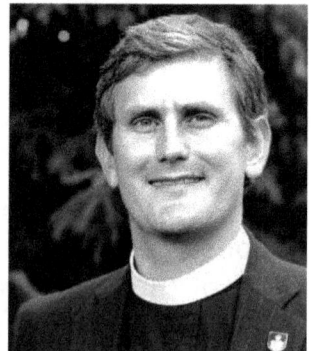

of *two* Episcopal priests and quipped that he was "doomed" to follow them into the family business.

Episcopal titles can be confusing to outsiders like me. Matt is a "priest," and a "reverend" and is addressed as "pastor," "father," "reverend" or even by his first name. In print, he is "The Rev. Matthew J. Lindeman."

Generally, a rector is the priest in charge of a self-supporting parish. The term is derived from the Latin word for "rule" and appears in such words as "correct" and "rectitude." A "rectory" is a house provided by a church for its rector. The title "rector" is also used for the supervisors of schools and universities, but generally not in the United States. Harry Potter's school, **Hogwarts**, was headed by a headmaster, not a rector.

An Episcopal rector has authority and responsibility for worship and the spiritual jurisdiction of the parish, subject to the rules of the church and the direction of the bishop. The rector is responsible for selection of assistant clergy, and they serve at the rector's discretion. The church and parish buildings and furnishings are under the rector's control. Administration at St. Peter's includes a Bishop, a Bishop Suffragan (assisting bishop), two Assisting Priests and others. Bishops don't have desks in the St. Peter's church offices but there is a "bishop's chair" in the sanctuary. A bishop also gets the title "Right Reverend," which sounds a bit fusty to me.

St. Peter's, like many Episcopal churches, has a conspicuous red front door. Rev. Matt said that red is an Episcopal "branding effort." The Episcopal coat of arms, flag, and religious clothing incorporate conspicuous red, too. He explained that "when people are ordained, we wear red, on feast days we wear red. Those are red-letter days."

The use of red doors on churches originated in England during the Middle Ages. It was a commonly recognized sign of sanctuary. If you were being chased by a robber or a sheriff, you would likely be safe if you could reach the red door. Red was also a reminder of Passover and God's covenant with the Israelites and is a symbol for the sacrificial blood of Jesus. It has also been said that church doors were painted red to indicate that their mortgage was paid off. (However, in symbolic financial terms, the church would then be "in the black," not "in the red.")

"I see a red door and I want it painted black."

Rolling Stones Mick Jagger and Keith Richards deny any connection between the lyrics of *Paint It, Black* and an Episcopal church door. But Rev. Matt said, "Who knows? Mick may have been onto something."

The Episcopal Church affirmed in 1976 that homosexual people are "children of God" deserving acceptance by the Church and equal protection by government; and a year later ordained its first openly gay priest, Ellen Barrett. In 2003, the church elected its first openly gay bishop, Gene Robinson, prompting a crisis in the American Episcopalian community and the wider Anglican world.

Leaders of the Anglican Communion's 38 member churches warned that Robinson's consecration would "tear the fabric of the communion at its deepest level." During his ordination ceremony, where his partner was present, Robinson wore a bullet-proof vest beneath his religious clothing and he received death threats following his installation.

In 2009, the Episcopal General Convention ordered theological and liturgical resources for same-sex blessings and gave bishops an option to provide "generous pastoral support," especially where civil authorities have legalized same-gender marriage, civil unions or domestic partnerships.

In the same year the Church's House of Bishops voted that "any ordained ministry" is open to gay men and women. In 2015, a resolution removing the definition of marriage as being between one man and one woman was passed by the House of Bishops. The Archbishop of Canterbury, Justin Welby, expressed "deep concern" over the ruling, and in 2016, Anglican leaders temporarily suspended the Episcopal Church from key positions in the global fellowship.

Disagreement over social issues including gay ordination led to the formation of the more traditional **Anglican Church in North America**, with over 1,000 parishes and 134,000 members. (The 'other' Episcopal Church has about 6,500 churches and 2 million baptized members, mostly in the United States, but about 3 million people self–identified as mainline Episcopalian/Anglican.)

Episcopal Church leaders, particularly former Presiding Bishop Katharine Jefferts Schori, opposed the separatists, with lawsuits against departing dioceses and parishes that have cost an estimated $60 million or more in court costs for both sides! (Perhaps the lawyers inherit the Earth.)

Litigation has mostly dealt with church properties, with the Episcopal leadership asserting ownership of buildings occupied by departing congregations. Schori forbade dioceses from selling parish property to departing groups, stating, "We do not make settlements that encourage religious bodies who seek to replace The Episcopal Church."

After the renegade South Carolina Diocese voted to withdraw from the national Church, it sued to retain control over its property. In the initial court ruling, it kept about

$500 million worth of property. Later, this ruling was substantially overturned by the South Carolina Supreme Court with a split decision that returned the property of 29 parishes plus a camp and conference center to the Episcopal Church in South Carolina, while seven parishes kept properties.

States along the American East Coast generally have a higher percentage of Episcopalians than other parts of the country. New York has the largest total number. The Church had significant growth in the first half of the 20th century, but like many "mainline" churches, it has had a decline recently. Episcopalians tend to be wealthier and better educated than most other religious groups in the United States, and have been disproportionately represented at the tops in American business, law and politics.

The Episcopal Church is decentralized, organized into dioceses led by bishops. The Presiding Bishop directs the national administrative headquarters at 815 Second Avenue in Manhattan, often referred to by Episcopalians simply as "815." This reminds me of the Chabad Jewish practice of referring to its headquarters at 770 Eastern Parkway in Brooklyn as "770."

I asked Rev. Matt if all of the Episcopal churches named "St. Peter's" are in a club. They are not.

Eleven American presidents (so far) have been Episcopalians—more than the followers of any other religion. Every "POTUS" has been a Christian of some type. JFK was the only Catholic.

(above) The Cathedral Church of Saint Peter and Saint Paul in Washington, D.C., is known as the **Washington National Cathedral**. It's not the only famous American Episcopal structure. Manhattan's **Cathedral of St. John the Divine** (below) has been famously under construction since 1892, and no completion date has been announced.

According to Rev. Matt, the ties between religion and government have been a "mixed blessing." "The Spanish Inquisition and the Crusades were geopolitical goals," he said, "under the guise of Christian faith. We live in a new time that our bishops describe as a 'new apostolic age.' In some ways we're back to the *Book of Acts*. We don't have to go to church anymore to succeed in society. A lot of the structural scaffolding that propped up Christendom is starting to erode."

The Episcopal Church is a worldwide religion, not strictly American, despite its founding in the USA. In some countries you might find an Episcopal church next door to an Anglican one. Rev. Matt told me that the Church's international success was one of the beneficial effects of British empire building "like the BBC." Part of the reason for the Episcopal church's worldwide growth, he pointed out, is the ability to "look at scripture, tradition and reason through the lens of experience over time."

The "lens of reason" is also important to Episcopalians. I asked if they accept the Bible literally and he replied, "What we say when we are ordained is that we affirm that the Bible contains all things necessary for salvation. That doesn't mean that I read the Bible cover-to-cover as one coherent document literally and believe that there was a six-day creation with a 26-hour break, just like I don't believe that the Trinity is two dudes and a bird."

The stories in the Bible, Rev. Matt continued, "speak to the character of God... and we are to be stewards of Creation and we are to recognize that the Divine has created and call 'good' everything on the planet, especially now as the Amazon is on fire and we are concerned more with creating shareholder value than we are with the enduring legacy of our planet." That's a very modern and enlightened attitude, especially for an ancient religion that once sanctioned slavery. I am impressed.

Anglican Priests Get Organized

According to one of Britain's largest unions, "Unite," there has been a rapid increase in the number of Anglican parish priests, or vicars, joining its specialist faith worker branch. Almost 1,500 priests plus a few rabbis and imams joined the union in 2018—an increase of 16 percent in 12 months.

The Anglican vicars are joining despite not having the usual British employment rights, because they are termed "officeholders" and cannot take their complaints to an employment tribunal. And while they cannot pursue rights they don't have as members of Unite, they can seek counsel and support there from others familiar with their travails.

Rev. Peter Hobson, who is head of the priests' Unite branch, the Church of England vicars are turning to the union because they are under pressure from all sides—from the people in the pews and from their bishops. "Although it is a vocation, it is also a very difficult role," Hobson said.

"The workload is enormous. In a consumeristic world, people expect you to deal with their needs instantly, and the bishop, while he is a pastoral figure, is also managerial. And the managerial approach is coming more and more to the fore," he said.

And Modernized

In July of 2019, the General Synod of the Anglican Church of Canada voted to remove a longstanding prayer from its liturgy that called for the conversion of the Jewish people to Christianity. The deleted wording will be replaced with a new invocation called: "For Reconciliation with the Jews." Thanks.

(From Religion News Service)

English King Henry VIII married two Annes, two Catherines, one Katherine and a Jane. Maybe he called them all "sweetheart," "darling" or "honey" to avoid fights after using the wrong name.

Henry VIII (previous page) was a Catholic King of England from 1509 until 1547. He is best known for his **six marriages** (to Catherine of Aragon, Anne Boleyn, Jane Seymour, Anne of Cleves, Catherine Howard, Katherine Parr), and the song *"I'm Henery the Eighth, I Am,"* a huge 1965 hit by Herman's Hermits.

Henry wanted to have his first marriage (to Catherine of Aragon) annulled so he could marry Anne Bolyn, whom he hoped would produce a male heir. The Church would not grant the annulment. His disagreement with the Pope led Henry to initiate the English Reformation, separating the Church of England from papal authority. He named himself the Supreme Head of the Church of England (a forerunner to the American Episcopal movement). Henry closed Catholic convents and monasteries, leading to his excommunication.

Anne had a daughter, the future Queen Elizabeth I, but did not produce a male heir and Henry had her committed to the Tower of London on a charge of adultery with various men and even incest with her own brother. She was convicted, and beheaded. The charges may have been false. Henry quickly moved on to wife-number-three, Jane Seymour (not to be confused with *two* actresses using that name), who gave birth to a male heir—the future King Edward VI.

Centuries after Henry's marital misadventures I knew a Catholic woman in the USA, stuck in an unhappy marriage to a Catholic man. She met and wanted to marry another Catholic man. Her local Catholic church, of course, would not grant a divorce. A diocese sometimes provides a "Decree of Nullity" (annulment), but this is uncommon. The woman begged her local parish and diocese and even offered lavish donations all the way up to the Vatican—but, as with Henry VIII, no annulment was provided.

Finally she and hubby got a civil divorce (a sin that would preclude a second wedding in a Catholic church). She and her second man then got married in an *Episcopal* church which, she explained to relatives, **"is almost as good as Catholic."**

She and the second husband slept in separate bedrooms, but that's a story for another book.

Chapter 10
My Muslim Cousins, & An Evil Priest

(Much of this chapter comes from the *Jewish Virtual Library*. I thank them.)

According to religious tradition, Jews and Muslims are sort of Semitic cousins, descending from the first monotheist, Abraham ("Ibrahim" for Muslims), who may have lived in what is now Iraq and Israel in the second millennium BCE.

The complex Biblical family tree reveals that Abraham had two wives who produced two sons: Ishmael (forefather of Muhammad), and Isaac (a Jewish patriarch).

I will not attempt to provide an extensive history of Islam (which was called "Mohammedism" when I was in school). I am more interested in the relations between Muslims and others, and the differences and similarities in traditions, beliefs and practices.

- The Muslim Quran and Jewish Torah have many similarities, and differences. For example, in the Torah, God created man in His own image. In the Quran, God says "There is nothing like unto Him." In the Torah, Noah's Ark settled on the mountains of Ararat. In the Quran, it settled on the hills of Mount Judi.

- Muslim and Jewish boys are circumcised: Jews on their eighth day and Muslims as early as the seventh day and as late as at the onset of puberty. Circumcision is optional for Christians, Hindus and others.

- Jewish dietary restrictions (*Kashrut*) and Muslim dietary restrictions (*Halal*) are similar—but not identical. Both notably forbid pork. Jewish law forbids shellfish but some branches of Islam permit it and others do not. In Islam, meat and dairy products can be consumed together and in Judaism they cannot. Muslim slaughter is accompanied by a prayer, Jewish slaughter does not require a prayer. When I lived in the Bronx in the early 1970s, a local kosher butcher had many Muslim customers because there was no nearby Halal meat market.

- Islam prohibits the consumption of alcohol. Judaism does not. In fact, wine is an important part of some Jewish rituals going back millennia. Even hard liquor is served in some synagogues on *Simchat Torah* ("Rejoicing of the Torah"), a holiday that marks the conclusion of the annual cycle of Torah readings, and the beginning of a new cycle.

- Some branches of Islam and Judaism require extremely modest dress for women, some branches of both religions do not. Mandatory modest dress is uncommon—but not unheard of—for Christians.

- Liberal Jewish congregations may have female leaders, as do liberal Muslim congregations.
- Muslim women have more freedom in Israel than in Muslim countries.
- The Jewish Sabbath (when work is prohibited) runs from Friday at sundown to Saturday at sundown. Muslims have a prayer day on Friday, but various Muslim communities may or may not permit work. Sunday is the Christian Sabbath.
- The Arabic and Hebrew languages are both Semitic, and have many similarities. The Hebrew *shalom aleichem* and Arabic *salaam alekum* both mean "peace to you." The word for "son" is *ben* in Hebrew and *ibn* in Arabic. One Hebrew word for house is *bayit*; in Arabic it's *bayt*.

Muslims have produced some magnificent literature such as the *Rubaiyat* by Omar Khayyam and *The Book of One Thousand and One Nights*. Most Islamic literature is unknown in the West where Christians, Jews and atheists dominate bestseller lists and book awards. However, Western authors have been influenced by Muslims. In Shakespeare's *Othello*, the title character is a Muslim.

Sadly, *The Satanic Verses* (1988) led to death threats against Indian Muslim author Salman Rushdie, including a *fatwā* calling for his assassination from Ayatollah Ruhollah Khomeini, Supreme Leader of Iran. Saudi Arabia is suspected of ordering the assassination and dismemberment of Muslim journalist Amal Khashoggi in 2018.

While the current strife between Israelis and Palestinians echoes troubles going back as far as the pre-Exodus enslavement of Jews in Egypt, there have been long periods of peace and cooperation between the faiths—and even incidents of personal sacrifice and heroism that cross cultures and borders. There have even been Muslim-Jewish marriages. For much of history Muslims and Jews lived together, or nearby, usually in harmony.

Perhaps the best example of cooperation and coexistence was in pre-Inquisition (1492 CE) Spain, in what may be considered a "**golden age**" for Jewish people. Spain hosted one of the largest, most prosperous and intellectually productive Jewish communities in the world. In the city and province of Cordoba, Muslims and Jews built a civilization called "Al-Andalus," which is the source of "Anadalusia," the label for the southern region of modern Spain. Cordoba was more advanced than other cities in Europe and by the tenth century had become the largest city in Europe.

Jewish spiritual, intellectual and economic life flourished and many Jewish people served in Spanish royal courts. Jews in Toledo translated texts into and from Arabic and were important in science, medicine, geography, mathematics, poetry and philosophy.

As mentioned previously, Moses ben Maimon—known as Maimonides and the acronym Rambam—was probably the most famous Jew of this period. He was a philosopher who became one of the most prolific and influential Torah scholars of the Middle Ages and was also an important astronomer and physician. A huge medical center in Brooklyn is named for him. In addition to being revered and respected by Jews, Maimonides is also important in Islamic and Arab sciences and philosophy.

During the golden age in Spain, according to Rebecca Weiner in *Jewish Virtual Library*, "Muslim and Jewish customs and practices became intertwined. For example, Arabic was used for prayers rather than Hebrew or Spanish. Before entering the synagogue, Jews washed their hands and feet, which is a practice done before entering a mosque. Arab melodies were used for

Jewish songs. Jews wore the clothing style of their Moorish neighbors, although they were not allowed to wear silk or furs.

Jews lived peacefully in Al-Andulus for 400 years. The Golden Age for Jewry in Muslim Spain declined after the Almovarids gained power in 1055 and continued to deteriorate after the Almohads came to power in 1147. Jews continued to work as moneylenders, jewelers, cobblers, tailors and tanners, however, they had to wear distinguishing clothing, such as a yellow turban.

The Christians conquered Toledo in 1098 and the Jews in Christian Spain prospered, while those in Muslim Spain suffered under the Almohad dynasty. Both Jews and Muslims were involved in the cultural, economic, intellectual, financial and political life of Christian Spain. By the mid-13th century, the Christians controlled most of Spain and increasingly forced Jews to convert to Christianity. Those who converted became known as Marranos or New Christians. Marranos are also known as crypto-Jews because they taught their children and practiced Judaism in secret."

The old Hebrew name for Spain was *Sepharad* and Jews from Spain and Portugal and their descendents are known as *Sephardim* or *Sephardi*. Their rituals, food, customs and language are distinct from the *Ashkenazim* from Eastern Europe who dominate American Jewish affairs and culture.

In 1391 anti-Jewish riots broke out in several cities in Spain, and Jews were tortured and killed in the Spanish Inquisition during the 15th century. The Inquisition was instigated by Father Tomas de Torquemada who convinced King Ferdinand and Queen Isabella that Jewish people were expendable. In 1492, the royal couple (who financed the exploration voyages of Italian Christopher Columbus) commanded that Jews who refused to convert to Christianity must leave Spain within just four months. About 100,000 Jews left.

Many exiles settled in Portugal, which was initially friendly to Jews—but just for five years. Many Jews from Spain and Portugal who did not convert relocated to North Africa and the Ottoman Empire, where they lived in peaceful coexistence with Muslims for many years—even in Palestine in much of the 20th century. In 1919 Emir Faisal of Iraq wrote a letter to U.S. Supreme Court Justice Felix Frankfurter supporting Zionism: "We Arabs...wish the Jews a most hearty welcome." However, a simmering Zionist fervor incited Arab jealousy and violence.

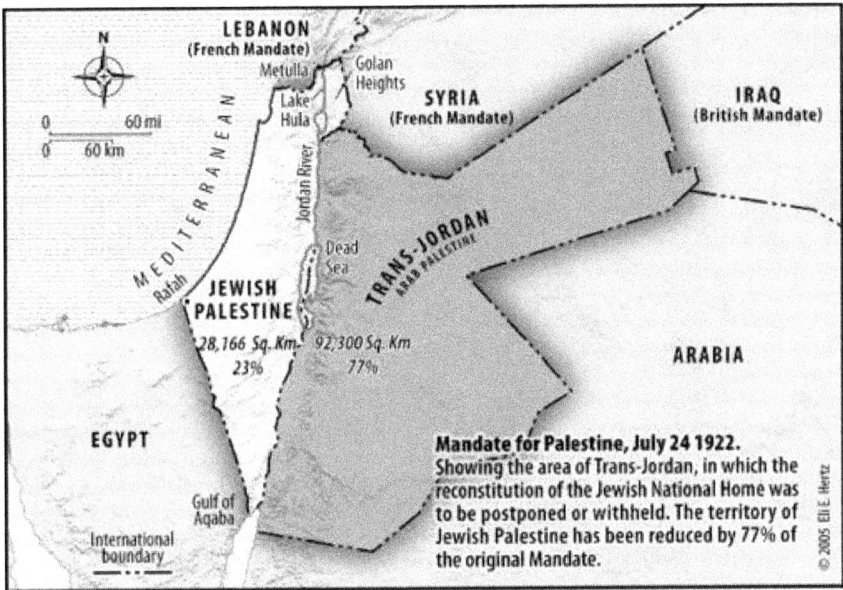

Mandate for Palestine, July 24 1922. Showing the area of Trans-Jordan, in which the reconstitution of the Jewish National Home was to be postponed or withheld. The territory of Jewish Palestine has been reduced by 77% of the original Mandate.

(Above) In the 1920s the League of Nations (a United Nations precursor) tried to separate the European-dominated "Mandates" in the region into separate Jewish and Muslim nations, but the plan failed. The League granted administration of the former Turkish territories of Syria and Lebanon to France; and Palestine, Transjordan, and Mesopotamia (Iraq) to Britain.

Muslim Transjordan was established with about 75% of the British Mandate area, forbidding Jewish immigration, and left about 25% for the new Jewish national homeland.

A British royal commission of inquiry traveled to Palestine to investigate causes of Arab-Jewish conflict and to propose solutions. In 1937 the commission recommended abolishing the Mandate and partitioning the country between the two peoples (a possible solution for Israel still being discussed as this book is being written).

Until the establishment of the two nations, the commission recommended that Jews should be prohibited from purchasing land in the area granted to the Arabs.

Again, in 1939, a British white paper called for the establishment of an Arab state in Palestine within 10 years, and for limiting Jewish immigration to no more than 75,000 over the following five years. Afterward, no one would be allowed in without the consent of the Arab population. Though the Arabs had been granted a concession on Jewish immigration, and been offered independence—the goal of Arab nationalists—they repudiated the white paper.

When the magnitude of the Holocaust became known as World War II ended, there was increased demand for a resolution to the Palestine issue so Holocaust survivors could have a sanctuary. The British tried to work out an agreement acceptable to both Arabs and Jews, but failed and turned the issue over to the United Nations in 1947. The conflicting national aspirations of Jews and Arabs could *not* be reconciled.

The Jews of Palestine were not satisfied with the small territory allotted to them by the UN Commission, nor were they happy that Jerusalem was severed from the Jewish State; nevertheless, they welcomed the compromise. Arabs rejected the UN' recommendations.

As the partition vote approached, it became clear that little hope existed for a political solution to a problem that transcended politics: the Arabs' unwillingness to accept a Jewish state in Palestine and the refusal of the Zionists to settle for anything less.

Arab League Secretary Azzam Pasha told Jewish Agency representatives David Horowitz and Abba Eban: "The Arab world is not in a compromising mood. It's likely, Mr. Horowitz, that your plan is rational and logical, but **the fate of nations is not decided by rational logic. Nations never concede; they fight**. You won't get anything by peaceful means or compromise. You can, perhaps, get something, but only by the force of your arms. We shall try to defeat you. I am not sure we'll succeed, but we'll try. We were able to drive out the Crusaders, but on the other hand we lost Spain and Persia. It may be that we shall lose Palestine. But it's too late to talk of peaceful solutions."

The proposed boundaries were based solely on demographics, with no consideration for security; the new Jewish state's frontiers were virtually indefensible. Though Jews were allotted more total land, the majority of that land was in the desert. Further complicating the situation was the UN's insistence that Jerusalem remain apart from *both* states and be administered as an international zone. This arrangement would leave more than 100,000 Jews in Jerusalem isolated from their country and surrounded by the Arab state—much as Berlin was within East Germany until reunification of the 'two Germanys.'

In the mid 20th century, Jewish residents of Palestine (who may be labeled as freedom fighters or terrorists, depending on your viewpoint), carried out many attacks against the British military forces.

On May 14, 1948 the State of Israel declared its independence. American President Harry S. Truman recognized

Israel within its first hour of existence and Arab armies invaded the new nation in a 14-month war. Since independence there have been major wars, frequent guerilla attacks, land grabs and failed peace talks.

After the Israeli independence, conditions for Jews in many Islamic countries grew uncomfortable—or unsafe. Few Jews remain in Yemen, Tunisia, Libya, Morocco, Syria, Iraq, Iran and Egypt—which once had large, flourishing Jewish communities. Interestingly, Israel now has mostly peaceful relations with Egypt, Jordan, Lebanon and Saudi Arabia. They all fear Iran.

As I was completing this book, Matti Friedman wrote in the *New York Times*: "No single episode has shaped Israel's population and politics like the wave of suicide bombings perpetrated by Palestinians in the first years of the 21st century. Much of what you see here in 2019 is the aftermath of that time, and every election since has been held in its shadow. The attacks, which killed hundreds of Israeli civilians, ended hopes for a negotiated peace and destroyed the left, which was in power when the wave began. Any sympathy that the Israeli majority had toward Palestinians evaporated."

My Plan for Mideast Peace
(for when I am king of the world)

1. Gaza and Golan become parts of Israel.
2. A chunk of the West Bank ("Judea and Samaria") becomes "Palestine," perhaps as a territory or protectorate of Jordan.
3. No homes are destroyed. Nobody has to move. Anybody can live anywhere with full citizenship rights.
4. Create lush resorts on the Mediterranean shore in Gaza, perhaps built and operated by casino billionaire Sheldon Adelson, a major supporter of Israel.

Although the last century has been fraught with frequent violence between Muslims and Jews, there have been noteworthy, encouraging exceptions.

- During the Holocaust, Muslims in Europe and the Middle East saved the lives of thousands of Jews, and some have been honored as "Righteous Among the Nations" in Israel's Yad Vashem Holocaust Memorial.
- Despite frequent cross-border attacks between Israel and its Arab neighbors, Israeli doctors frequently have treated and saved the lives of 'enemy' soldiers and civilians.
- It's not unusual to find businesses in Israel operated by Jews and Muslim partners.
- In the United States, after terrorist attacks on mosques and synagogues, Muslims and Jews quickly helped each other with money, marchers and prayer space.
- Canadian and American synagogues recently helped to resettle hundreds of Muslim refugees from Afghanistan and Syria.
- New York City's oldest Jewish bagel shop was rescued by two Muslim men. Peerzada Shah and Zafaryab Ali took over the 91-year-old "Coney Island Bialys and Bagels." Ali once worked as a baker there and contacted Shah when he heard the shop was closing. Sadly, the rescue was apparently short-lived.
- However, in Montreal, Canada, Falafel St. Jacques seems to be thriving, and is described as "one-part Jewish, one-part Muslim, and equal parts healthy(ish) and delicious. Everything is vegetarian and the fake meat shish taouk is almost as perfect as the falafel, which is arguably the most perfect in town."
- Abu Dhabi, capital of the United Arab Emirates—which has no official relationship with Israel—announced the construction of a multi-faith complex called the "Abrahamic Family House" which will include a synagogue.
- Morocco has restored Jewish historical sites and encourages Jewish tourism.

Chapter 11
Do Methodists Use
The Method?

We need to clarify some things to eschew ambiguity.

Method acting is a collection of techniques for actors, intended to encourage sincere and emotionally expressive performances, based on a system conceived by Russian actor and director Konstantin Stanislavski. It was further developed by Lee Strasberg, Stella Adler and Sanford Meisner in the United States. In 1951 Strasberg became director of the nonprofit Actors Studio in Manhattan, considered to be "the nation's most prestigious acting school" and in 1966 he helped launch Actors Studio West in Los Angeles.

Strasberg's students include many prominent American actors of the latter half of the 20th century, including Marilyn Monroe (shown on the previous page), Paul Newman, Al Pacino, George Peppard, Dustin Hoffman, James Dean, Jane Fonda and Jack Nicholson.

Rhythm Method is a birth control system favored by the Catholic Church. It aims to avoid pregnancy by limiting sexual intercourse to times each month when a woman is considered infertile. The Church taught that all other methods of birth control were sinful, and the rhythm method was a main form of birth control available to Catholics for a long time.

Most menstrual cycles have several days at the beginning that are infertile, a period of fertility and then several days just before the next menstruation that are infertile.

To use the rhythm method, a woman is required to know the details of her menstrual cycles, which can vary.

Imperfect uses of the method include not correctly tracking the length of a woman's cycles or of having unprotected intercourse on a fertile day. The discipline required to keep accurate records of menstrual cycles, and to abstain from unprotected intercourse, lead to a typical failure rate of 25% per year. Many babies have been born due to failures of the rhythm method.

JOKE TIME:
(Q) What do you call a woman who uses the rhythm method?
(A) "Mommy"

Methodism is a Protestant denomination based on teachings of John Wesley, Charles Wesley and George Whitefield—students and friends at Oxford in the 1700s. They became known as "Methodists" because of the methodical way in which they carried out their Christian faith, and John Wesley later used the term "Methodist" for their methodical pursuit of biblical holiness.

Methodism originated as a revival movement in the Church of England and became a separate denomination after John Wesley's death in 1791. Methodism spread in the British Empire, North America and beyond because of vigorous missionary work.

There are about 80 million Methodists worldwide and Methodism is reportedly the second largest Protestant group in the United States (after Southern Baptists), with 8 million adherents.

Methodist theology—according to Wesley—focuses on sanctification and the effect of faith on the character of a Christian. Doctrines include **new birth** ("that great change which God works in the soul when he brings it into life, when he raises it from the death of sin to the life of righteousness"), **assurance** ("neither more nor less than hope; or a conviction, wrought in us by the Holy Ghost, that we have a measure of the true faith in Christ..."), **imparted righteousness** (the gracious gift of God given at the moment of the new birth which enables a Christian disciple to strive for holiness and sanctification), the possibility of **entire sanctification** (a work of grace received by faith that removed inbred or original sin, and this allowed the Christian to enter a state of perfect love—"Love excluding sin"), **works of piety**, and the **primacy of Scripture.**

Most Methodists accept that Jesus Christ was the Son of God, died for all of humanity and that salvation is available for all. This rejects the Calvinist position that God has pre-ordained the salvation of a select group of people. However, Whitefield and several other early leaders of the movement were considered to be "Calvinistic Methodists."

Methodism emphasizes charity and support for the sick, the poor and the afflicted through the works of mercy. These ideals are known as the **Social Gospel** and have led to establishment of hospitals, orphanages, soup kitchens and schools to spread the faith and serve all people.

Early Methodists came from all levels of society, including the aristocracy—but preachers sought laborers and criminals likely to be unreached by other religions. In the United States, Methodism became the religion of many slaves who later formed black Methodist churches.

Denominations that descend from the British Methodist tradition are generally less ritualistic, while American Methodism is more so. Methodism is known for its rich musical tradition, and Charles Wesley wrote many hymns.

My local Methodist church goes back to 1836. **Mary Taylor Memorial United Methodist Church** is named to honor Mary Anna Meyer Taylor, the first wife of Henry Augustus Taylor (1839-1899), a wealthy New York businessman.

The Late-Gothic-Revival-style church is notably warm and inviting. It says: "Our welcome knows no boundaries. We recognize and celebrate the diversity of God's creation and God's gifts. As disciples of our Lord, we publicly acknowledge, welcome and support people of all races, genders, sexual orientations and gender identities, ages, nationalities, ethnicities, abilities and socio-economic situations. We are committed to follow Christ's teaching and example by heeding his call to feed the hungry, welcome the stranger, preach the good news, teach our children and youth, and visit the sick, homebound and imprisoned."

Methodists have great diversity, including "people with a wide range of understandings and what joins us together is a commitment to grow in grace and in the knowledge of God and a further commitment to serve our sisters and brothers, whoever they may be, in the name of Jesus Christ."... "This is not a 'creedal' church, which is to say that there is not one particular creed or formula of faith to which one must agree in order to become a member. At Mary Taylor Memorial, we recognize that people are at all stages of their Christian journey. We invite all to find a spiritual 'home base' in our church community."

The Mary Taylor pastor is a woman, Kristina Hansen. The church has a colorful sign that, reads, "To be clear if you are queer LGBTQIA+ you are affirmed here!" It was posted shortly after the United Methodist Church voted to bolster its ban on gay clergy and same-sex marriages.

While I was writing this book, a man from Tennessee was arrested for damaging the Connecticut church. Police reported that he told them he entered the building and damaged a door because he thought that the pastor and the church as a whole were supporting and pushing the LGBT agenda. Charges filed include hate crime, burglary and criminal mischief.

John Wesley Hardin (1853 –1895) was an American Old-West thief and multiple murderer. His father was a Methodist preacher who named him after **John Wesley**. *John Wesley Harding* (with the improper "g" in the name) is a superb album by Bob Dylan, from 1967. The title track starts, "John Wesley Harding was a friend to the poor. He trav'led with a gun in ev'ry hand all along this countryside. He opened many a door but he was never known to hurt an honest man."

John Wesley Harding is the stage name of an English singer-songwriter-author, born in 1965.

Chapter 12
My Debt To Christianity

For nearly 2,000 years many Christians refrained from eating the meat of warm-blooded land animals such as cows and pigs on Fridays. There are several explanations for this.

- One is that it's an act of penance.
- There is advice that the money saved from buying expensive food should be given to the poor.
- According to Pope Peter of Alexandria, the Friday meat fast commemorates the crucifixion on Good Friday.
- A more cynical explanation is that another pope instituted the rule to boost the income of fishermen.

So, what is my debt to Christianity? On Fridays I can always get clam chowder in diners, and I *love* clam chowder.

Although Friday meat abstinence remains the law of the Catholic Church, many national bishops' conferences—including the U.S. bishops—make exceptions in their jurisdictions, permitting Catholics to choose another form of penance instead. In England and Wales in 1984 the rules were relaxed allowing Catholics to choose a different form of penance, such as offering extra prayers.

While fish, lobster and other shellfish are not considered meat and can be consumed on days of abstinence, indulging in the lavish buffet at your favorite seafood place sort of *misses the point*.

In 2010, Archbishop of New Orleans Gregory Michael Aymond clarified that **alligator is considered seafood**, saying "the alligator's considered in the fish family, and ... God has created a magnificent creature that is important to the state of Louisiana, and it is considered seafood."

In 1966, the National Conference of Catholic Bishops issued a "Pastoral Statement on Penance and Abstinence" in which they declared, among other things: Among the works of voluntary self-denial and personal penance which we especially commend to our people for the future observance of Friday, even though we hereby terminate the traditional law of abstinence binding under pain of sin, as the sole prescribed means of observing Friday, we give first place to abstinence from flesh meat. We do so in the hope that the Catholic community will ordinarily continue to abstain from meat by free choice as formerly we did in obedience to Church law.

Eastern Christians, both Catholic and Orthodox, still observe abstinence on Fridays (and on Wednesdays, as Catholics once did—and their abstinence is sterner than ours, excluding fish, dairy, and other animal products).

In anti-Catholic times, on the modest end of the spectrum, Catholics were mocked for avoiding meat, for example with slurs like "fish-eaters" or "mackerel snappers" that Catholics have claimed as badges of honor.

- In 2009 Bishop R. Daniel Conlon, then of the Diocese of Steubenville, Ohio, encouraged Catholics of his diocese to resume abstaining from meat on all Fridays as a form of pro-life witness and penance.
- In 2011 the bishops of England and Wales restored meatless Fridays for the faithful in their jurisdictions.
- Responding to the restoration of Friday abstinence in England and Wales, in 2011 New York's Cardinal Timothy Dolan published a reflection on the value of external markers of religious identity, wondering whether Catholics "threw out the baby with the bathwater" and whether the English bishops were "on to something."
- In 2012 Cardinal Dolan, then president of the United States Conference of Catholic Bishops (USCCB), invited the nation's bishops to reflect on "re-embracing Friday as a particular day of penance, including the possible re-institution of abstinence on all Fridays of the year, not just during Lent."
- Later in 2012 came the USCCB "pastoral strategy" noted above, which included recommending fasting as well as abstinence on Fridays. Since then, the USCCB has published weekly prayer intentions for Friday abstinence and fasting. You can get these via email or text message.
- In 2013 Bishop Edward Weisenburger of the Diocese of Salina, Kansas asked the faithful in his diocese to re-embrace year-round Friday abstinence.

- In 2014 several Australian bishops indicated their support for reestablishing year-round Friday abstinence.
- In 2015 Bishop Early Boyea of Lansing, Michigan raised the topic of year-round Friday abstinence, alluding to the collapse of Friday penance in general and referring to an increased desire among the faithful for the restoration of Friday abstinence.
- Also in 2015, Bishop Glen John Provost of Lake Charles, Louisiana wrote a pastoral letter asking for a "renewal of the sense of Fridays" as a day of penance and highlighting abstinence from meat as a form of penance encouraged in canon law "to this day."

I have nothing important to put in this valuable space, so instead you get a funny story:

A few years ago in October, at the time of the Jewish New Year (*Rosh Hashanah*), I had an appointment with one of my doctors.

At the end of the examination I wished him a Happy New Year (*l'shanah tovah* in Hebrew).

He smiled, thanked me and asked, "How did you know I'm Jewish?

I said, "(1) You're a doctor, (2) your first name is Harvey, and (3) I saw a diploma from the Bronx High School of Science on your wall."

It was a safe bet.

Chapter 13
Denominations & Divisions

"In mathematics, the **lowest common denominator** (or least common denominator) is the lowest common multiple of the denominators of a set of fractions." [Wikipedia]

"It's an obnoxious person one encounters in extremely large groups. Because there are so many people, there is a significantly higher probability of idiotic people." [Urban Dictionary]

Religions get divided into **denominations**, and even sub-denominations and sub-sub-denominations. No license is required to open a house of worship, or even to start a new religion, as Mormon Joseph Smith did in 1884. In some parts of New York City, tiny churches (many of them shuttered and abandoned) are as common as bodegas.

Protestant Christians include Presbyterians, Episcopalians, Baptists, Lutherans, Methodists, Oneness Pentecostals, Premillenial Dispensationalists, Amish, Mennonites, Hutterites, Old German Baptist Brethren, and *many* more. There are divisions within the Lutherans (Missouri, and Wisconsin Evangelical Lutheran Synod and others) and Baptists ("Southern," "Convention of Baptists in Portugal" and more).

    Catholic Christians include Roman (also called "Latin" or "Western") Catholic, Eastern Orthodox and unaffiliated congregations.

    Mormons consider themselves to be Christians, but *not* Catholic or Protestant.

    Jews include Reconstructionist, Reform, Conservative and Orthodox groups—with dozens of variations. There are also groups that consider themselves to be Jewish—such as Messianic Jews and Sicarii Black Hebrew Israelites—that are *rejected* by mainstream Jews.

    Within Judaism are individuals and organizations that consider themselves to be "**post-denominational.**" The online **Pluralistic Rabbinical Seminary** says it is "is a pioneer in post-denominational rabbinical training. Our Jewish educators and professionals come from a wide variety of countries, careers, and backgrounds. The *smicha* committee (beit din) at PRS includes Reform, Conservative and post-denominational rabbis who act as mentors throughout a student's education." [Note the absence of Orthodox participants, despite the strong commitment to technology by the Orthodox Chabad movement.]

Outside the USA—particularly in Asia—are many more religions (not "denominations"), including Hinduism, Buddhism, Jainism, Sikhism, Confucianism, Taoism, Zoroastrianism and more.

In Christianity, there is a growing number of "**non-denominational**" churches, including some huge "**megachurches**" with thousands of members. They usually reject certain key philosophies or rituals of traditional denominations, and have been accused by some of promoting a "lite" version of Christianity.

"Everybody knows that the so-called 'mainline' is now the sideline," according to sociologist Rodney Stark. "The United Church of Christ, Presbyterians, Methodists and the Episcopalians have been shrinking at a rather prodigious rate. But that isn't because people left church, it is because people left THOSE churches. Groups like the Assemblies of God have doubled and redoubled in size in the same period of time." The flight from mainline churches, Stark says, has been going on since the 1800s. It wasn't really noticed until the 1960s because overall population growth made it look like mainline churches were growing, while all along their percentage of the population was dropping.

Part of the reason Stark thinks denominations are declining is that they used to be, at least partly, connected to a person's ethnic identity. "My generation is much less concerned to be Lutheran than my parents—and especially my grandparents—were because they were Norwegians and

Swedes and immigrants. And being Lutheran was part of the package."

In *Deseret News*, Timothy Dalrymple, associate director of content at Patheos.com and an evangelical columnist, said "American Christianity is a vital open marketplace of religious ideas in churches. Non-denominational churches can try 100 things and find a model that works."

The model may include a well-defined conservative version of Christianity that contrasts with more moderate theology of mainline churches. Dalrymple said this "dissipation" of mainline churches' theology is part of the reason why people are leaving. "They became less committed to traditional Christian teaching regarding the authority of scripture, regarding salvation in Christ alone, and so forth."

Dalrymple says that part of the weakness of mainline churches is that they became centers of liberal political activism. "That may be where the leadership was, coming out of the seminaries, but that was not where the congregations were." However, he recognizes that people are now more open to churches that have a commitment to social justice. "The more successful of the non-denominational churches right now are those that bring together solid Biblical teaching with dynamic social activism. And they may do it in ways that remain socially and culturally conservative."

Some non-denominational churches are considered to be "**megachurches**," with at least 2,000 congregants. Joel

Osteen is an American pastor, televangelist and author, based in Houston, Texas. Osteen's televised sermons are seen by over 20 million monthly in over 100 countries and are on satellite radio around the clock. He is senior pastor of Lakewood Church, and, since joining Lakewood, attendance has grown from

5,000 to 43,000. Osteen has been complained about for promoting the "prosperity gospel," the belief that material gain is the will of God for all pious Christians. He has an estimated net worth of $40 million.

Preachers at other megachurches (and some small churches)—such as Benny Hin, Paula White and Creflo Dollar—have been criticized for religious heresy, unpaid bills, dishonest biographies, phony healing and lavish lifestyles.

- Televangelist Jesse Duplantis asked viewers to donate money so that he could replace his Dassault Falcon 50 jet with a fancier $54 million Falcon 7X.
- Jimmy Swaggart had a huge $150 million annual salary in the 1980s. Sex scandals ended his career and salary.
- Televangelist Leroy Jenkins sold "miracle water" that contained coliform (poop!) bacteria. His marriage to an elderly woman was annulled because he apparently married her for her $6 million lottery prize.
- Peter Popoff is a televangelist and notorious con man. He was exposed in 1986 for using an earpiece to receive radio messages from his wife, who gave him names, addresses and ailments of audience members during religious services. Popoff falsely claimed God revealed this information to him so that Popoff could 'cure' them with fake faith healing. He went bankrupt but made a comeback in the late 1990s. Popoff bought TV time to promote useless "Miracle Spring Water" on infomercials.
- When Billy Graham died, he left nearly $25 million.
- A brawl broke out at in Detroit's Great Faith Ministries International when Bishop Wayne T. Jackson—the wealthy pastor who drives a Bentley and lives in a mansion—asked for thousand-dollar donations. The church is in a very poor neighborhood.

Chapter 14
Religion & Women

Hijab, $9.50   Sheitel, $2150

Females make up a little bit more than half of the world's human population. If there were no women, there would be no men. Despite this, some religious groups treat girls and women as second-class, or second-rate.

In **Islam,** the Christians' Virgin Mary is highly revered, according to my "Muslim friend," attorney comedian broadcaster Dean Obeidallah, Sadly, Mary's status has not lessened the oppression of many Islamic women—forced to cover their hair with *hijabs* or hide within tent-like *burkas* and forbidden to go shopping, drive cars or run for political office.

Business Week recently said that "religious police roamed the streets shouting at women to cover up" in Saudi Arabia and "unmarried couples can face arrest." The *New York Times* reported that "Middle-aged Moroccan men drink in bars with their mistresses but teenagers are detained for kissing in a park. Women hesitate to report rapes lest they be accused of having sex outside marriage. When these laws are applied, women are disproportionately penalized, legally and socially."

In Syria, Iraq and Afghanistan, Muslim ISIS fighters used rape as a weapon against women, and women have been held as sex slaves for warriors. The victims and their children often face discrimination. In Nigeria, the Muslim Boko Haram have kidnapped and raped girls and kept them captive.

The **Jewish** Torah is filled with protective, perceptive, sacrificing, wise and heroic women—some of them tough warriors such as Deborah and Yael. Modern Israel was led by a tough Jewish grandmother, Prime Minister Golda Meir, from 1969 to 1974. The USA has had female Jewish politicians (and one Jewish Miss America). The liberal branches of Judaism have female rabbis.

However, some Orthodox Jewish groups separate the sexes in synagogues, demand female modesty (hair covered with a *sheitel* (wig), no exposed elbows or knees) and men cannot dance with women except their wives or listen to women sing. In Ultra-Orthodox Jerusalem neighborhoods women are banned from certain sidewalks, and buses have had separate male and female sections. Women were not allowed to pray at parts of the holy Western Wall—but some Ultra-Orthodox women work to support their families while their husbands spend most of their lives studying texts.

According to *Modern Jewish Library*: "Jewish feminism has also posed challenges to the traditional Jewish God. Contemporary feminist thinkers like Judith Plaskow and Rachel Adler have noted that the images of God in traditional

Jewish literature and liturgy are almost exclusively male. However, this is only the surface of the problem. The real issue is that a religious community's descriptions of God represent the attributes and values that it holds dearest. Thus, by depicting God as only male, Judaism implicitly values men over women. The feminist critique of Jewish theology cannot be resolved by simply adding female God pronouns to Jewish liturgy. Conceptions of God need to be molded out of female as well as male experiences of Judaism. Some Jewish feminists, including liturgist Marcia Falk and many within the Jewish renewal movement, revisit and make expansive use of the few traditional female images of God (like the *Shekhinah* of *kabbalah*), and experiment with new ways of envisioning and naming God in light of Jewish women's experiences and contemporary feminist insights."

Like Israel, predominantly **Hindu** India has been led by a female Prime Minister: Indira Ghandi from 1966 to 1977 and again from 1980 until her assassination in 1984. However, in a powerful, disturbing scene in 1956's *Around the World in 80 Days*, a young widow was expected to burn to death on her husband's funeral pyre. (She was saved by the travelers.)

Christianity certainly reveres Mary, the mother of Jesus. She is considered by millions to be the most important saint and she is said to have miraculously appeared to believers many times over the centuries, sometimes providing cures. Catholic, Anglican, Eastern and Oriental Orthodox, and Lutheran churches believe that Mary, as mother of Jesus, is the Mother of God. The Catholic Church proclaims her Immaculate Conception, her perpetual virginity and her Assumption into heaven. (When I was I kid in New Haven I attended an annual fair presented by the Santa Maria Assunta Society, which honors the Assumption.) Mary's image is widespread, institutions and countless girls are named after her—but the

168

reverence is not universal within Christendom. Many Protestant churches are led by women, but so far there are *no* female Catholic priests, bishops, cardinals or popes.

Although they are in the minority, there are several sexually assertive women in the Bible. Ruth sought the advice from her mother-in-law, Naomi, for seducing husband Boaz. Naomi told Ruth to wait until Boaz was drunk and sleepy and "go in and uncover his feet [meaning genitals], and lay thee down."

But most sex in the Bible was performed by men on women. Jacob asked Laban for his daughter Rachel so he could "go in unto her." Moses ordered the men of Israel to "come not at your wives" before he went up Mount Sinai.

Satmar Jewish Women Are Second-Class

Jewish author Deborah Feldman, a former Satmar member, said that the Satmars established an extremely rigid community in Brooklyn to appease God to avoid a second Holocaust. They believe that the Holocaust was God's punishment for assimilation and Zionism.

"God exists only to be feared," she said, "women need to be controlled to secure the future of the community. Satmars believe the female body is dirty, sexuality is evil and a threat to the community. Women are disgusting, but their bodies are vital to the community."

In 2016 it was learned that the Satmar sect issued a decree warning that university education for women was "dangerous." Written in Yiddish, the decree warned:

"It has lately become the new trend that girls and married women are pursuing degrees in special education. Some attend classes and others online. And so we'd like to let their parents know that it is against the Torah.

We will be very strict about this. No girls attending our school are allowed to study and get a degree. It is dangerous. Girls who will not abide will be forced to leave our school. Also, we will not give any jobs or teaching position in the school to girls who've been to college or have a degree.

We have to keep our school safe and we can't allow any secular influences in our holy environment."

Some liberal Jews describe Satmars as "kosher Taliban."

Chapter 15
Christ & Antichrist

I am a Jew and have been called both a "Christ killer" and the "Antichrist." I vociferously denied the first accusation, but had to do some investigation before I could respond to the second.

During his 2008 campaign for the American presidency, Barack Obama was accused of being the Antichrist. Neither of us are that, but he is a Christian (who has been accused of being a secret Muslim). One smear email said, "According to The Book of Revelations the anti-christ will be a man, in his 40s, of MUSLIM descent, who will deceive the nations with persuasive language, and have a MASSIVE Christ-like appeal.... the prophecy says that people will flock to him and he will promise false hope and world peace, and when he is in power, he will destroy everything is it OBAMA?"

PolitiFact.com analyzed the claim and debunked it completely. The word "Antichrist" does not appear in the Book of Revelation (it does refer to "The Beast"). The Book of Revelation never mentions the Beast's age, nor does it state "Muslim descent," as the religion of Islam was not founded until hundreds of years after the book was written.

Some Protestant theologians have accused Catholic popes of being the Antichrist.

In Christian theology the Antichrist or ("anti-Christ") is a being that fulfills Biblical prophecies predicting one who will oppose Christ and substitute himself in Christ's place before the Second Coming.

The term is found five times in the New Testament, solely in the First and Second Epistle of John, described as the one "who denies the Father and the Son." I have never done that.

The similar term *pseudokhristos* or "false Christs" is found in the Gospels. In Matthew (chapter 24) and Mark (chapter 13), Jesus alerts his disciples to not be deceived by the false prophets, which will claim themselves as being Christ, performing "great signs and wonders." Two other images often associated with the Antichrist are the "little horn" in Daniel's final vision and the "man of sin" in Paul the Apostle's Second Epistle to the Thessalonians.

In Islamic theology, Al-Masih ad-Dajjal is an anti-messiah figure (similar to the Christian concept of an Antichrist) who will appear to deceive humanity before the second coming of "Isa," as Jesus is known to Muslims.

The concept of an Antichrist is absent in traditional Judaism, although in some medieval texts the symbolic figure Armilus appears. According to the *Jewish Encyclopedia*, Armilus is "a king who will arise at the end of time against the Messiah, and will be conquered by him after having brought much distress upon Israel."

Here's a funny, important and unrelated story:

A man was driving past a mental asylum and got a flat tire. He stopped the car and went out to change the tire and saw about a dozen people on the other side of the fence jumping up and down, waving their arms and babbling incoherently.

After a while one of them calmed down and began watching him intensely. Nervous and trying to work quickly, the driver jacked up the car, took off the wheel and put the lug nuts into the hubcap. He accidentally bumped into the hubcap, sending the lug nuts clattering into a sewer.

The mental patient was still watching him through the fence. The driver desperately looked into the sewer but the lug nuts were gone. The patient was still watching. The driver paced back and forth, trying to think of what to do. (This was before cellphones.)

The mental patient said, "Take one lug nut off each of the other wheels and you'll be able to have three lug nuts on each of the four wheels and you can drive to the auto parts store in the next town and get more lug nuts."

"That's brilliant!," said the driver. "What are you doing in an asylum?" Lesson: **Just because someone is crazy doesn't mean she or he is stupid or ignorant.**

Chapter 16

Mixed Marriages & Conversions

Jewish people have been loving and marrying gentiles since Biblical times (even Moses married a non-Jew). As with many things, the Bible provides mixed messages about mixed marriages.

From Deut. 7:3: "neither shalt thou make marriages with them: thy daughter thou shalt not give unto his son, nor his daughter shalt thou take unto thy son." This has been interpreted to mean that marriage with a non-Jew is forbidden. However, since the passage refers to "seven nations" (Hittites, Girgashites, Amorites, Canaanites, Perizzites, Hivites and the Jebusites), some scholars maintain that the prohibition applies only to intermarriage with those seven nations.

Others say that the prohibition applies to all gentiles because after the prohibition "neither shalt thou make marriages" the biblical passage continues: "for he will turn away thy son from following after Me" (Deut. 7:4), which serves "to include all who would turn [their children] away."

This is traditionally attributed to Moses, shortly after the Exodus in the 13th century, BCE. However, it was apparently written later, between the 7th and 5th centuries BCE.

The following is older, from the **Book of Ruth**, going back to approximately 1000 BCE: "And Ruth said, 'Intreat me not to leave thee, or to return from following after thee: for whither thou goest, I will go; and where thou lodgest, I will lodge: **thy people shall be my people, and thy God my God.**"

The Bible and later media are filled with stories of marriages between Jews and gentiles. Some of the relationships turned out fine, some terrible, some funny (Stiller and Meara, *Bridget Loves Bernie*, *Abie's Irish Rose*, *Brooklyn Bridge*).

A mixed marriage between, say, a Presbyterian and a Congregationalist, requires minor accommodation and could be stress-free. A Jewish/gentile marriage—because of insurmountable disagreement about the divinity of Jesus—requires a great degree of compromise, or *silence* by one partner. I'm personally aware of several marriages where one person converted before a wedding. In each case, the conversion was based on love of the future spouse or even desire to please future in-laws—*not* infatuation with the new faith.

Other converts are quite sincere, and famous. **Sammy Davis Jr.** nearly died in an automobile accident in 1954 in California. During the previous year, he had become friendly with Jewish entertainer Eddie Cantor, who had given him a *mezuzah* (a piece of parchment with a Jewish prayer in a decorative case). Instead of putting it at his door, per tradition, Davis wore it around his neck for good luck. The only time he forgot it was the night of the accident—when Davis lost his left eye to the car's bullet-shaped horn button.

Eddie Cantor talked to Davis about similarities between Jewish and black cultures. Davis had a Catholic mother and Baptist father, but began studying Jewish history and converted in 1961. He said, "After the accident I needed something desperately to hold onto. I found myself being more and more convinced that Judaism was it for me. I know there's sort of a kinship between the plight of a Negro and the plight of a Jew: the oppression, the segregation, the constant trying to survive and trying to achieve dignity." Davis liked to describe the time he was playing golf with Jack Benny and was asked what his handicap was. He responded: "Handicap? I'm a one-eyed Negro Jew."

There were some cruel remarks about the Jewish "nigger," but most of the jokes were more affectionate, such as the one attributed to [wife May] Britt. When it became public that she would marry the entertainer, she was asked if her parents back home expressed any objection to the match.

"Why should they?" she supposedly responded. "There is no antisemitism in Sweden."

Britt was converted at Temple Israel in Hollywood and, if anything, took her new faith even more seriously than did her husband.

In later years, Davis visited Dachau and admitted that he became as prejudiced against Germans as some whites are against blacks. In a visit to Israel, he expressed his delight at encountering so many dark-skinned Jews.

When *Fiddler on the Roof* became a musical hit, there was talk of mounting an all-black version and Davis was asked whether he would accept the role of Tevye. He declined, saying, "There has to be respect for certain things, and a black Tevye would be stretching it too far."

After a while, the jokes about Davis's Jewishness stopped as his friends realized how committed the entertainer was to his faith.

An example is seen in Davis's face-off with the imperious (Jewish) movie mogul Samuel Goldwyn. When Goldwyn insisted on filming through the High Holy Days, Davis asked for 24 hours off. Goldwyn scoffed at the request but relented when Davis assured him that he would spend the entire time in a synagogue.

"All right," Goldwyn finally agreed. "But I'll check up on you. I hope I'll be able to recognize you in shul."

According to a 2015-'16 exhibition called *Becoming Jewish: Warhol's Liz and Marilyn* at New York's Jewish Museum, for **Elizabeth Taylor** the loss of (Jewish) Mike Todd more than her scandalous marriage to his Jewish best friend, Eddie Fisher, led to her conversion. Following Todd's death, Taylor began seeking spiritual counseling from his rabbi, Max Nussbaum of Hollywood's Temple Israel. She began studying with Nussbaum, who oversaw her conversion and performed her 1959 marriage to Fisher. "It was something I had wanted to do for a long time," Taylor said of her decision to convert and choose "Elisheba Rachel" as her Hebrew name. She continued her devotion to Israel, Judaism and Jewish causes long after her marriages to Jews disintegrated.

Bob Dylan was born as Jewish Robert Zimmerman in 1941. Over the years his musical style shifted, as did his theology. In the late 1970s, Dylan converted to Christianity. From January to March 1979, Dylan attended the Vineyard Bible study classes in California and considered himself to be "born again," a term used by Evangelicals.

By 1984 Dylan was distancing himself from the "born again" label. He told Kurt Loder of *Rolling Stone* magazine: "I've never said I'm born again. That's just a media term. I don't think I've been an agnostic. I've always thought there's a superior power, that this is not the real world and that there's a world to come." In response to Loder's asking whether he belonged to any church or synagogue, Dylan laughingly replied, "Not really. Uh, the Church of the Poison Mind."

In 1997, he told David Gates of *Newsweek*: "Here's the thing with me and the religious thing. This is the flat-out truth: I find the religiosity and philosophy in the music. I don't find it anywhere else. Songs like *Let Me Rest on a Peaceful Mountain* or *I Saw the Light*—that's my religion. I don't adhere to rabbis, preachers, evangelists, all of that. I've learned more from the songs than I've learned from any of this kind of entity. The songs are my lexicon. I believe the songs."

In 1997 in the *New York Times* Jon Pareles reported that "Dylan says he now subscribes to no organized religion." Dylan has supported the (Orthodox Jewish) Chabad Lubavitch movement, and has privately participated in Jewish religious events, including the Bar Mitzvahs of his sons, and attended a Chabad Lubavitch religious school. In 1989 and 1991 he appeared on Chabad telethons. On Yom Kippur in 2007 he attended Congregation Beth Tefillah in Atlanta, where he was honored with an *aliyah* (chanting blessings before and after reading Torah portions).

Dylan has performed gospel songs in concert, but apparently no Jewish songs). In a 2004 interview on *60 Minutes*, he told Ed Bradley that "the only person you have to think twice about lying to is either yourself or to God." He explained his constant touring schedule as part of a bargain he made a long time ago with the "chief commander—in this earth and in the world we can't see."

In a 2009 interview with Bill Flanagan promoting Dylan's Christmas LP, *Christmas in the Heart*, Flanagan acknowledged the "heroic performance" Dylan gave of *O Little Town of*

Bethlehem and that he "delivered the song like a true believer." Dylan replied: "Well, I am a true believer." So, is Dylan now a Christian or a Jew? Or something else? Who knows? He has always been cryptic.

I ntermarriage has always been a danger to the Jewish People, notes the Jewish Virtual Library. "Any group that lives as a minority has the potential of being absorbed by its host society. Some contact among the groups within a society is inevitable, but that contact can take many forms as relations among groups are played out—not always in consistent patterns—along several dimensions: cultural, institutional, residential, social, and familial."

- Intermarriage is seen as the very antithesis of Jewish continuity. ... exogamy was one of the most energetically discouraged and forcefully condemned acts that a Jew could perform.
- Until the 1980s, men were twice as likely as women to marry non-Jews. In later years, however, the gap has narrowed considerably.
- It used to be that intermarriage was most frequent among Jews with the highest educational and income levels, but recent studies call this pattern into question. Jews at the top of the socioeconomic scale turn out to be less likely to intermarry than those toward the middle, but the differences are small.
- The older Jews are at the time of their first marriage, the more likely they are to be exogamous.
- Second marriages after divorce are also much more likely than first marriages to involve a non-Jewish partner.
- Generally, areas of high Jewish concentration have less intermarriage, but some cities with large Jewish populations have very high intermarriage rates (San Francisco, Denver, and Washington, DC, are examples).

- The less traditional the religious "movement" with which a Jew identifies, the more likely that Jew is to intermarry, with the highest rates of intermarriage among those who claim to be "just Jewish."
- During most of the 1980s it was generally believed that in about one-third of the marriages between Jews and partners born non-Jews, the originally non-Jewish partner converted to Judaism according to the norms and practices of one of Judaism's religious movements, either before or after the marriage. The most recent studies show that a much smaller proportion of intermarriages is conversionary than had previously been thought to be the case.
- Recent studies show that far fewer than half of the children of intermarriage identify as Jews, even by the most liberal criteria. Moreover, those who do consider themselves Jews have weaker Jewish identity on the whole than do born Jews, and they are themselves far more likely to intermarry.
- The organized Jewish community in North America is expressing renewed alarm over intermarriage. Not only has the rate risen dramatically over the last decades, but the demographic impact is seen as more threatening than had been hoped. Many Jewish organizations have begun to address what they articulate as the problem in "Jewish continuity." Jewish organizations have been encouraged to strengthen programs that contribute to Jewish identity, and funds are being allocated for activities designed to enhance Jewish continuity.

Steven Carr Reuben, a Reconstructionist rabbi, says: "As a rabbi who has officiated at interfaith ceremonies for over 37 years I have watched as the rate of intermarriage has risen every year so that today more Jews may actually marry non-Jews than Jews and I see no reason to believe that this trend will reverse itself any time soon. I have always considered finding non-judgmental ways of supporting every couple and family, regardless of the religious lifestyle that they choose to create for themselves, as one of my most important challenges."

- I believe that religious consistency promotes emotional stability, especially for young children. Children are very flexible and they have no trouble saying, "My mom is one religion and my dad and I are another and we get to celebrate mommy's holidays with her, too."
- What is most difficult for children is when they are put into a situation where they have to say, "I know what my mommy is and I know what my daddy is but I don't know what I am. So the best decision is usually to give your children an identity to call their own.
- Telling children that they can make up their minds about which religion to be is putting an unfair and emotionally difficult burden on them.
- All children have the same needs—to feel that both of their parents love them and will protect them and keep them safe from life's fears. The last thing that children want is to be in a position where they are asked to choose between one parent and another.
- Regardless of how they choose they will inevitably feel that they are betraying one parent or another and thereby risking that parent's love and affection.
- All of us have the ability to choose which religion or spiritual tradition we will follow or embrace when we become adults and millions of people change from one religious tradition to another every year, regardless of how they were raised.
- My best advice is to raise your children in a consistent religious tradition, whatever that may be, so that they will have a sound, emotionally secure religious identity out of which they can make decisions for themselves.
- Interfaith couples have both the opportunity and responsibility of creating their own unique religious lifestyle together which requires patience, tolerance, flexibility and an openness to experiencing life in a different way from which they were raised.

- Ultimately one person in each couple will inevitably take the lead in creating the religious celebrations and experiences of the family, but the most successful interfaith families are those in which both partners are willing to share the experiences together and find a way to create a stable and consistent sense of religious identity for their children."

Children of mixed marriages may choose no religion, or form identities based on each parent's heritage. I know a man, a third-generation mixture, who describes himself as a "spic-a-heeb-a-wop" (Hispanic, Jewish, Italian).

Recently retired Rabbi Alan Alpert converted about 36 people to Judaism over 20 years. The procedure usually takes 12-18 months and involves study, meetings, synagogue attendance and more. He said, "If a person studying for conversion feels that Jesus remains an important part of her or his life, this candidate is not viable for conversion."

Rabbi Alpert told me of some converts with impressive sincerity, who did not convert in order to have an easier marriage to Jews:

1. One woman convert changed her first name to seem more Jewish. She became an expert Torah reader, has a magnificent voice, and could be a cantor.
2. Another woman with four children all converted. She raised her kids Jewishly while her parents lived nearby and celebrated Easter and Christmas. She taught at a Jewish religious school and became an expert on *kashrut* (kosher cooking and eating).

The late Rabbi William Cohen of Congregation Shalom in Orlando would perform interfaith marriages for older couples who do not expect to have children. "Two adults simply by themselves could go to synagogue every day and to church every day, but when you've got to answer a little four-year old, then it's a little difficult," he said, noting he won't marry couples who do not plan to raise their children in the Jewish faith.

A traditional approach to Jewish conversion has been for a rabbi to turn away a seeker three times before accepting that the seeker truly wants to convert. Recently, the Rabbinical Assembly of Conservative Judaism has repudiated that process in favor of welcoming seekers and non-Jewish partners in interfaith marriages (although it is still not Conservative Jewish practice to proselytize).

Gary A. Tobin wrote a book called *Opening the Gates: How Proactive Conversion Can Revitalize the Jewish Community*. He said, "in order to rebuild and revitalize Judaism in this country we must rethink our religion as something both born Jews and converts must actively choose and stop blaming intermarriage for Judaism's decline. We must abandon the paradigm that our children and grandchildren may become Gentiles and promote the thought that America is filled with millions of potential Jews."

If a man has not been circumcised, he must have the procedure before the conversion is complete. If he had been circumcised, he will need to lose just a bit of blood from the glans of his penis. Both males and females must immerse in a *mikveh* (ritual bath). Prospective Jews must write an essay detailing their reasons for wanting to become Jewish and how they've been putting their new Jewish knowledge into practice. The essay is given to a *beit din* (three-person religious court) for consideration and the

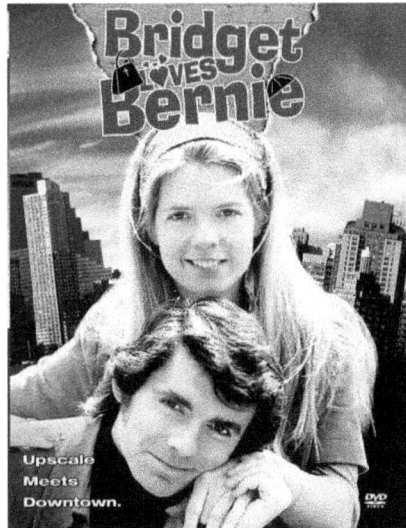

Upscale
Meets
Downtown.

183

three will meet with and question the applicant. According to Rabbi Al-pert, in his experience, rejection is very unusual.

The procedure is simpler for children and prospective Reform and Reconstructionist Jews, and more complicated for prospective Orthodox Jews.

In 15th-century Spain, Jews chose between conversion and death. The Second Vatican Council (1962-'65) stressed that "Jews do not need to convert to Christianity in order to be saved. They already are saved. Thus, the Church's approach to Jews cannot be to proselytize or try to convert them. It must be one of dialogue between two Peoples of God who are bound together by a common Bible, the Hebrew Scriptures, and the fact that Jesus lived and died a faithful Jew."

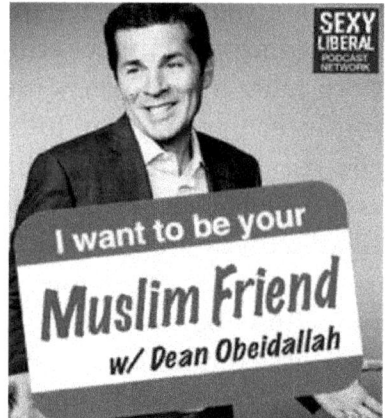

Dean Obeidallah is the host of a show on SiriusXM satellite radio and has contributed to CNN, *New York Times*, *Los Angeles Times* and *Newsweek*. His father is a Palestinian Muslim, his mother is an Italian-American Catholic and he considers himself to be a Muslim. He co-created the comedy show "Stand up for Peace" with Jewish comic Scott Blakeman that they perform at colleges, in support of understanding between Jews and Muslims. In the Middle East, Dean has performed in both Israel and in Muslim countries.

Clichés often influence the quest for mates. The sexy blonde gentile woman (*shiksa* or "trophy wife") is a persistent meme, as is the concept of the Jewish husband as stable, sober, loyal and a good provider. My wife's mother was Jewish, her father (whom I never met) was a lapsed Catholic. He advised my wife to marry a Jewish man—and I'm pleased that she did.

Some intermarriages are barely noticed and some are very newsworthy, e.g., Caroline Kennedy (at right) and Jack Schlossberg, Chelsea Clinton and Marc Mezvinsky, Ivanka Trump and Jared Kushner. Ivanka converted, so technically hers is not a mixed marriage, but still it's been subject to much gossip.

Hollywood has been the scene of scores of Jew-gentile marriages since its earliest days, involving studio owners, creative people and entertainers—with some conversions. Jewish George Burns married Catholic Grace Ethel Cecile Rosalie Allen. George said, "I'm the only Jew in the family. Because of Gracie, the two children were raised as Catholics and I've got seven Catholic grandchildren and five great-grandchildren. I used to eat fish every Friday, but always with my hat on."

Unlike Gracie, Marilyn Monroe converted to Judaism to become Mrs. Arthur Miller. Egypt then banned her movies. Intermarriage occurs in politics, too. Gentile U.S. Senator Kamala Harris's husband is Jewish attorney Douglas Emhoff.

Ellen on Facebook wrote: "I have known of a couple of people who converted to Judaism and when they were dying, they chose to convert back to the religion to which they were born!" To counter that, I offer this joke:

A rabbi is on his deathbed, and a friend asks him if he has any last requests. The rabbi asks his friend to find him a Catholic priest, so that he might convert.

A priest is summoned and spends several days teaching and praying and performs a quick conversion. When the rabbi's death is imminent, the priest asks, "Rabbi, why? You have been a great teacher and leader of your congregation, and you have led a good and honorable Jewish life. Why would you want to become a Catholic now, before you die?"

The rabbi says, "Well, if someone has to die, it's better that it's one of you than one of us."

I attended a wedding with a Jewish bride and a Catholic groom where both a rabbi and a priest officiated. Some rabbis refuse to participate in weddings like this. I know one rabbi who refused to even be a *guest* at the mixed marriages of relatives—so great was his disapproval. He said he'd gladly marry "a woman and a man, two women, two men, even a porpoise and a squirrel—as long as both are Jewish."

However, there are a few Jewish rabbis who actively seek 'business' in performing mixed marriages. Rabbi "Marrying Sam" Silver (1912-2008) was a pioneer in interfaith marriages, according to the *South Florida Sun Sentinel*. "When other rabbis were shunning the practice, Rabbi Silver was performing the ceremony for thousands of mixed-faith couples. 'He was devoted 100 percent to humanism,' his son said. 'It was unheard of. He did thousands of weddings and never charged a fee. He loved what he did. He loved Judaism. He thought it was a wonderful influence on people. He loved to talk and to help people become better.'"

The Jewish woman I mentioned who was married by a priest and a rabbi had two Jewish parents in a minimally Jewish home. She said that her mother did not have any Jewish knowledge to pass along and that the family never went to synagogue. I asked her what being Jewish meant to her and she quickly replied, "the food." She added that "one of my fondest memories was having Italian food on one of the

[Jewish] holidays. It may have been Rosh Hashanah or Yom Kippur. We ate lasagna."

Her children are being brought up with no religion, but she feels bad about it. "My kids are confused," she says. "They used to ask, 'am I Jewish? am I Catholic?' They don't ask much anymore. They know they're both." I asked if when she was "at the mating age" if she sought a Jewish husband. She said she had no preference.

Her husband's large Catholic family seems to have a strong influence on the kids. It's hard to deny children a Christmas tree when cousins and friends have them. Christmas has become a pervasive secular holiday. The photo at the right shows me with Santa Claus in around 1950. I'm the one on the left. I have no idea why I wore a gun to visit Santa.

While researching this book I interviewed a newly-wed woman, in her late 20s. She has a not-very-Jewish father and a Catholic mother and was raised as a Catholic—but has been an atheist since her teens.

Her new husband is a Jewish atheist (son of a Jewish-born father and a mother who converted to Judaism). They had a Jewish wedding and plan to raise any children as Jewish. Despite their non-belief, she said they think it's important to give kids a religious foundation and to replenish the Jewish people. That's nice—and shows the strength of a tribal connection even if there is a theological lapse. I have both.

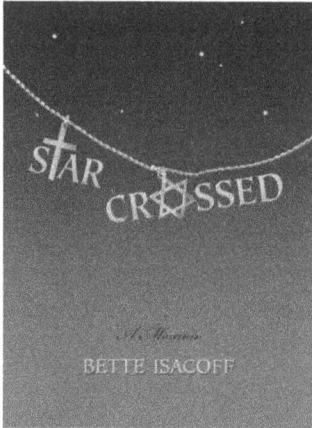

Star Crossed is a superb book about a Catholic-Jewish romance and marriage, written by Bette Isacoff. It's a love story (i.e., "chick lit") that even a *man* can enjoy reading. Men who read this book may be jealous of Bette's husband, Richard, because of Bette's mixture of love *and* writing ability. I wish someone would write a book like this about me.

Set in New England in the late 60s, *Star Crossed* is the poignant, funny and inspirational chronicle of an interfaith courtship at a time when interfaith relationships were exotic and sometimes forbidden by parents.

When Bette met Richard in 1968, he was a 17-year-old Jewish high school kid. She, at 21, was a Catholic college senior doing a practice-teaching assignment at his school. Seven weeks later, they were engaged. To say that their two-year courtship was ill-received is an understatement.

After graduation Bette moved home to parents determined to break up the couple. She was denied all contact with Richard and he was told to find a Jewish girl. The harder their families tried to pull them apart, the tighter they clung together.

This couple faced not one impediment to marriage, but *four*: religion, age (at a stage when it is significant), education level, and the tenor of the times—a culture in which Jews and Catholics rarely married "outside."

Added to the negativity were outraged parents, scornful siblings, snickering friends, legal obstacles, uncooperative clergy, and yet they persevered. With secret post office boxes, clandestine meetings and Bette's extended family—who conspired with Richard against their own relatives—the odd relationship was nurtured; and it has lasted. (By the way, Bette gets extra points for a perfect cover image that reinforces the book title much better than the images on most of the books I see.)

Once a Jew, always a Jew.

While many people change political parties, nationalities and religions, it just may not be possible to exit from Judaism.

Chabad Rabbi Schneuer Wilhelm told me that "a Jew can't get rid of his or her *neshama* (Jewish spirit) even if converting to another religion. It's the essence of a Jew."

Author (and former speechwriter for both Obamas) Sarah Hurwitz wrote, "there is a Yiddish phrase for this: "*dos pintele yid*," which literally means "that little point of a Jew" and refers to that spark of Jewishness in each of us that we can't quite manage to ignore, no matter how hard we may

Mazel Tov!

The son of a Catholic man and a Jewish woman was going to be married to a Catholic woman in the office of a Justice of the Peace. The son was not religious, but was 'officially' Jewish because of his maternal connection to the tribe.

Mama noticed that the Justice had a Jewish name and told him that she had always wanted her son to have a Jewish wedding.

The J.P. smiled, opened a desk drawer and took out a *kippah* (skull cap).

He put it on his head and performed the civil ceremony. The Catholics were not offended and Mama was happy.

Chapter 17
Memorable Bible Quotes

(These are inspiring and otherwise, in no particular order, some with comments, from various translations. One quote is a parody—from the *Blasphemous Bible*. Can you find it?)

- In [the] beginning God created the heavens and the earth. [A good place to start, but maybe a Big Bang did it.]
- And Jacob said to Rebekah his mother, "Behold, Esau my brother is a hairy man, and I am a smooth man" [One of my favorites, best said by a powerful Bible-thumper at random times.]
- Thus saith the LORD, "Let my people go." [Without this powerful command, there would be no Exodus, no Passover, no matzo ball soup, maybe no Golden Globe nomination for Charlton Heston, who played Moses.]
- Hear, O Israel, the Lord is our God, the Lord is one. [Basic monotheism, and basic Judaism]
- Whither thou goest, I will go; and where thou lodgest, I will lodge: thy people shall be my people, and thy God my God. [A love story, with religion. Ruth, from the pagan land of Moab, married Boaz, a Jewish man, and became great-grandmother of Israel's great King David.]
- How are the mighty fallen in the midst of the battle!
- He said, "I was born with nothing, and I will die with nothing. The Lord gave, and now he has taken away. May his name be praised!"
- To every thing there is a season, and a time to every purpose under the heaven.

- A wise son brings joy to his father, but a foolish son brings grief to his mother. [Ancient sexism, but probably realistic]
- Those who spare the rod of discipline hate their children. Those who love their children care enough to discipline them.
- Even a fool who keeps silent is considered wise; when he closes his lips, he is deemed intelligent.
- If you have to choose between a good reputation and great wealth, choose a good reputation.
- Behold, a great flood of our boiling blood will go and consume all the idols, the brothels, the groves, the unholy altar and the temples to false gods.
- Therefore the Lord Himself shall give you a sign: behold, the young woman shall conceive, and bear a son, and shall call his name Immanuel. [This is a Jewish translation from Isaiah. Christian Bibles say "virgin," not "young woman." That's a BIG difference. Also, why "Immanuel," and not "Jesus?"]
- When they sow the wind, they will reap a storm! A field of grain that doesn't ripen can never produce any bread. But even if it did, foreigners would eat it up.
- If a man lies with a male as with a woman, both of them have committed an abomination; they shall surely be put to death. [Lesbian sex, however, is apparently OK with God.]
- The Lord is slow to anger and great in power, and the Lord will by no means leave the guilty unpunished. [Maybe God should not be slow to anger. Why did it take so long for the Nazis to be defeated?]
- Love your enemies, bless them that curse you, do good to them that hate you, and pray for them which despitefully use you, and persecute you. Judge not, that ye be not judged. Ask, and it shall be given you; seek, and ye

shall find; knock, and it shall be opened unto you. [This is from the New Testament and very foreign to me. I *hate* my enemies, would *never* bless them, I *always* make judgments, and lots of things I've asked for have not been given to me.]

- It is easier for a camel to go through the eye of a needle, than for a rich man to enter into the kingdom of God. [Did sewing needles exist back then?]
- Render to Caesar the things that are Caesar's, and to God the things that are God's. [I'm tempted to insert a funny line about Caesar dressing, but I won't.]
- For God so loved the world, that he gave his only begotten Son, that whosoever believeth in him should not perish, but have everlasting life. [The "begotten" has been the source of conflict between Jehovah's Witnesses and more traditional Christians. I'll stay out of it. However, I do not believe in everlasting life.]
- The wages of sin is death; but the gift of God is eternal life through Jesus Christ our Lord. [Immortality again. I'm still not convinced.]
- Put on the whole armour of God, that ye may be able to stand against the wiles of the devil. [What about people who don't think the devil is real?]
- Set your affection on things above, not on things on the earth. [Good for astronomers and astronauts.]
- The day of the Lord so cometh as a thief in the night. (Is that good?)
- How beautiful are your tents, O Jacob; how lovely are your homes, O Israel! [Ancient real estate assessment?]
- Your two breasts are like two fawns, twins of a gazelle, which feed among the lilies. [The *Song of Solomon* has some soft-core porn. Enjoy.]
- There is no new thing under the sun. [The author's father insisted that "There are no new jokes."]

Chapter 18
Eating Animals, Being Buried

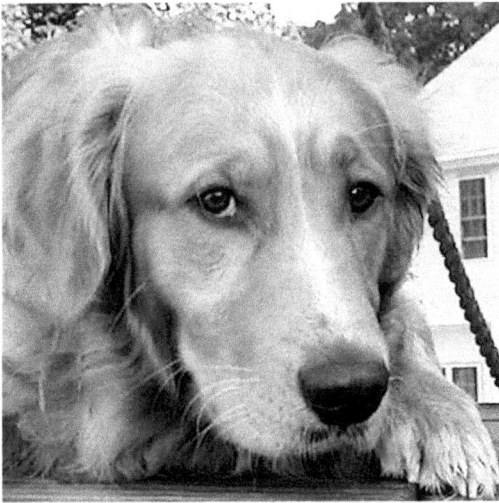

The photo shows Hunter J. Marcus, my four-legged son (a golden retriever, officially) who died in 2017 at the age of 15 years and a few months. He gave and received a lot of love. I could not have loved him more if he was a human child.

In my home he had all the rights and privileges granted to homo sapiens—and even more. (My wife is nice even to *insects*. If she finds a fly in the house, she'll open a window and politely encourage it to leave. I, however, would kill it.)

Our kitchen table has a stainless-steel top. It's nearly indestructible and cool like a veterinarian's exam table. Hunter often used it as a place to relax—sometimes with a friend.

First-time visitors to our home may have thought that it was strange for a 75-lb. furry critter to be standing or snoozing on the kitchen table. In some parts of the world a dog would be on the table not because he liked it there but because he was a *meal*. Yes, in China, Korea and other parts of Asia people eat dogs—and monkeys and other mammals that are regarded as near-humans elsewhere.

I would never eat a dog or a monkey, but I have no problem eating pieces of cows, pigs, chickens, flounders or lobsters. What's the difference? Should there be a difference?

The difference is cultural, *and* moral. I used to think it was just cultural, and health-related.

The Jewish *kashrut* rules for eating are commonly thought of as a means to avoid illness (e.g., un-refrigerated pork in an ancient desert could cause trichinosis, or pigs and shellfish are "dirty")—but there is a *strong moral aspect* about what makes food kosher or not.

According to Dennis Prager and Joseph Telushkin: "The Jewish ideal is that we not kill for food. Its compromise, known as kashrut, places a strict limit on the number of animal species which Jews may kill to eat, and legislates a uniquely humanely manner in which to kill the permitted animals." ... "The Torah, therefore, prohibited the Jews from consuming animals that eat other animals so that we do not ingest a killer instinct. [This seems like voodoo or witchcraft!] It is not a coincidence that every kosher animal is herbivorous, and that every carnivorous animal is nonkosher." ... "Judaism is uniquely preoccupied with life." ... "Judaism asks us to separate meat (death) from life (milk). One proof of this explanation is that only milk-producing animals may not be eaten with milk. We are allowed to eat fish and milk together because fish do not produce milk. Milk does not represent life with regard to fish, as it does with regard to mammals."

Vegans and vegetarians (I can never remember the distinction) pride themselves in not consuming other life forms, or only some other life forms. In India, many emaciated holy cows roam the streets.

Well, folks, we all consume other life forms—*constantly*. Even if you shun beef, poultry and sea creatures, and eat nothing but kale and radishes raised in your own garden, you are still killing things. (Experiments, particularly in Russia, have shown that plants can experience pain.)

And every time you inhale air, you inhale, kill and incorporate within your own body, the bodies of countless mini-size munchies you neither see nor taste. When you walk, you probably step on bugs. When you drive, your windshield shows the splattered evidence of countless insects violently executed by your vehicle—and you never even get to eat them.

All life forms cause the deaths of other life forms, often accidentally, and often deliberately.

In Genesis, very early in the Bible, God allegedly said about the new human creations, "let them have dominion over the fish of the sea and over the birds of the heavens and over the livestock and over all the earth and over every creeping thing that creeps on the earth." Also: "Behold, I have given you every plant yielding seed that is on the face of all the earth, and every tree with seed in its fruit. You shall have them for food. And to every beast of the earth and to every bird of the heavens and to everything that creeps on the earth, everything that has the breath of life, I have given every green plant for food."

That sounds like animals are supposed to eat just green plants, but maybe not. Like much of the Bible, this is ambiguous.

We homo sapiens may think we are "top dogs," but we are merely *part of the food chain*, and if attacked by hungry dogs, maybe not the top.

Clearly, we are not supposed to starve to death. But if we eat, we stop other creations from living. That's just the way it is.

MyPyramid
STEPS TO A HEALTHIER YOU
MyPyramid.gov

GRAINS · VEGETABLES · FRUITS · MILK · MEAT & BEANS

The U.S. Department of Agriculture has published various "food pyramids" over the years that show "goals for both nutrient adequacy and moderation."

I think there is a parallel to the traditional pyramid of recommended nutrients. To me, we rank potential animal-based foods based on how important it is to let them live.

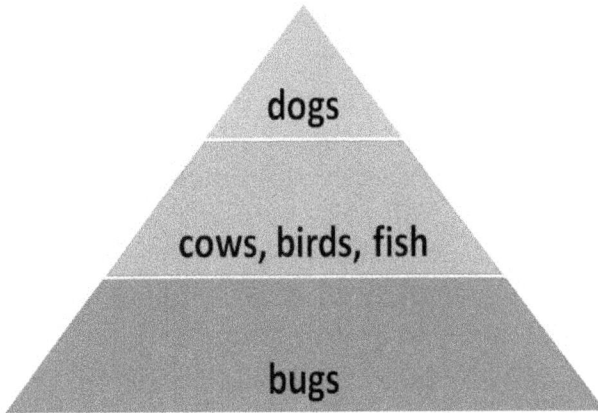

Near the top we encounter creatures with admirable intelligence and utility, particularly pets (I *hate* that word) and working or entertaining animals. In western cultures, most of them don't get eaten by human beings.

In the middle are mammals bred to be food, plus birds and wet creatures that swim, crawl on the bottom or burrow in the mud. A dolphin is more 'worthy' than a snail. I won't complain if you eat predatory alligators, especially if you eat one that tried to eat you.

On the very bottom are annoying bugs like house flies and mosquitoes that may be necessary in the overall ecosystem, but few humans would miss (or eat).

I've never been a farmer but I've observed farm life and culture. I'll never understand how farm kids can lovingly raise chickens, ducks, pigs, lambs and cattle from birth to maturity—and willingly allow them to be *slaughtered*. The Supremes sang in 1964, "Where Did Our Love Go?"

As I said, I believe that we are all part of the food chain. I don't preach that we should strip naked and go for a swim in a shark-infested sea or a gator-filled river, but *we should become food when we no longer need our bodies.*

Any organs or tissue that can be used to extend the lives of others, or educate future doctors, should be promptly divested.

The rest should *not* be cremated. Cremation cheats the system and avoids paying the debt incurred by eating. *It is our solemn duty to decompose.* By becoming worm food, we fertilize the plants that feed animals that feed other animals, and maybe even feed people. It's only fair. (Also: Cremation is a *violation of Jewish law.* It is opposed by many Jewish people, particularly those who are aware of the Nazis' cremation of Jews—both dead and alive—during the Holocaust.)

Luther Turmelle, writing in the *New Haven Register,* said: "according to the Wisconsin-based National Funeral Directors Association, burials represented 53.3 percent of all disposal of remains in the United States in 2010. This year [2019], the burial rate in this country is expected to drop to 39 percent, according to the NFDA. By 2040, cremation is expected to account for 78.7 percent."

According to Nicole Wetsman in *Popular Science,* "The practice of filling bodies with chemicals like formaldehyde to preserve them dates back to ancient Egypt, but it caught on stateside in the mid-1800s as a way to transport fallen Civil War soldiers. Today, U.S. morticians embalm roughly 1 million people every year. It takes between 3 and 4 gallons of chemicals to preserve the average body. That's a lot of carcinogens to leave floating around for the sake of the dead.

The ripple effects are numerous and nasty. Conserved corpses can go on display in caskets that, collectively, use tons of wood and steel, which we then bury in concrete containers. Instead of returning bodily nutrients, like potassium and calcium, to the ground, we slowly molder while shielded from the dirt. Lack of oxygen causes wasting flesh to release methane, a greenhouse gas more potent than the carbon dioxide we'd produce in open air."

Chapter 19
Abortion

Planned Parenthood®

I have neither vagina nor ovaries. I have never been pregnant and probably will never be pregnant. However I have strong opinions on Planned Parenthood.

I fail to see why anyone would oppose Planned Parenthood. Clearly, it is *much* better than unplanned parenthood.

Children should be planned, and should arrive in families with love, time, health, intelligence, space and financial resources that will make it likely that the new arrival will survive and thrive until adulthood.

Unplanned children are often neglected or abused. I can't imagine how a raped woman could feel compassion for a baby who looks like her rapist.

Abortion is birth control, but more attention must be paid to *conception control*. Sadly, no method is foolproof. I know a family with three children—all born after the failure of a different contraception method.

A fetus is *not* a child, *not* a human being.

It is a *potential human being* but can't have a Social Security number or life insurance, can't own property or provide a tax deduction.

Sure, a nearly born fetus could probably survive outside its mother; but that doesn't matter. *Birth* determines the beginning of human life. You can say it's arbitrary, unscientific, illogical, immoral or something else, but it's the law. "Beginning" has to happen at a legally defined point.

Some on the right insist that life begins at conception and have promoted "fetal heartbeat" bills in several states to block abortions. But conception has never been defined to satisfy everyone. Does conception occur when sperm enters a vagina, when a sperm cell is attached to an egg, when a zygote (fertilized egg) implants in a uterus—or another point?

Abortion is unpleasant and not to be decided on casually. But it is legal in the USA and many other countries. It should be legal, rare, available and safe for the mother.

Planned Parenthood, of course, provides a wide array of needed health services and must not be the target of conservative politicians or crazed, murderous right-wingers.

If you don't want to have an abortion, don't have one. It's simple.

For *The Atlantic*, Emma Green interviewed Jes Kast, a United Church of Christ pastor. She supports abortion rights, and is representative of her denomination on this issue. According to the Pew Research Center, 72 percent of people in the UCC, think abortion should be legal in all or most cases. Kast also serves on the clergy-advocacy board of Planned Parenthood.

She grew up in a conservative Christian community, attended an evangelical church as a teenager, and participated in anti-abortion protests. Her process of coming to support abortion rights has been long, and definitive: Kast no longer believes there are any circumstances under which it is immoral to get an abortion. She said (slightly edited):

The first protest I ever went to was when I was 12. It was an anti-abortion protest. When I was in a private Christian college in Michigan, I began to understand myself as a woman in ministry. I began to see myself as this Christian feminist. I began to own my voice differently, and to question the rules of engagement of Christianity that I was raised with.

I began saying "Why is abortion the only issue that my family really cares about?" Like many millennials coming out of evangelicalism, I began to care about the Earth, racial justice, interfaith justice and abortion.

I began questioning: What about bodily autonomy? Isn't that justice? How would God infringe upon that? Why is it that it's almost always white, straight, Christian men who are the loudest?

I believe reproductive rights and bodily autonomy are deeply important. I believe that is faithfulness to Christianity. I believe in access to safe and legal abortions. I believe that the person who can best make these decisions is the person who's considering these decisions.

I have known people who have accessed abortion and reproductive care. Some haven't had any emotional turmoil over it; it has been more like celebration for them. And I know people who saw it as a hard decision.

I believe every person I encounter, including myself, has the right to their body. When that bodily autonomy is taken away, that is against the Gospel I believe in.

We're not puppets controlled by God. We have freedom. That's what's really clear to me: freedom.

Encouraging someone to carry a fetus and give birth might not be the most life-giving decision. Take a 12-year-old who gets raped. It's evil to ask that 12-year-old to carry the baby. I don't think that's life. I don't think that's valuing a 12-year-old's life.

For me, it's a health-care issue. The best person to make that decision is the person who has to decide that. And if that person believes it's immoral for them, then I would have to honor the conscience of that person and walk with them through what they would choose. I value a more nuanced conversation. I value thoughtfulness a lot. And I wish those who are considering the choices in front of them were honored and respected, and that government and institutions and even God doesn't have the final say over how we make the choices that are best for us."

Generally, Orthodox Jewish authorities approve of abortion only when a pregnant woman's life is at risk. Liberal Jews are less restrictive, assuming that a fetus does not achieve personhood until birth, so abortion is *not* murder.

If pregnancy endangers a woman, the fetus must be destroyed to save her. Once it starts to emerge, however, it becomes a human life, and mother and child have equal value and both should be saved—if possible. If the woman already has a child to care for, some rabbis give her priority.

As I was completing this book, a new Guttmacher Institute report said that the U.S. abortion rate again hit an all-time low.

- The **number of abortions** had a 19% decline from 2011 to 2017.
- The **abortion rate** (the number of abortions per 1,000 women aged 15–44) fell by 20%.
- The **abortion ratio** (the number of abortions per 100 pregnancies) fell 13%.

The report said that this period coincided with an unprecedented wave of new abortion restrictions: 32 states enacted 394 new restrictions.

According to the Institute, reducing abortion by shuttering clinics and erecting logistical barriers for patients is in direct conflict with sound public health policy, and the debate should not be framed based on the false premise that any reduction in abortion is good. Timely and affordable access to abortion should be available to anyone who wants and needs it. Obstructing or denying care in the name of reducing abortion is a violation of individuals' dignity, bodily autonomy and reproductive freedom.

Chapter 20

Michael on Miracles

News media frequently describe unusual events, such as the rescue of a missing person who was lost in the wilderness, as a "miracle."

In its extensive report on the fire at the Notre-Dame Cathedral in Paris, the *New York Times* said, "**Miraculously**, no one was killed.

In 1987, 18-month-old Jessica McClure fell into an 8-in.-wide, 22-ft.-deep abandoned well. After 58 hours she was finally rescued. *Time* magazine labeled the rescue a "**miracle**."

Time also classified the 2009 repair of the Hubble space telescope as a "**miraculous** rescue."

In 2015 Louis Jordan lived 66 days clinging to his capsized boat off Cape Hatteras, North Carolina. *Inside Edition* called him a "**Miracle** Survivor." Some cynics have expressed doubt about the story.

Shopping districts in California, New York, Florida and elsewhere have been labeled the "**Miracle** Mile."

Multiple movies have "**miracle**" in their titles.

The American men's hockey team's victory over the heavily favored Soviet team in the 1980 Winter Olympics was dubbed the "**Miracle** on Ice."

In 2019 when Popeye's introduced a fried chicken sandwich, food website *Thrillist* called it a "tiny **miracle**."

In 2009 US Airways Flight 1549 struck a flock of geese, lost engine power, and pilots Chesley Sullenberger and Jeffrey Skiles "ditched" the plane in the Hudson River off Midtown Manhattan. All 155 people aboard were rescued by nearby boats and there were few serious injuries. The accident came to be known as the "**Miracle** on the Hudson."

Two sisters, ages five and eight, were found safe after spending 44 hours in California woods in 2019. They said they had gotten lost following a deer trail and survived by drinking water from huckleberry leaves. County Sheriff William Honsal said their discovery was a "**miracle**."

In Nebraska in 2019, T. Scott Marr's children decided to "pull the plug" after he was declared brain-dead and was unconscious for two days. He unexpectedly woke up after his doctors thought there was no hope of recovery and his breathing tubes were removed. He recovered and said, "This whole thing has been a **miracle** from God."

During a night shift in 2018 Connecticut paramedic Chris Cabral became the patient when he suffered a stroke while driving an ambulance. Because of quick action by his partner Ray Berwick, he was quickly on the way to a full recovery. "It is a true **miracle**," Cabral said.

A split-second decision during the 2018 Thanksgiving holiday saved Bill Casselman, 58, of Missouri, who had been waiting for a donor kidney for nearly four years. Bill and his wife Angela were visiting relatives in Kansas, but news of an oncoming blizzard made them decide to go home early. When they arrived home they received a phone call saying that a donor kidney was ready. Casselman said, "Too many things fell into place all at once for this to be anything other than a **miracle**." *Readers Digest* wrote of a stroke patient: "One side of his body was paralyzed. He walked out less than a month later. No [physical] therapy and no permanent damage. Guy is over 80. This case is one of the most **miraculous** medical miracles of the year."

In *Fireislandandbeyond.com* we learned of the heroic actions of Danny Wakefield. "He pulled all three kids out from under the boat," she said. "I tried myself but wasn't strong enough. Their life vests were keeping them up and they were holding onto whatever they could reach to keep their own heads up in the air pocket. And Jamison kept the girls calm under there," she added. "It is absolutely **miraculous** we all survived."

When kayakers in Lake Michigan escaped being buried in a cliff collapse in Lake Michigan, an NBC reporter said it was a "**miracle**."

In an article in *Mysterious Ways*, a nurse who had suffered with a lifelong disease visited a church to hear a 'healer' speak. She said, "folks all around me were speaking of the **miraculous** healings they had received, everything from relief from shortness of breath to the reversal of paralysis.

Relief from paralysis is a common miracle scam demonstrated in churches, and exposed on television.

Christians seem obsessed with alleged miracles, starting with the "virgin birth" of Jesus—but other religions have **miracle** stories, too. Some Muslims believe that Muhammad split the Moon, but NASA disagrees.

In a 2019 report on the crash of a private jet carrying the family and dog of auto racer Dale Earnhart, Jr., an NBC reporter said that their survival was "**miraculous**."

Jewish tradition includes alleged miracles, too. One of the most prominent—which many Jewish children absorb quite early—involves the holiday of Chanukah (also spelled in other ways).

Chanukah is sometimes referred to as the "Jewish Christmas" because it is often celebrated near Christmas (and may overlap) and gifts are given in many families.

Chanukah commemorates the rededication of the Second Temple in Jerusalem at the time of the Maccabean Revolt against Greeks in around 160 BCE. According to tradition, the victorious Maccabees could find only a small jug of uncontaminated oil to sustain the oil lamp in the Temple for one day. It allegedly lasted for *eight days*, until more oil could be obtained, and this was a **miracle**.

Children play with (and adults gamble with) a *dreidel*, a four-sided top that shows the Hebrew letters that stand for the words **nes gadol hayah sham** ("a great miracle happened there").

Because Chanukah may be called the Jewish Christmas, Christian kids are often jealous of Jewish friends who get presents on "eight crazy nights" (as Adam Sand-ler sang).

Jewish kids often get clothes on Chanukah. Since I was the son of a retailer and had an almost unlimited clothing budget throughout the year, there was no point in giving me a sweater or shirt for the holiday.

I started asking my parents for a toboggan when I was about 12. I got it when I was 17—the same time my best friend, Howie, got a nice green British sporty car. Did he deserve a miracle more than I did? Probably not.

Well, folks, there are NO miracles.

There are:
1. highly unusual events
2. unexplained events
3. inaccurate observations
4. misinterpretations
5. faulty memories
6. frauds
7. dreams
8. desires to make something ordinary seem special
9. strange coincidences
10. counterfeit evidence

Here's something funny that does not relate to this chapter but it fills up space and it does relate to religion:

What a putz!

In the Pennsylvania Dutch dialect, a *putz* is a three-dimensional nativity scene—a crèche.

In Jewish slang, however, the word is the equivalent of "schmuck," and means both "penis" and "fool."

The Christmas customs in Bethlehem, Pennsylvania attracted the attention of a women's magazine in the late 1960s. It described the special meals and music, the decor, and the elaborate putzes assembled in many homes.

The small Jewish community in Bethlehem had a good laugh at the magazine's suggestion that tourists might "knock on any door in town and ask to see the family putz."

Oh Uncle Herman! There's someone here to see you!

Chapter 21
In God I Trust?

E Pluribus Unum (Latin for "out of many, one") was a perfectly good national motto for the United States of America. The phrase comes from the concept that *the union of the original thirteen colonies produced a new single nation.* It is on the Great Seal of the United States and was on both American metal and paper money for a long time, starting in 1795.

However, President Theodore Roosevelt strongly objected to using it on coinage.

In 1907 he said: "My own feeling in the matter is due to my very firm conviction that to put such a motto on coins, or to use it in any kindred manner, not only does no good, but does positive harm, and is in effect irreverence, which comes dangerously close to sacrilege. ... Any use which tends to cheapen it, and, above all, any use which tends to secure its being treated in a spirit of levity, is from every standpoint profoundly to be regretted. ... it seems to me emi-

nently unwise to cheapen such a motto by use on coins ... In all my life I have never heard any human being speak reverently of this motto on the coins or show any signs of its having appealed to any high emotion in him, but I have literally, hundreds of times, heard it used as an occasion of and incitement to ... sneering." ... Everyone must remember the innumerable cartoons and articles based on phrases like 'In God we trust for the 8 cents,' ... Surely, I am well within bounds when I say that a use of the phrase which invites constant levity of this type is most undesirable. ..."

Although it was never made a law, *E Pluribus Unum* was considered a de facto motto of the USA until 1956 when Congress passed an act adopting *In God We Trust* as the official motto. A similar phrase is in "The Star-Spangled Banner," written in 1814 by Francis Scott Key (and adopted as the U.S. national anthem in 1931 by President Herbert Hoover). The song says, "And this be our motto: 'In God is our trust.'"

The change from *E Pluribus Unum* to *In God We Trust* was popular at the time, due to the influence of organized religion and Cold War politics. The 1956 law was one of several legislative actions Congress took to differentiate the United States from atheistic communism. Earlier, a 1954 act added the words "under God" to the Pledge of Allegiance. There were few complaints at the time, but some non-believers now refuse to say the Pledge, or they say it without the added words. I personally think its fine to express allegiance to people, but not to a textile assemblage.

Favoring *In God We Trust*

Some American states adopted mottos with religious overtones during the Cold War, such as Ohio's *With God, all things are possible*. Multiple states—particularly in the South—have put *In God We Trust* on state seals and license plates. The phrase is common on the walls of government buildings, and even appears on law enforcement vehicles.

Christian nationalist zealots (more later) have been pressing for wide use of the phrase. In 2001 Rev. Donald Wildmon, who runs the **American Family Association**, came up with what he believes is a can't-miss idea: States and local school boards should pass laws requiring public schools to post signs reading *In God We Trust*. He said, "The ACLU and liberal judges may not allow the posting of the Ten Commandments, but they cannot prohibit the posting of our national motto!"

As reported by Virginia's DailyPress.com, the "**York-Poquoson Sheriff's office** announced that its patrol cars now bear a decal reading *In God We Trust*. Sheriff J.D. "Danny" Diggs, a Christian, who announced the move, said the decision was made in an effort to honor God by acknowledging him for his blessings upon us and it shows our patriotism by displaying our national motto. Diggs ordered about 100 decals for the department's 50 marked patrol cars. Diggs said he paid for the decals, which cost about $1,480, out of his own pocket. "It doesn't say 'in Jesus we trust.' ... Everybody has a God—the Jews and the Muslims have a God. Hindus and Buddhists and everybody else has a God, except, let's say, atheists," Diggs said. "I don't get why atheists would be so threatened by something that doesn't exist to them. Local nonbelievers found decals offensive.

Aiden Barnes, an atheist who lives in the area, thinks the decals will worsen the trust issues and tension between citizens and law enforcement that has been a growing issue all over the country. 'What was wrong with 'To Protect and Serve'?" Barnes asked. "This is a government office showing preference for a belief in a deity.... That says to me, as a resident of the area, that since I don't believe in God I'm not as valued to these people."

The Original Motto Project offered to provide stickers reading *E Pluribus Unum* in Bonifay, Florida where the police put on *In God We Trust* stickers. "We feel that this phrase will provide an inclusive statement to the citizens of the city of Bonifay," group president Robert Ray said.

Some say that the "God" slogan is a problem on government property. "Society works better when state and church are kept separate because it creates a fair and equal place for all of us to live," said Wesley Wilson, who organized a protest of the use of the religious motto by the Bonifay Police Department. "The saying *In God We Trust* that has been put on public property violates that.... Law enforcement is here to serve everyone, and that saying [isn't representative] of all who live here."

(ahead) The seal of Florida's Seminole tribe of Native Americans incorporates the "God" text, presumably inspired by the Florida seal. Interestingly, the Oklahoma Seminole seal does not mention God, nor do the seals of other tribes I've found.

The **Freedom From Religion Foundation** and four of its members sued in 2016 after commissioners of Lehigh County, Pennsylvania declined its request to stop using a seal which contains an image of a cross behind the county courthouse, plus other images related to farms and industries. The seal was adopted 75 years earlier and is used on the county's flag, vehicles and website.

According to Adelle M. Banks writing for Religion News Service, a Federal Appeals Court ruled in favor of the seal, citing a recent Supreme Court decision, and overturned a lower court decision that found the seal violated the establishment clause of the First Amendment.

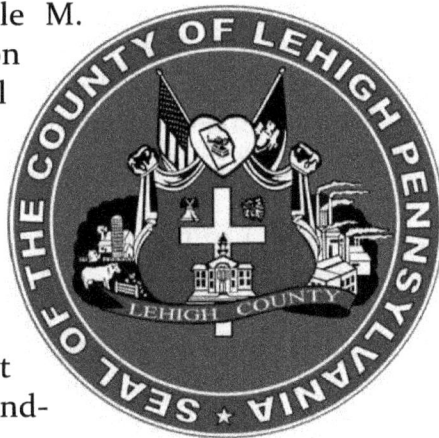

The Appeals Court said the seal is not a constitutional violation. "The Latin cross at issue here no doubt carries religious significance," reads the opinion written by Circuit Judge Thomas M. Hardiman. "But more than seven decades after its adoption, the seal has become a familiar, embedded feature of Lehigh County, attaining a broader meaning than any one of its many symbols."

The Appeals Court opinion said the district court applied a three-pronged test used since the 1971 Supreme Court decision in the Lemon v. Kurtzman case. The Lemon test has been used to determine whether a government agency has a secular purpose for a religious symbol, while requiring that it primarily "neither advances nor inhibits" religion nor fosters "an excessive government entanglement with religion."

The Appellate Court ruled the Lemon test, which it noted has been ignored in some similar past cases, does not apply in the seal case.

The seals of nearby Bethlehem Township and the City of Bethlehem ("Christmas City"—where I went to college) also contain crosses. The patch worn by Bethlehem City cops has a Bible as well as the cross.

The U.S. Supreme Court ruled in 2019 that the "Peace Cross" in Bladensburg, Maryland, which was dedicated by the American Legion in 1925 and stands in a traffic circle, *is constitutional.*

Students returning to public schools in South Dakota at the time this book was published saw new signs reading *In God We Trust* in their school buildings.

A new law signed by Republican Governor Kristi Noem required that the phrase be posted in schools in prominent locations before the 2019-20 school year began. According to CBS News: "Supporters say the phrase will instill patriotism. It's unclear how a motto that is clearly religious in nature will do this. Public school displays that included the U.S. Constitution, the Declaration of Independence and other historic documents might give students a better appreciation for our country's foundations and thus foster patriotism, but a religious phrase—even if it is the national motto—can never do that. Patriotism and religious belief are not one and the same. A firm atheist can be just as patriotic as the most ardent believer.

In fact, legislators in South Dakota and other states that have considered these bills have been clear about the religious motivation behind them. In Nebraska, state Senator Steve Erdman explained he wants to put up the motto because 'we have taken God out of everything' and we should 'let people see it.' He continued, 'The society we live in today is not as good as when we had school prayer and we had God in things.'

State Rep. Brandon Reed in Kentucky opined that 'we need God in our schools now more than ever' to combat 'rampant drug use, increasing school violence, and mounting cases of suicide.' He added, 'We are one nation under God, and that reality should be reflected in public life, including in the buildings where our children are being educated.'

In Illinois, Rep. Darrin Bailey issued a press release asserting that his bill will 'put God back in our schools ... and help give a moral compass to young people.' He also said that he introduced the bill because he believes 'there is power in honoring the name of God' and that 'as a God-fearing Christian, I believe that the lack of [Christian principles] is the problem in our country today.'"

Franklin Graham—evangelist, son of Billy and head of the Billy Graham Evangelistic Association—cheered South Dakota on Facebook: "Way to go South Dakota! When you think about it, this simple four-word historic motto is so profound. The only hope for the future of our nation is in Almighty God. This should not only be the motto on our country's currency, but the motto of our families, lived out every day. Maybe we should take a lesson from South Dakota schools and stencil it in our homes—and in our hearts."

Christian nationalism is a conservative ideology that seeks to establish the United States as a Christian nation. It encourages pro-Christian laws and displaying Christian religious art and symbolism in public areas, such as the Ten Commandments and "In God We Trust."

The **Foundation for Moral Law** was founded for this purpose in Alabama in 2003 by Republican politician Roy Moore. He was ousted as Chief Justice of the state's Supreme Court in that year for refusing to comply with a federal court order to remove a Ten Commandments monument from the grounds of the Alabama Judicial Building. In 2013, Moore was again elected to the Court, but was suspended in 2016 and resigned in 2017 after ordering Alabama probate judges to ignore federal court decisions on same-sex marriage.

Moore Money

Moore said he did not draw a "regular salary" from the foundation, but the *Washington Post* reported that he had an annual salary of $180,000, and from 2007 to 2012 collected more than $1 million, an amount that far surpasses what the foundation declared in public filings. Also, the *Post* reported that in 2012 when the charity could not pay his full salary, Moore received a note promising that he would get the salary in back pay or a stake in the assets of the foundation. The foundation paid for Moore's health-care costs, travel expenses and bodyguard, and the foundation's website promoted his speeches and book. The foundation employed Moore's wife and at least two of his children. The *Post* noted considerable overlap between the charity and Moore's political activities, with top officials of the charity leading Moore's 2017 Senate campaign and the charity and campaign using the same fundraising firm. The IRS warned the foundation about discrepancies.

216

Christian Nationalists also advocate bans on abortion and same-sex marriage, and support Sunday blue laws. The **Lord's Day Alliance** (LDA) was organized for this purpose in 1888. In 2018, the **Congressional Prayer Caucus Foundation** began **Project Blitz** to achieve those goals.

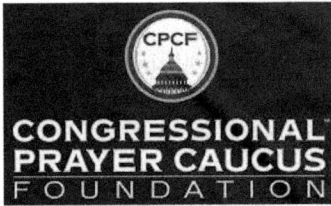

The **National Reform Association** (NRA), founded in 1864, seeks to make the USA Christian with an amendment to the Constitution acknowledging "Almighty God as the source of all authority and power in civil government, the Lord Jesus Christ as the Ruler among nations, His revealed will as the supreme law of the land, in order to constitute a Christian government..." It opposes drinking of alcohol, and even Sunday newspapers.

The NRA gained the support of churches. The **Wesleyan Methodist Church**, in its 1896 *Disciple,* contained a section, which continues to be retained by its successor, the **Allegheny Wesleyan Methodist Connection.** Its recent 2014 *Discipline* said: "It shall be the duty of the ministers and members ... to use their influence in every feasible manner in favor of a more complete recognition of the authority of Almighty God, in the secular and civil relations, both of society and of government, and the authority of our Lord Jesus Christ as King of nations as well as King of saints."

In 1895, the anti-liquor **Woman's Christian Temperance Union,** which was at that time the largest women's organization in the United States, proclaimed its solidarity with the NRA "whose efforts are parallel to ours on many lines." The WCTU passed a resolution: "God in Christ is the King of Nations, and as such should be acknowledged in our government; and His Word made the basis of our laws."

Opposing A Christian Nation

There is considerable opposition, by individuals and organizations, to the United States being recognized as or becoming a Christian Nation.

A group called **Christians Against Christian Nationalism** states: "As Christians, our faith teaches us everyone is created in God's image and commands us to love one another. As Americans, we value our system of government and the good that can be accomplished in our constitutional democracy. Today, we are concerned about a persistent threat to both our religious communities and our democracy—Christian nationalism.

Christian nationalism seeks to merge Christian and American identities, distorting both the Christian faith and America's constitutional democracy. Christian nationalism demands Christianity be privileged by the State and implies that to be a good American, one must be Christian. It often overlaps with and provides cover for white supremacy and racial subjugation. We reject this damaging political ideology and invite our Christian brothers and sisters to join us in opposing this threat to our faith and to our nation.

As Christians, we are bound to Christ, not by citizenship, but by faith. We believe that:
- People of all faiths and none have the right and responsibility to engage constructively in the public square.
- Patriotism does not require us to minimize our religious convictions.
- One's religious affiliation, or lack thereof, should be irrelevant to one's standing in the civic community.

- Government should not prefer one religion over another or religion over non-religion.
- Religious instruction is best left to our houses of worship, other religious institutions and families.
- America's historic commitment to religious pluralism enables faith communities to live in civic harmony with one another without sacrificing our theological convictions.
- Conflating religious authority with political authority is idolatrous and often leads to oppression of minority and other marginalized groups as well as the spiritual impoverishment of religion.
- We must stand up to and speak out against Christian nationalism, especially when it inspires acts of violence and intimidation—including vandalism, bomb threats, arson, hate crimes, and attacks on houses of worship—against religious communities at home and abroad.

Whether we worship at a church, mosque, synagogue, or temple, America has no second-class faiths. All are equal under the U.S. Constitution. As Christians, we must speak in one voice condemning Christian nationalism as a distortion of the gospel of Jesus and a threat to American democracy."

Americans United for Separation of Church and State is a nonpartisan educational and advocacy organization dedicated to advancing the separation of religion and government as the only way to ensure freedom of religion, including the right to believe or not believe, for all.

It says: "All students should feel welcome at and included in extracurricular events and clubs at their public schools. Public schools must treat all student-led groups equally. Religious student clubs must not be given preference by the schools or be exempt from nondiscrimination policies. In addition, public school officials may not use religion as a basis to bar students from starting clubs.

Public school assemblies, graduation ceremonies and foot-ball games may not include school-sponsored prayer, even if student led. It inevitably makes some students feel excluded.

No student should feel like an outsider in his or her own school. That's why Americans United fights to ensure students of all backgrounds and beliefs can participate in student-led clubs and attend extracurricular events without fear of having to participate in religious activities.

The wall of separation between church and state protects us all. It makes our country more fair, more equal and more inclusive. We envision a nation where everyone can freely choose a faith and support it voluntarily, or follow no religious or spiritual path at all, and where the government does not promote religion over non-religion or favor one faith over another.

Project Blitz is part of a larger national trend to redefine religious liberty as a sword used to harm others instead of a shield that protects people. Its organizers' strategy is to pass an increasingly ambitious set of state laws, starting with bills that require prominently displaying *In God We Trust* and establishing Bible classes in public schools and escalating to laws that would permit religion to be used to justify discrimination.

Some people behind the drive have argued that the phrase *In God We Trust* isn't really religious, and one hears more than an echo of that in the assertion from South Dakota that it's merely patriotic. Such claims, to be blunt, are ridiculous. *In God We Trust* sends a series of religious messages: It says there is one God (not five, not 20, not no God); it asserts that the nation trusts in this God, and you should too. After all, that's what *real* Americans do. If you choose not to, you're not only a lesser-type of citizen, your very loyalty may be suspect."

IN SCIENCE
WE TRUST

FFRF.org

The previously mentioned **Freedom From Religion Foundation** is a national organization incorporated in 1978. Members include approximately 32,200 "freethinkers, atheists, agnostics and skeptics of any pedigree." The Foundation and its staff attorneys act on countless violations of separation of state and church on behalf of members and the public including: prayers in public schools, payment of funds for religious purposes, government funding of pervasively sectarian institutions, and the ongoing campaign against civil rights for women, gays and lesbians led by churches.

In *The Founding Myth*, FFRF constitutional attorney Andrew Seidel discusses religion's role in America's founding: From a scholarly standpoint, the idea of a single 'Judeo-Christian tradition' is a myth.

One Jewish theologian stated the problem plainly: "Judaism is Judaism because it rejects Christianity, and Christianity is Christianity because it rejects Judaism."

"Judeo-Christian" is slippery because it is more a political invention than a scholarly description. It originated at the close of World War II when Christian exclusivity was too threatening. After "the Nazi death camps, a phrase like 'our Christian civilization' seemed ominously exclusive," explained Prof. Mark Silk. But the term didn't gain prominence until the fight against communism, during which some religion, any religion, was better than atheistic communism.

Eisenhower was probably the first president to use the term, explaining to a Soviet general in 1952 that the American "form of government has no sense unless it is founded in a deeply felt religious faith, and I don't care what it is. With us of course it is the Judeo-Christian concept."

President Harry Truman stated, more than once, that "the fundamental basis of all government is in this Bible right here, and it started with Moses on the Mount," and "the fundamental basis of our Bill of Rights comes from the teachings we get from Exodus and Saint Matthew, from Isaiah and Saint Paul."

The ill-defined term becomes clearer in light of these statements; Judeo-Christian principles can be derived from Mosaic Law, such as the Ten Commandments.

The term has the benefit of sounding inclusive to a broad audience while actually speaking directly to conservative Christians who hear only the second part of the term, "Christian." Robert Davi, the actor, Bond villain and frequent contributor to the conservative website Breitbart.com, gave this game away. Writing about the imaginary "War on Christmas," Davi argued that removing a nativity scene from government property is part of "a systematic attack on Judeo-Christian values that our country was founded on."

Davi knows that the nativity scene features the birth of Jesus as savior, something Judaism rejects. The nativity is Christian, not Judeo-Christian.

The Judeo-Christian Voter Guide website provides local resources, but prior to the 2016 election, they were nearly all Christian. In the state with the highest number and percentage of Jewish citizens, New York, the state guide linked to groups such as the Christian Coalition and the American Family Association, whose goal is "to be a champion of Christian activism."

It did not link to a single Jewish group. The site even had an identical twin, the "Christian Voter Guide" website, which was the same in every respect except that it lacked that crumb of inclusion: "Judeo-."

Christian nationalists are bent on "restoring" America to the principles on which they wish it were founded. They believe that secular America is a myth, and under the guise of restoration they seek to press religion into every crevice of the government. They not only think it appropriate for the government to favor one religion over others, but also believe America was designed to favor Christianity. To them, America is a Christian nation founded on Christian principles, and promoting that belief is a religious duty.

Christian nationalism's fabricated history conceals an important historical truth: religion and government are best kept on either side of an impregnable wall, as the founders intended.

Some people, *including me*, question the constitutionality of the "God" motto because of the separation of church and state provided for in the First Amendment. Sadly, in 1970, in *Aronow v. United States*, the United States Court of Appeals for the Ninth Circuit ruled that the motto does not violate the First Amendment.

The Court tacitly approved the motto in 2019 by dismissing a case brought by atheist Michael Newdow, arguing on behalf of a group of atheists. He claimed that the motto is a government endorsement of religion and violates the First Amendment. He argued that "by mandating the inscription of facially religious text on every coin and currency bill, the government was turning atheists into political outsiders." Newdow lost cases in lower courts, including an attempt to remove "under God" from the Pledge of Allegiance. According to the Christian Broadcasting Network, "He also tried to keep government leaders from saying the phrase 'So help me God' in the 2009, 2013, and 2017 presidential inaugurations."

Newdow is an attorney and physician and the son of Jewish parents. He said, "I was born an atheist."

The constitutionality of *In God We Trust* has been upheld by the Supreme Court under the judicial interpretation of *accommodationism:* the entrenched practice of using the motto has not historically presented any constitutional difficulty, is not coercive, and does not prefer one religious denomination over another. In *Zorach v. Clauson* (1952), the Supreme Court also wrote that the nation's "institutions presuppose a Supreme Being."

I resent the new motto and the phrase "under God" that was added to the Pledge of Allegiance during Cold War fever in the 1950s. The USA is *not* a theocracy. We are not and should not be a nation under God. Our freedom of religion includes freedom *from* religion.

I particularly resent people such as Dr. Russell Moore of the Southern Baptist Convention and Moral Majority founder Jerry Falwell, who claim that the USA is a "Christian nation." The nation was founded to provide religious freedom to *all* immigrants.

According to Mokhtar Ben Barka, in *The European Journal of American Studies:* "One of the Religious Right's most visible spokesmen, evangelist-psychologist James Dobson, distributes through his Focus on the Family history lessons that seek to show that "the Constitution was designed to perpetuate a Christian order." Many of America's disorders, Dobson says, stem from abandoning this unity of state and church." Beverly LaHaye, chair of Concerned Women of America, affirms that "America is a nation based on biblical principles.... Christian values dominate our government. Politicians who do not use the bible to guide their public and private lives do not belong in government."

Chapter 22
Yom Kippur for the Non-Observant Jew
How to observe the Day of Atonement?

Today (12 October 2016), like any other day, I turned on my bedroom TV to watch *Morning Joe*. And like any other day, I will not fast or pray. Both are customary activities on this Jewish "Day of Atonement."

I was a bit surprised to see Jewish Mark Halperin doing his usual work. Although I know nothing about his personal religious practices, I do know he is Jewish. Other Jews recognize his Jewish name, but perhaps non-Jews do not. It's not as obvious as Schwartz, Cohen or Katz.

Of course, names are not conclusive. Reagan's Secretary of State Caspar Weinberger was Episcopal. (His paternal grandparents converted from Judaism.)

CBS newsman Walter Cronkite—regarded by many as the most-trusted person in America—was widely assumed to be Jewish. Maybe it was because he was in the media, maybe because "Uncle Walter" was smart and personable, like so many Jews are. His name certainly sounds Jewish. Walter told a story about taking a cab to the CBS building on Yom Kippur. The cabby, of course, recognized him; and berated the "King of the anchormen" for working on a highly holy day. Walter explained that he was not Jewish.

I used to hate Yom Kippur as a child. Not only did I have to wear a tie, but the B'nai Jacob service was even longer and more boring than Sabbath services. My parents said that in order to take the day off from school, we kids had to go to services. Having the day off from school was not a suitable reward for the agony.

I fasted between breakfast and lunch. My father skipped breakfast and lunch some years.

Pop's retail stores were open, with gentiles taking care of business. He explained: "People have religions. Businesses do not." (This was before Ultra-Christian Hobby Lobby and Chick-fil-A.)

My own business will function today. My Jewish employee will be praying at a synagogue (and will get paid for not working). I will answer phone calls and email, but there will be fewer of both than on a normal day. Some customers know that AbleComm, Inc. is a Jew-owned business, but most customers and prospective customers do not. Observant Jews will probably not try to do business with me today. That's OK (but it hurts after doing little business on Columbus Day).

"Respect," Los Angeles Dodger baseball player Sandy Koufax responded when asked by *Jewish Week* why he sat out a World Series game on Yom Kippur in 1965. For the same reason, and to show solidarity with my tribe, I will not make my customary dozens of Facebook posts today or publish my two online political newspapers.

UPDATE: In 2019, as this book was nearing completion, I realized that I had scheduled my car for an oil change on Rosh Hashanah. I canceled the appointment for the same reason that Sandy Koufax did not play ball: Respect.

Chapter 23

Old Testament God Vs. New Testament God

The deity of the Torah era ("Old Testament" or "Old Covenant") is sometimes described as being tougher than the nice guy deity of the "New Testament" or "New Covenant."

Atheist Richard Dawkins wrote in *The God Delusion*, that the God of the Old Testament is "arguably the most unpleasant character in all fiction: jealous and proud of it; a petty, unjust, unforgiving control-freak; a vindictive, blood-thirsty ethnic cleanser; a misogynistic, homophobic, racist, infanticidal, genocidal, filicidal, pestilential, megalomania-cal, sadomasochistic, capriciously malevolent bully."

Got AnswersMinistries says: "In the New Testament, God's loving-kindness and mercy are manifested even more fully through the fact that 'God so loved the world that he gave his one and only Son, that whoever believes in him shall not perish but have eternal life.'"

In reality, the Gods written about in *both* books exhibit a wide range of personalities: from **violent, jealous and irrational** to **helpful, kind and loving**. Neither God is a "better" God, and those same personality traits also apply to human beings.

According to Focus on the Family (a conservative website I would normally avoid), "To say that the God of the Old Testament is wrathful and punishing while the God of the New is loving and kind is a gross oversimplification. The God of the Old Covenant is anything *but* the relentlessly bad-tempered taskmaster some people make Him out to be. The Old Testament Scriptures are forever describing Him as merciful and gracious, slow to anger, and abounding in mercy. They refer to Him as a God who has not dealt with us according to our sins nor punished us according to our iniquities."

Rev. Adam Eckhart of my nearby First United Church of Christ pointed out that the God of the Torah era is "not all bad" and that the New Testament has "plenty of fire and brimstone."

Chapter 24
B.C. & A.D.

No. Those abbreviations do not stand for "Before Christ" and "After Death," as I often heard when I was a kid in the 1950s.

They do stand for the Latin words *Anno Domini* (AD) and the English words Before Christ (BC) and are used to label or number years in the Julian and Gregorian calendars. The term *Anno Domini* is Medieval Latin and means "year of the Lord," but is often defined using "our Lord" instead of "the Lord," taken from the full original phrase "*anno Domini nostri Jesu Christi*," which translates to "in the year of our Lord Jesus Christ."

This calendar era is based on the traditionally calculated year of the conception or birth of Jesus, with *AD* counting years from the start of this epoch, and *BC* denoting years before the start. There is no year zero in this scheme, so the year AD 1 immediately follows the year 1 BC. This dating system was devised in 525 by Dionysius Exiguus of Scythia Minor, but was not widely used until after 800.

The Gregorian calendar is the most widely used calendar in the world today. For decades, it has been the unofficial global standard, adopted in the pragmatic interests of international communication, transportation, and commercial integration, and recognized by international institutions such as the United Nations.

Traditionally, English followed Latin usage by placing the AD abbreviation *before* the year number and BC is placed *after* the year number (for example: AD 2019, but 68 BC), which also preserves logical order.

The abbreviations are also widely used after the number of a century or millennium, as in "fourth century AD" or "second millennium AD" (although conservative usage formerly rejected such expressions).

Because BC is the English abbreviation for *Before Christ*, it is sometimes incorrectly concluded that AD means *After Death*, i.e., after the death of Jesus. However, this would mean that the approximate 33 years commonly associated with the life of Jesus would neither be included in the BC nor the AD time scales.

Terminology that is viewed by some as being more neutral and inclusive of non-Christian people is to call this the *Common Era* (abbreviated as CE), with the preceding years referred to as *Before the Common Era* (BCE). Astronomical year numbering and ISO 8601 avoid words or abbreviations related to Christianity, but use the same numbers for AD years.

[Most of the above comes from Wikipedia. I thank them.]

Chapter 25
Salad Dressing & Faith

I asked a Catholic friend to explain the Trinity to me. He said that he accepts it on faith.

I accept *almost nothing* on faith. The things I accept on faith are based on *experience in the physical world.*

- I have faith that the sun will rise tomorrow morning—just as it always has in the past. (Yes, I know that the sun doesn't really rise. It just seems to rise because of the Earth's rotation, but don't try to distract me.)
- I have faith that the pizza prepared for me at my favorite pizzeria, Papa's Pizza, will be perfect—just as it always has been in the past. I want and will receive a large pie with eggplant and onions, heavy on the sauce, light on the cheese, crisp but not burned.
- I have faith that if I open the door to my refrigerator I will find between two and eight bottles of salad dressing—because they have always been there before.
- Do I have faith in the existence of a Supreme Being? Not without evidence.

A funeral can be funny.

My wife and I once attended a funeral about 50 miles away from home, in a city we were not familiar with.

The proceedings started with a religious service in a synagogue, and then there was a long procession of about 20 vehicles that meandered through the city streets to the cemetery for the burial.

Our car was near the end of the line. When we reached the cemetery, we sensed that something was wrong.

Instead of familiar Jewish stars, most of the gravestones were engraved with crucifixes, and we saw lots of statues of Jesus and Mary.

Apparently as some of the cars navigated through a complex intersection, we separated from the main group and merged into a *different dead person's* procession.

We never found the right cemetery, but we had a very nice lunch at Bertucci's.

Chapter 26

Aging (& T-Shirts)

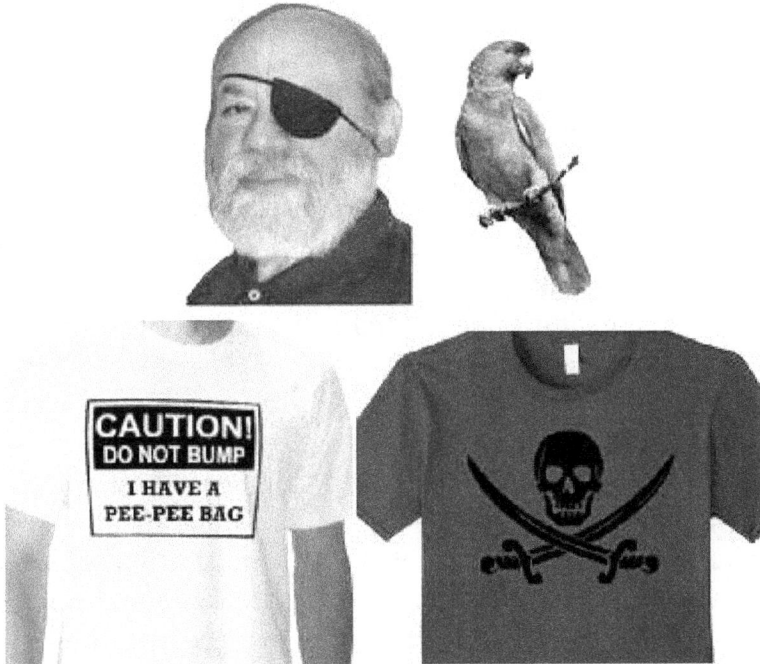

I saw a preview for an HBO special with Carl Reiner, Mel Brooks, Dick Van Dyke and others praising the joys of being 90 or older. I recently passed my 73rd birthday and I spend a lot of time contemplating being old. But, *I'm* still middle-aged, of course. "Old" doesn't start until people begin shoveling dirt on top of you.

Young people eagerly contemplate becoming 5, 10, 13, 16, 18, 21 and—if they have presidential pretensions—35. The following decades don't mean much until age 65 for Medicare and 62 to 70 for Social Security. Social Security works like putting quarters into a slot machine for five decades and then—KA-CHING—coins start flowing out.

I had foolishly and eagerly thought that SocSec would buy me a second home and worldwide travel. Sadly, it's used for such frivolities as food, medicine and taxes.

After finance, physical and mental health are the big issues for senior citizens. Lots of body parts no longer work as well or as often as they used to—or at all. Every year I add more *ologists* to my list of medical specialists.

I'm a wreck, physically. (Mentally, not yet so bad.) Some people deal with pain and dysfunction with increasing amounts of drugs, or acupuncture, spirituality and other conventional or exotic remedies.

So far I've been able to deal with my failing body by combining conventional medicine with disobedience, egomania and self-deprecating humor.

In my world, *everything* is a proper subject for laughter, and I have *no* secrets.

I recently told the world (at least the Facebook world), that I had peed in my pants while rushing to the men's room in a supermarket. I was *amazed* by the number of men and women who confessed to the same malfunction.

Someone said that "the eyes are the window to the soul." I think that T-shirts do the job quite well.

A few years ago I expected to have surgery for kidney stones. I ordered and wore a shirt that proclaimed "**CAUTION! Do Not Bump. I Have A Pee-Pee Bag.**" It turned out that I did not need the bag, but I wore the shirt to the hospital and to other places since then. People's reactions vary. Some gasp. Some giggle. Some turn away. Some ask where they can buy a shirt like mine.

In 2016 I had diplopia ("double-vision") for four months. I wore an eye patch to compensate by blocking one eye. I also often wore a pirate T-shirt and sometimes put a fake parrot on my shoulder. When kids asked me if I was a real pirate, of course I responded "aaaarrrggghh." Can dysfunction, illness and inadequacy be funny? Sometimes. (But *please* don't make fun of other people.)

Back in the 70s I was an "award-winning Madison Avenue advertising copywriter." One of my favorite mediums (not "media" in this usage) was the T-shirt. The objective was to turn millions of human bodies into mobile billboards. To get those millions to carry our messages, each wearer of the shirt had to become *part of the message*, maybe part of a joke.

At that time Castrol introduced a new motor oil designed to stand up to the high temperatures of small, high-RPM car engines. I devised a shirt with a slogan that proclaimed, "**I Don't Stop When I Get Hot**." The oil and sexy shirt were very successful—and I saw some of the shirts being worn even 30 years later.

Back to health: I am able to deal with incontinence, diabetes, neuropathy, skin pre-cancer, arthritis, sleep apnea, swollen feet, atrial fibrillation, hand pain, missing teeth, fading memory, trouble typing and other issues. (However, I did eliminate nosebleeds and outgrew migraines.)

Photos reveal that I have lost the hairs that used to sprout from my arms and legs. I can accept the loss of hairs, but what scares me is the loss of my mind!

Is trouble thinking of a word—or typing a wrong word—no big deal? Or is it the onset of the **dementia**?

I produced this book with a 12-year-old version of *Microsoft Word*. It works as well as it did when it was brand-new, back in 2007—and that's good enough.

Chapter 27

I Don't Want To Be A Jewish Mouse For An Evangelical Cat

Evangelical Christians frequently express their support (and even "love") for both the country of Israel and the Jewish people. Evangelical groups make pilgrimages to Israel, support American political candidates deemed to be pro-Israel, donate money to Israel, and some evangelists are more fervent Zionists than many American Jews are. The Christian Broadcasting Network's website has an extensive section of news about Israel. An article in July of 2019 celebrated

"Prophecy Fulfilled: Hundreds of Jewish Immigrants Come Home to Israel this Summer."

Some Christians believe that the return of the Jews to the Middle East and the establishment of the state of Israel in 1948 were in accordance with Bible prophecy. Some believe that the gathering of the Jews in Israel is a prerequisite for the Second Coming of Jesus. Since the Reformation in the 16th century, many Protestant Christians actively supported the Jewish return to the Israel and encouraged Jews to become Christians as a means of fulfilling Biblical prophecy.

According to a poll released by the Brookings Institution, 53 percent of American evangelicals supported Trump's decision to move the American embassy in Israel from Tel Aviv to Jerusalem, while just 37 percent of all Americans supported the decision.

Why the big difference?

Elizabeth Oldmixon is a politics professor at the University of North Texas. She studies the alliance between evangelical Christians and Orthodox Jews who are strongly pro-Israel. She told Sean Illing of Vox.com: "These are the folks who believe that there will be a millennium in the future, a golden age, where Christ reigns on Earth, [and] they believe that before Christ will return, there will be a tribulation where Christ defeats evil. There will be natural disasters and wars, and perhaps an Antichrist, as the book of Revelations notes. Then at the end of that period, the people of the Mosaic covenant, including the Jews, will convert. Then after their conversion, the great millennium starts.

You have this group of people looking around for signs of the end time, and in the 20th century when Israel was founded, this was seen as a major sign. This was electrifying for that community because the gathering of all the Jews in exile to the Holy Land is a prerequisite for all of these events unfolding. So for the subset of evangelicals in the 20th century, support for Israel became a really, really important political position.

[Orthodox Jews have] an understanding that the Messiah will come, but it won't be a second coming of the sort Christians believe in. But the state of Israel has welcomed the political support of evangelical Christians nevertheless. They even encourage Christians to visit Israel, to tour the holy sites.

If Evangelicals want to absorb Jews, to use us as a kind of spiritual cannon fodder in a war with Satan, I have to conclude that *evangelicals love Jews like cats love mice.*

In ExploreGod.com, Barry Cooper wrote: Satan's "concern for our well-being is much the same as a shark's concern for a sardine—nonexistent. In fact, he would gladly devour us." To me, this is another animal equivalent of the relationship between Evangelicals and Jews.

In yet another analogy, Donald Trump has used American Jews as non-volunteer partners in his war against the "Squad" of four congresswomen of color who Trump told to go back to their home countries in mid-2019. He repeatedly exaggerated about their antisemitism and anti-Israel leanings (e.g.: "I can tell you that they have made Israel feel abandoned by the U.S."). Presidential sycophant Senator Lindsey Graham proclaimed that "AOC and this crowd are a bunch of communists" who hate their own country and Israel. "They're antisemitic. They're anti-American."

Trump's line of attack—instructing a group of American citizens to 'go back to where they came from'—is one that has often been aimed at Jews. Jewish Senator Brian Schatz of Hawaii criticized Trump for citing the women's views on Israel as justification for his ire. "You really have to leave us out of your racist talking points. You are not helping us, you are not helping society, you are not helping Israel."

I am one American Jew who does not want to be part of Trump's war, or the evangelical final solution. I am too smart to be a "useful idiot."

According to the *Christian Post* (edited): There is outrage brewing over comments made by the Palm Beach County Democratic Party Chairman during the Democratic National Convention in which he states that Christians want to "slaughter" Jews so there can be a "second coming of Christ."

Mark Alan Siegel, Palm Beach County Democratic Party Chairman, accused fundamentalist Christians of not being real friends of Israel and holding alternative motives to advance their agenda. "Christians just want us to be there so we can be slaughtered and converted and bring on the second coming of Jesus Christ."

"They're not our friends. They want Israel to pursue policies which are antithetical with its security and existence," Siegel said. "The worst possible allies for the Jewish state are the fundamentalist Christians who want Jews to die and convert so they can bring on the second coming of their Lord. It is a false friendship. They are seeking their own ends and not ours."

Scottie Neil Hughes, a reporter for PatriotTV and the Tea Party News Network, revealed that: "I have heard from both Christians and members of the Jewish faith who are upset and ashamed of this man's comment ... I find it ironic that while we here at a convention focused on unity, the first quote I get is filled with so much hate." However, she did see where Christians and Jews could disagree, especially when it came to politics regarding Israel.

"I noticed a man with a Hebrew pin which was obviously for Obama ... I simply asked him, 'As a man of Jewish faith, why do you support Barack Obama for a second term when the DNC platform almost completely ignores Israel?'"

According to Jonathan Weisman, in *Semitism: Being Jewish in America in the Age of Trump*: "To stand against Israel is to stand against God," [Moral Majority founder] Jerry Falwell declared. Pat Robertson's 700 Club extolled the virtues of the Jewish state, a redoubt of democratic ideals and Judeo-Christian values in a sea of Muslims.

Christian tourism in the Holy Land brought a steady stream of Middle America to that small island of recognizable civilization in the Middle East, about the size of New Jersey. Amid M16-wielding Israeli soldiers and wary Palestinians, pilgrims from Wisconsin and Kansas wearing Bermuda shorts and church-issued matching T-shirts carried crosses through the Old City of Jerusalem, tracing Jesus's path on the Via Dolorosa.

Savvy Jewish leaders understood that this affection for Israel was not exactly geopolitical. Christian fundamentalists saw the founding of the Jewish state and the ingathering of Jews in the Holy Land as an important step toward the New Testament's prophesied Armageddon and the eventual return of Jesus Christ.

The Jews all might die, slaughtered in the battle of the faithful against the faithless, incinerated in the Tribulation or left behind by the Rapture—"How's it gonna end? Isn't gonna be none too pretty," Pat Robertson warned—but for now they were friends. The Jews would have to put up with some inconvenient theology—and some distasteful cultural appropriation—but it was in the service of the Jewish state.

In 1981, after Israeli warplanes bombed a nuclear reactor in Iraq, Israeli prime minister Menachem Begin called Falwell to rally a favorable response from the American public. Thirty-six years later, a staunchly conservative congressman named Clay Higgins journeyed from his home state of Louisiana to the gas chambers of Auschwitz-Birkenau to videotape himself preaching the gospel of raised drawbridges. "It's hard to walk away from gas chambers and ovens without a very sober feeling of commitment, unwavering commitment, to make damn sure that the United States of America is protected from the evils of the world," Higgins intoned, not seeing the irony of a nationalist message filmed at the site of the National Socialists' greatest crime. The Jews largely held their tongues.

Whores In The Bible

There have always been horny men so it should not be a surprise that women indulged in "the oldest profession" even in Biblical times.

When I was in high school I encountered the work of folk singer and connoisseur of dirty songs **Oscar Brand**. He recorded a song with lyrics like these:

Once on a time there lived a dame
Who plied a trade of ancient fame
She was a girl of ill repute,
In fact she was a prostitute.
Hi, Ho Kafoozalum
The harlot of Jerusalem;
Hi, Ho Kafoozalum
The daughter of the rabbi.

In the song an aroused priest aimed his penis poorly and inadvertently engaged in anal intercourse. Kafoozalum flatulated strongly, propelling the priest "like a dart, Sailing o'er Jerusalem."

There are several versions of the song. Some say "baabaa," not "rabbi" and the customer was a prince, not a priest.

Anyway, getting back to serious business: the "Whore of Babylon" (shown on the previous page) is a symbolic female figure and also a place of evil mentioned in the Book of Revelation, the final book in the New Testament. Her full title is *Mystery, Babylon the Great, the Mother of Prostitutes and Abominations of the Earth.*

17:4   And the woman was arrayed in purple and scarlet color, and decked with gold and precious stones and pearls, having a golden cup in her hand full of abominations and filthiness of her fornication:

17:5   And upon her forehead was a name written, Mystery, Babylon the great, the mother of harlots and abominations of the earth.

17:6   And I saw the woman drunken with the blood of the saints, and with the blood of the martyrs of Jesus: and when I saw her, I wondered with great admiration.

According to the *Jewish Virtual Library*: The prostitute was an accepted though deprecated member of Israelite society in the Torah era. The Bible refers to Tamar's temporary harlotry and to the professional harlotry of Rahab without passing any moral judgment. Samson's visits to the harlot of Gaza are not condemned, but go with his roguish life.

Harlots had access to the king's court; but harlotry was a shameful profession, and to treat an Israelite girl like a prostitute was considered a grave offense. The Israelites were warned against prostituting their daughters, and priests were not allowed to marry prostitutes.

The punishment of a priest's daughter who became a prostitute, thus degrading her father, was death by fire. According to the talmudic sages, however, this law applies only to the priest's daughter who is married or engaged.

Prostitutes might be encountered in the streets, calling out to potential customers. They sang, played harps and bathed publicly. Men were warned about their glances and smooth talk—much like sailors in Greek mythology who were warned about the **Sirens**, dangerous creatures who lured sailors with their enchanting music and voices to shipwreck on the rocky coast of their island.

In various parts of the ancient Middle East, "temple women" may have served as sacred prostitutes. In ancient Israel the sacred prostitutes were condemned for their connection with idolatry. Deuteronomy forbids Israelite men and women to become sacred prostitutes, and states that their wages must not be used for paying vows.

In the New Testament Mary Magdalene was a Jewish woman and frequent companion to Jesus who is said to have witnessed his crucifixion and resurrection. Some people have claimed that she was a prostitute. The 2007 documentary *The Lost Tomb of Jesus* proposed that evidence existed to show that Jesus was married to Mary Magdalene and that their son was named Judah.

Is Celibacy Its Own Punishment?

My maternal grandmother ("Gramma Del") was born in 1898 in what was then called "Hell's Kitchen" on Midtown Manhattan's West Side. The young Jewish Adele Schwartz took piano lessons from a nun at a nearby Catholic church. Gramma told me that she once arrived early for her lesson and saw a nun and priest embracing and kissing.

The clerical couple was doing what comes naturally to most human beings, and other life forms—but is frowned upon by the Catholic Church. The usual escalation from making out to outright sexual intercourse is forbidden for most Catholic priests and nuns.

Helen Prejean is an author, anti-capital-punishment activist, and a nun. In an interview with Terry Gross on NPR she revealed a romance she had with a highly attractive priest when she was in her 20s. He wanted to 'go all the way' and even marry her, but she stayed true to her vow of celibacy, and the couple decided to just be friends. She

described a party attended by nuns and priests with "beer, wine and hard liquor" and romantic music, and "the attraction was there. We couldn't help it."

For many years, Catholic priests were allowed to marry, but the rules for Roman Catholics changed in 1139, under Pope Innocent II. (Priests in "Eastern Rite" Catholic churches may marry prior to ordination.)

Over 800 years later, in 1980, the rules for Roman Catholics changed again. Married non-Catholic clergy were allowed to remain married (and sexually active) after converting to Catholicism and being ordained as Catholic priests.

Thus, a current Catholic priest who wants to get married must choose between marriage and the priesthood, while a married Lutheran minister or Episcopal priest can become a Catholic priest and *keep his wife*. This seems unfair to some Catholic priests who left the clergy to marry. Some priests who married continue to function as "independent" priests, defying the Vatican.

In the fall of 2019 Pope Francis opened a meeting of bishops that would debate whether the Church should loosen its requirement of celibacy for priests. The meeting, called a "synod," dealt with "new paths for the church" in South America's Amazon region, particularly deforestation and other threats to indigenous communities.

According to Francis X. Rocca in the *Wall Street Journal*: "The potentially momentous debate pits those who say ordaining married men could relieve the church's clergy shortage against those who warn that doing so would undermine the distinctive character of the priesthood.

The most controversial 'new path' scheduled for discussion was the possibility of ordaining married men to serve as priests in the sparsely populated region, where Catholic parishes sometimes go for months without a visit from a priest.

The Pope has said that the 'door is always open' to married priests in remote places such as the Amazon or the Pacific islands. The ratio of Catholics to priests in South America is 7,200 to one, almost four times the ratio in North America, according to Vatican statistics for 2017. In parts of the Amazon, the ratio is more than 8,000 to one. The world-wide ratio has risen sharply in recent decades, to about 3,200 to 1 from 1,900 to 1 in 1980."

Many of the apostles were married. Seven popes were married. Thirteen popes were sons of priests. Six popes fathered children after the 1139 Celibacy Law. Pope Alexander VI had grandsons who became cardinals. (Info from FutureChurch.com, and other sources)

A Rabbi and a Priest were talking

Priest: "So tell me, Rabbi, have you ever eaten ham?"

Rabbi: "Yes, once, just to see what it was like. What about you? Have you ever been romantic with a woman?"

Priest: "Well, I entered the priesthood later in life and before that, I confess, I did have girlfriends."

Rabbi: "It's a lot better than ham, isn't it?"

In *Back to Basics: God's Word vs. Religion*, Messianic Jew Steven R. Bruck told the joke above and more seriously deals with the apparent dichotomy between Church-imposed celibacy and God's commandment, early in the Torah: "be fruitful and multiply."

Bruck says, "that one command is not only the easiest to obey, but (probably) the most enjoyable one for us, as well. ... I feel that the celibacy issue is so important and so far from God's commands about relationships, that it needs to be covered. Another reason to discuss this is because there is not one commandment or regulation in the Manual [Bible] that prohibits men in the priesthood from marrying. The celibacy requirement is a religious requirement, and this book exists to show the difference between the Word of God and the regulations and requirements of religion. ...

In the early days of the church (which means around the 3rd Century) a priest to be ordained could already be married, as many of the men were already older (maybe that's where we get the term 'elders'). However, they were required to refrain from conjugal relations with their wives. Apparently this didn't work very well (big surprise there, right?) so the church split down its East-West axis. The Western church decided it would not ordain married men and made the new priest take a vow of celibacy. The Eastern Church continued to allow marriage, and eased the regulation of abstinence to only a short time before the Eucharist.

The "Official" Reason one of those sites justified celibacy of the Priesthood by referring to the fact that Jesus (Yeshua) didn't marry and lived His life devoted only to God and to doing His will. This is true. He did, indeed, live His life totally devoted to doing God's will. As a sample of total devotion, He set the bar pretty high. However, is it correct to compare us to Him? After all, we are all born into original sin. We are born to live a human lifetime, and commanded to be fruitful and multiply. This is a purpose for which God created us. That's the one side.

On the other side, we have Yeshua. Yeshua was not born of humans, but of the Spirit through a human. Therefore, He was not born into original sin. He was not born to live a complete human life (He came here to die for us, remember?) and he was destined to die without any descendants (Isaiah 52). For Yeshua to even consider marriage and family, when all the time He knew that He would be making His wife a widow and His kids fatherless, would have been a sin, would it not? At the very least, it wouldn't have been very nice. In fact, one of the very last things He did, just before He gave up His spirit, was to (essentially) disown His mother.

In the Gospel of Yochanon (John) 19:25-6, He calls Miryam (Mary) and Yochanon to the execution stake and says, "Woman, this is your son. Man, this is your mother." Yeshua knew that He was here for a purpose, and that purpose had nothing to do with being fruitful and multiplying.

The truth is that Yeshua didn't live a celibate life solely for the purpose of devoting it entirely to God; He lived a celibate life to fulfill prophecy and His purpose for existing as a man, which required that He remain single and unattached. Therefore, to say that a priest should not marry because Yeshua didn't marry is not only an unfair comparison, but (I think) shows a lack of understanding of the very reason Yeshua took on the mantle of flesh. Another justification given for a priest to live a celibate life is that marriage and family would be a hindrance to the Priest's ability to give his all to serving God. How can you disagree with that? Isn't it a truism that if a person has no life of their own they can devote 100% of it to something else? If we take that thought a little further, then businesses that hire high profile executives that need to be available around the clock shouldn't hire married men or women.

Oh, yeah—doctors should be single, as well as anyone who wants to devote themselves to their career. I know that God is much more important than a worldly career, but there are many people who do a lot of really good work that is not directly devoted to God and they are married. For my money, anything we do should be devoted to God and done to glorify Him. Anything we do, not just clerical duties.

The Reasons for Shaul's (Paul) Celibacy In Chapter 7 of 1st Corinthians, Shaul (Saul) stated it was his wish everyone could be like him, living exclusively and singly to serving God (BTW…when you read this chapter Saul also is very clear to separate his ideas from God's commandments). The problem with Saul's idea about everyone being like him is that it is self-defeating to have a generation of celibate Believers. Let's get real, Folks! If everyone was celibate they would be, by definition, the last generation to practice celibacy because they would be the last generation, period!

Assorted comments:

- Many thousands of clergy people in various faiths—as well as physicians, psychiatrists, attorneys, mechanics, statesmen, architects, coaches and other advisers—are able to serve those who need them even if the advisers are married.

- A clergyperson may be able to give better advice to married people if the clergyperson is married and has experienced first-hand the issue being asked about. "He no play-a da game, he no make-a da rules," said U.S. Secretary of Agriculture Earl Butz in 1974, reacting to Pope Paul VI's opposition to using artificial contraception.

- Sexual activity is a primal urge for most species. If the urge is suppressed, it's possible that the suppressed people will react in unhealthy, immoral, illegal ways, such as child molesting. The Catholic Church has generally refused to fire pedophile priests until recently, and has paid billions to settle lawsuits from victims. As this book was nearing completion, NPR reported that "Missouri Attorney General Eric Schmitt announced Friday he is referring 12 former priests for criminal prosecution on charges of sexual abuse of minors following a 13-month-long investigation of church personnel records dating back almost 75 years. The investigation, detailed in a 329-page report, covered more than 2,000 priests who have served in Missouri since 1945, and included some 300 deacons, seminarians and religious women in that state's four dioceses. The investigators also spoke with survivors of clergy abuse and their families. The inquiry found 'credible allegations of 163 instances of sexual abuse or misconduct by Catholic diocesan priests and deacons against minors.' Of those, 83 have died. The statute of limitations has run out on 46 crimes allegedly committed by the 80 who are still alive, Schmitt said in a St. Louis news conference. 'The betrayal of trust and of innocence is devastating and in many instances incomprehensible,' said Schmitt. The investigation found church officials 'refused to acknowledge the victims and instead focused its efforts on protecting its priests,' by relocating priests without notifying law enforcement or the offending priest's old and new parishes."

- Opus Dei ("work of God") is an international Catholic organization [some call it a cult] involved in charity and educational work with about 100,000 priests and lay members. It is beyond the scope of this book to provide a detailed analysis of the organization, but I will point out that about 30% of members are *celibate*, and many live in sex-segregated Opus Dei centers. I used to service the telephone system for a large Opus Dei campus. The men were uniformly knowledgeable, intelligent and friendly—but very uncomfortable on those occasions when my wife accompanied me. I'm not sure if the presence of a female invoked suppressed feelings of temptation. Strangely, in men's bathrooms that were large enough to accommodate several people, there were signs limiting occupancy to one person at a time.

Well, maybe not...

When Josh Harris was 21, he wrote *I Kissed Dating Goodbye*—an **abstinence manifesto** and courtship manual that convinced a generation of conservative Christian teenagers that avoiding premarital sex was more than a good idea or even God's plan—it was a holy calling and a prerequisite to a good marriage. More than a million copies were sold. Josh became a celebrity in evangelical circles and got married at age 23. In 2019 he and his wife announced they were separating after 19 years of marriage.

According to Ruth Graham, writing in *Slate.com*, "Josh's early career was built on the promise that there might be a formula to building a permanent and happy Christian marriage. He has also spent the past few years publicly reckoning with the legacy of his youthful certainty and the pain that critics say he caused. The end of the Harrises' marriage is a coda of sorts to the 'purity culture' he helped inspire.

His teenage readers had grown up, and many of them were sharing stories online about their experiences. Not all participants in the abstinence movement regret it, but many readers shared stories of shame, disillusionment, sexual dysfunction, and divorce. Harris started soliciting stories on his own site, and heard from disenchanted readers directly. In 2016, he told me that he was reconsidering his role in the purity movement: 'It's like, well, crap, is the biggest thing I've done in my life this really huge mistake?' he asked."

Chapter 30

What Happened To All The Protestants?

Since shortly after protester **Martin Luther** (above) nailed his *Ninety-five Theses* to the door of All Saints' Church in Wittenberg, Germany in 1517 Christianity seemed to be divided into Catholics and Protestants. The Protestants were further divided into Lutherans (of course) Baptists, Episco-palians, Methodists, Moravians, Quakers, Congregational-ists, Mormons, Seventh Day Adventists, Jehovah's Witnesses and many others.

I don't know why, but at around the beginning of the 21st century, the term "Protestant" seemed to disappear, or at least become strongly repressed. Maybe the term "protest" bothered people. At any rate, the new umbrella term for eve-ryone from proper New England Congregationalists to rural venom drinkers was "CHRISTIAN."

I see nothing wrong if these folks prefer a less con-frontational label, but the usurpation of "Christian" strange-ly excludes the Catholic religion, which some might say is the most Christian religion there is—and the inspiration for Martin Luther's protest.

Why has "Protestant" faded away? I asked in an inter-faith group on Facebook and got these un-edifying replies:

- We have grown in our understanding of Christianity. Most now believe that there will always be those more loyal to denominations than Christ, He's calling us out.
- In Germany I'm called "evangelisch" (which is not evan-gelical) when I'm Protestant. We don't really use the word Protestant here. I first heard of it when I started to learn English.
- Most have become complacent so if they used the term Protestant they would have to take a more active role for what the bible teaches and the word means. Like the Catholic churches do today.

Author **Xavier Clayton** says: Protestantism is full of rituals that spread Light, joy and kindness. The feeling of being in a dynamic spiritual community of like-minded spiritualists is very evident in the way we practice it. We perform with others the many acts of compassion that The Master Christ demonstrated in his lifetime. Helping the homeless awakens our Protestantism.

Catholicism is more ritualized. Many rites are done to symbolize our connection to The Master Christ, to our highest virtues and to God. Through symbolism, we remember our Divinity. We can then go out into the world find these symbols and will immediately remember what they represent. A White Dove landing on our window sill awakens our Catholicism.

For hundreds of years, these two faiths have been at war. Even though they both follow the same Master, millions of people have died, been tortured or imprisoned because of this war. Would Jesus Christ tell a Protestant he was wrong to practice charity? Would Jesus Christ tell a Catholic she was wrong to remember the power of The Sacred Heart?

Protestantism is a condensed form of Catholicism.

Catholicism is an expanded form of Protestantism.

In every Catholic Mass, there are several moments of transcendence; the moments we are praying, the moments we are tithing, the time we are listening to the sermon, and the moments we are having communion. However, it can be argued that the highest and most auspicious moment the priest asks us to "turn to your neighbor and spread the word of Peace." We can feel the energy of the church change. It changes more dynamically than at any other time during the mass. Before the priest even says it, we feel the JOY building throughout the hall. We feel our hearts leaping. We feel every cell of our being vibrating with UNIVERSAL LIGHT!

When we Catholics then turn to all of the people sitting around us to shake their hand, hug them or to say "Peace be with you!," at that moment, we are practicing PURE PROTESTANTISM.

So, why hate? Acts of Kindness are better than war.

The sentiment is nice, but my question remains unanswered.

Chapter 31
Could I Wear Mormon Underwear?

Followers of different religions often wear distinctive clothing. Orthodox Jewish men wear fringes and cover their heads; and their wives are very modest—even hiding elbows and knees. Muslim women may cover their heads or entire bodies. Sikh men wear turbans. Male Jehovah's Witnesses wear business clothing including neckties—even in oppressive heat. Clergy of most faiths have distinctive garb.

Probably no religious apparel is subject to as much interest and speculation as the Mormon "temple garments." They are sometimes derisively dismissed as "magical underwear" but a Mormon video states that there "is nothing magical or mystical about temple garments."

The Mormon Church achieved national attention with the Republican presidential candidacy of Willard ("Mitt") Romney in 2012. He was apparently the first Mormon nominated for the presidency by a major American political party. Romney has also been a governor, senator and successful businessman, and served as a Mormon missionary in France for a few years.

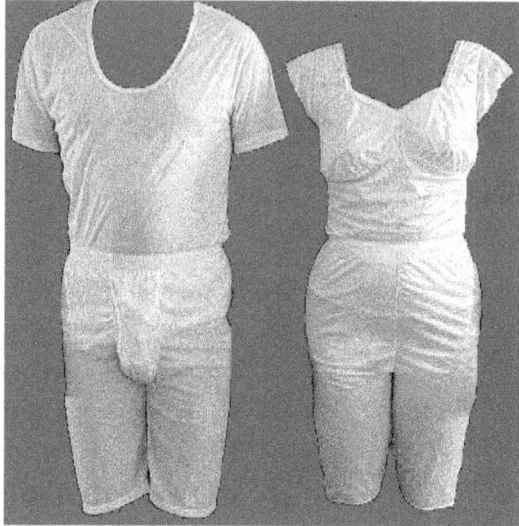

Temple garments are simple, white underwear composed of a top piece similar to a T-shirt and a bottom piece similar to shorts that nearly reach the knees. The garments are worn underneath regular clothes. According to the LDS Church, the garment provides the member with "a constant reminder" of the covenants made in the temple, and "provides protection against temptation and evil." Mormons are supposed to wear the garments day and night but are permitted to swim without them.

According to LDSendowment.org, "Traditionally, the temple garment was a white, one-piece undergarment not unlike a union suit. It originally extended to the wrists and the ankles, had a collar, and closed with strings. In the 1920s, Church leaders authorized a shorter garment that extended to the elbows and knees, had no collar, and closed with buttons. A two-piece garment was introduced in 1979, resembling a t-shirt and long boxer briefs. A women's garment has a somewhat lower neckline and shorter sleeves." Garments are available in 10 different fabrics. Latter-day Saints serving in the armed forces can obtain garments in a military-approved shade of brown. Customized garments are available for people with special needs, even a garment designed like a hospital gown for those restricted to bed.

The Mormon religion (officially the Church of Jesus Christ of Latter-Day Saints, or **LDS**) is a 'new' religion, formed in the USA in 1830. I don't know any Mormons and there are no Mormon temples or churches near me, so my research for this chapter relies on the web.

I learned that "The Church of Latter-day Saints is a Christian church but is *neither Catholic nor Protestant*. Rather, it is a **restoration of the Church of Jesus Christ as originally established by the Savior in the New Testament of the Bible**. The Church does not embrace the creeds that developed in the third and fourth centuries that are now central to many other Christian churches."

The founder of The Church of Jesus Christ of Latter-day Saints, Joseph Smith, wrote, "The fundamental principles of our religion are ... concerning Jesus Christ, that He died, was buried, and rose again the third day, and ascended into heaven; and all other things which pertain to our religion are only appendages to it." In addition to the above, Latter-day Saints believe unequivocally that:

1. Jesus Christ is the Savior of the world and the Son of our loving Heavenly Father. Latter-day Saints believe God sent His Son, Jesus Christ, to save all humankind from their sins. God is a loving Heavenly Father who knows His children individually, hears and answers their prayers and feels compassion toward them. Heavenly Father and His Son, Jesus Christ, are two separate beings but, along with the Holy Spirit, are one in will, purpose and love. Latter-day Saints worship Jesus Christ as their Savior and Redeemer. He is central to the lives of Church members. They accept His grace and mercy, and they seek to follow His example by being baptized; praying in His holy name; partaking of the sacrament, or communion; doing good to others and bearing witness of Him through both word and deed.

2. Christ's Atonement allows humankind to be saved from their sins and return to live with God and their families forever. Latter-day Saints believe that God has a plan for His children to return to live with Him and become "joint-heirs with Christ." For members of the Church, Jesus Christ's sacrifice is central to God's plan for our happiness. Although humans make mistakes and sin, Latter-day Saints view this mortal life as an opportunity to progress and learn. By following Christ's teachings, embracing His mercy and accepting baptism and other sacraments, Latter-day Saints believe they are cleansed from sin through Christ's grace and can return to live with God and their families forever.

3. Christ's original Church as described in the New Testament has been restored in modern times. Members believe that Christ established His Church anciently on the "foundation of the apostles and prophets" with "one faith, [and] one baptism." They believe this foundation of "one faith" was gradually undermined after the death of Christ's apostles. As a result, the original foundation of authority to lead the Church was lost and needed to be restored. Today members preach that the Lord has indeed restored His Church with living apostles and prophets, starting with the founding prophet of The Church of Jesus Christ of Latter-day Saints, Joseph Smith. Church members understand that families are the most important unit of society. Accordingly, those who follow Christ and keep His commandments are promised that they will live with their families forever in Divinely instituted eternal relationships.

The religious experience of Church members is based on a spiritual witness from God that inspires the heart and mind, creating an interpersonal relationship directly with God. The Church's role is to aid its members in their quest to follow Christ's teachings. Therefore, the Church's core doctrines align with Christ's teachings as outlined in the Bible and other sacred scripture, including the Book of Mormon.

Latter-day Saints believe God sent His Son, Jesus Christ, to save all humanity from death and their individual sins. Jesus Christ is central to the lives of Church members. They seek to follow His example by being baptized, praying in His holy name, partaking of the, doing good to others and bearing witness of Him through both word and deed. The only way to salvation is through faith in Jesus Christ.

God is often referred to in The Church of Jesus Christ of Latter-day Saints as our **Heavenly Father** because He is the Father of all human spirits and they are created in His image. It is an appropriate term for God, who is kind and just, all-wise and all-powerful. God the Father; His Son, Jesus Christ; and the Holy Ghost constitute the Godhead, or Trinity, for Church members. Latter-day Saints believe God is embodied, though His body is perfect and glorified.

Latter-day Saints believe God the Father, Jesus Christ and the Holy Spirit are separate personages, but one in will and purpose—not literally the same being or substance.

For Latter-day Saints, mortal existence is seen in the context of a great sweep of history, from a pre-earth life where the spirits of all humankind lived with Heavenly Father to a future life in His presence where continued growth, learning and improving will take place. Life on earth is regarded as a temporary state in which men and women are tried and tested—and where they gain experiences obtainable nowhere else. God knew humans would make mistakes, so He provided a Savior, Jesus Christ, who would take upon Himself the sins of the world. To members of the Church, physical death on earth is not an end but the beginning of the next step in God's plan for His children.

The Church reveres the Bible as the word of God, a sacred volume of scripture. Latter-day Saints cherish its teachings and engage in a lifelong study of its Divine wisdom. Moreover, during worship services the Bible is pondered and discussed. Additional books of scripture—including the *Book of Mormon*—strengthen and reinforce God's teachings through additional witnesses, and they provide moving accounts of the personal experiences many individuals had with Jesus Christ.

In addition to the Old and New Testaments of the Bible, the **Book of Mormon**, named after one of its ancient prophets, is another testament of Jesus Christ. It contains the writings of prophets, giving an account of God's dealings with the peoples who lived anciently on the American continent. For Latter-day Saints it stands alongside the Old and New Testaments of the Bible as holy scripture.

In temples, members of the Church make covenants, or promises, with God to live a virtuous and faithful life. They also participate in ordinances on behalf of their deceased ancestors. Temples are also used to perform marriage ceremonies in which the faithful are promised eternal life with their families. Family is of central importance.

When Latter-day Saints speak to God, they call it prayer. When God responds through the influence of the Holy Spirit, members refer to this as **revelation**. In its broad meaning, it is Divine guidance or inspiration; it is the communication of truth and knowledge from God to His children on earth, suited to their language and understanding. It simply means to uncover something not yet known. Latter-day Saints believe that Divine guidance generally comes quietly, taking the form of impressions, thoughts and feelings carried by the Spirit of God.

Most often, revelation unfolds as an ongoing, prayerful dialogue with God. When a problem arises, we study out its dimensions and we ask God our questions. If we have sufficient faith, God leads us to answers, either partial or full. Though ultimately a spiritual experience, revelation also requires careful thought. God does not simply hand down information. He expects us to figure things out through prayerful searching and sound thinking.

All women are daughters of loving Heavenly Parents. Women and men are equal in the sight of God. From the beginning of The Church of Jesus Christ of Latter-day Saints, women have played an integral role in the work of the Church. While worthy men hold the priesthood, worthy women serve as leaders, counselors, missionaries and teachers and in many other responsibilities. They routinely preach from the pulpit and lead congregational prayers in worship services. They serve both in the Church and in their local communities and contribute to the world as leaders in a variety of professions. Their vital and unique contribution to raising children is considered an important responsibility and a special privilege of equal importance to priesthood responsibilities.

The practice of polygamy was discontinued in 1890.

The gospel of Jesus Christ is for everyone. The *Book of Mormon* states, "Black and white, bond and free, male and female; ... all are alike unto God." People of all races have always been welcomed and baptized into the Church since its beginning. In fact, at the end of his life in 1844, Joseph Smith, opposed slavery. During this time some black males were ordained to the priesthood. The Church unequivocally condemns racism, including any and all past racism by individuals inside and outside the Church.

Jesus Christ taught that "except a man be born of water and of the Spirit, he cannot enter into the kingdom of God." For those who have passed on without the ordinance of baptism, proxy baptism for the deceased is a free-will offering. According to Church doctrine, a departed soul in the afterlife is completely free to accept or reject such a baptism—the offering is freely given and must be freely received. The ordinance does not force deceased persons to become members of The Church of Jesus Christ of Latter-day Saints, nor does the Church list deceased persons as members of the Church. In short, there is no change in the religion or heritage of the recipient or of the recipient's descendants—the notion of coerced conversion is utterly contrary to Church doctrine.

Proxy baptism for the deceased is nothing new. It was mentioned by Paul in the New Testament and was practiced by early Christians. As part of a restoration of New Testament Christianity, Latter-day Saints continue this practice. All Church members are instructed to submit names for proxy baptism only for their own deceased relatives as an offering of familial love.

Alcohol, tobacco, tea, coffee and illegal drugs are forbidden. A 14-year UCLA study, completed in 1997, tracked mortality rates and health practices of 10,000 members of The Church of Jesus Christ of Latter-day Saints in California, indicating that members who adhered to the health code had one of the lowest death rates from cancer and cardiovascular disease in the USA. It also found that Church members who followed the code had a life expectancy 8 to 11 years longer than the general white population of the United States.

LDS doctrine does not subscribe to traditional creedal trinitarianism. That is, the LDS do not believe the extra-biblical doctrines which surround many Christians' ideas about God, such as expressed by the [Catholic] Nicene Creed. Specifically, the LDS do not accept that Jesus Christ and the Holy Spirit are "of one substance with the Father," as the Nicene Creed declares.

Rather, LDS doctrine teaches that God the Father is physically and personally distinct from Jesus Christ, His Only Begotten Son. The Father is understood to be the literal father of His spirit children.

LDS believe that Jesus Christ's role is central to our Heavenly Father's plan. Christ is unique in several respects from all other spirit children of God:
- Jesus was and is perfect
- Jesus is God.
- Jesus is the Creator.
- Jesus obeyed the Father in all things.
- Jesus was chosen and foreordained to be the Redeemer.
- Jesus is the Mediator between God and.
- Jesus was "the Only Begotten"—only He, of all God's children, had a physical inheritance in His body from God the Father. All other mortals have two mortal parents, and Satan and his followers never receive physical bodies at all.

God the Father also had many other **spirit children**, created in His image and that of His Only Begotten. These children include all humans born on the earth. Some of God's children rebelled against Him, and contested the choice of Jesus as Savior. The leader of these children was Lucifer, or Satan. Those spirit children of God who followed Satan in his rebellion against Christ are sometimes referred to as demons or devils. Thus, it is technically true to say that **Jesus and Satan are brothers**, in the sense that both have the same spiritual parent, God the Father.

ReligionNews.com published **How to be Mormon, in just 73 easy steps!** by Mette Harrison. Here are some:

- Never use the word "Mormon" in describing anything Mormon. Doing so is a win for Satan.
- Drink no coffee, tea or alcohol.
- Eat meat sparingly. (Actually, scratch that. It's in the Word of Wisdom, but no one pays attention to it anyway, so bring on the burgers. You're going to need to keep your strength up for keeping all the other rules.)
- Eat a lot of vegetables and fruits in their season. And yes, Funeral Potatoes totally count as a vegetable.
- Go to church every Sunday, even when you're on vacation. God gives you extra credit for this.
- Never use a curse word. If you need a library of faux swear options, watch *Napoleon Dynamite* multiple times and absorb its vocabulary.
- Feed the missionaries—hefty portions. You don't want emaciated elders or sisters around.
- Volunteer to clean the church/temple when the signup sheet goes around. Remember to wear clothes you can get dirty in. You're keeping the church clean, not yourself.
- Keep a year's supply of food in your basement, even if you never eat any of it. The family with the most wheat wins.
- Do regular disaster planning with your kids, from fire drills to flood plans. You can never be too prepared for the end of days.
- Know how to make important knots with rope. No one knows why this matters, but it does.

- Learn how to build a fire without a match.
- Know the stories of your pioneer ancestors, if you have them, to tell your children on Pioneer Day. (Don't worry about the gruesome details—kids will love them!)
- Invite non-members to attend church meetings and activities. Repeatedly.
- Figure out how to use beans in fudge making and wheat in chili-making.
- Help with local fundraising activities for the youth, like allowing them to put a flag in your yard even if they break your sprinkler system.
- God expects you to be happy.
- Eat "better than sex" chocolate cake.
- Drink sparkle punch.
- Know how to cook a marshmallow properly to make S'mores. They're practically a Mormon invention.
- Be able to make seven different kinds of Jell-o salad, at least one with carrots.
- Wear makeup, because even an old barn looks good with a little paint on it.
- Do not nurse at church except in the mother's lounge in the women's bathroom, which will also be where children's dirty diapers are changed and disposed of. But modesty!
- (Men) You can have up to one ear piercing per God's instructions. Getting double-pierced ears is beyond the pale, so don't push it.
- Sacrament must be administered and passed by young men in white shirts, only using their right hands. The patterns may vary from ward to ward, but are secret and only for men to know.
- Do not shed tears in any scenario ever, except during testimony meeting, when it is 100% acceptable for you to cry.
- Do play church ball hard enough to get injured or injure someone else. Unless someone winds up in the hospital, the Spirit hasn't spoken strongly enough.

- Facial hair was fine for Jesus but not for you. The clean-cut look is definitely the ~~Mormon~~ Latter-day Saint look. Oh, and man buns are flat out.

In August, 2019, the official Mormon *New Era* magazine, clarified the LDS position on drinks and products tied to substances banned by the religion.

The religion forbids tobacco, tea and coffee. The *New Era* article points out that "most vaping pods contain nicotine, which is highly addictive, and all of them contain harmful chemicals."

It may be difficult to know which drinks sold by a coffee shop have coffee in them, according to the magazine, so "if you're in a coffee shop (or any other shop that's well-known for its coffee), the drink you're ordering probably has coffee in it, so either never buy drinks at coffee shops or always ask if there's coffee in it." ... "Anything with green and black tea, including iced tea, are against the *Word of Wisdom*, as are any drinks that have tea in them."

Marijuana and pain medications, such as opioids, "should be avoided except under the care of a competent physician, and then used only as prescribed."

Vaping is forbidden and substances such as marijuana and opioids should be used only for medicinal purposes as prescribed by a competent physician."

(from Religion News Service) LDS updated its policy on firearms, moving from a recommendation that lethal weapons, including guns, were considered "inappropriate" on church property to an outright prohibition of them, except for current law enforcement officers."

So, what's the answer to the question that provides the title of this chapter? I *could* wear it, but don't want to.

There Are *Two* Books of Mormon

The Book of Mormon is a sacred text which Mormons believe contains writings of ancient prophets who lived on the American continent from approximately 2200 BCE to CE 421. It was first published in March, 1830 by Joseph Smith as *The Book of Mormon: An Account Written by the Hand of Mormon upon Plates Taken from the Plates of Nephi.*

According to Smith the book's narrative, the *Book of Mormon* was originally written in otherwise unknown characters referred to as "reformed Egyptian" engraved on golden plates. Smith said that the last prophet to contribute to the book, a man named Moroni, buried it in present-day Manchester, New York before his death, and then returned to Earth in 1827 as an angel, revealing the location of the plates to Smith, and instructing him to translate the plates into English for use in the restoration of Christ's true church in the latter days. Critics claim that it was authored by Smith, drawing on material and ideas from contemporary 19th-century works rather than translating an ancient record

The Book of Mormon is also the name of a musical comedy. First staged in 2011, it is a satirical examination of Mormon beliefs and practices that ultimately endorses the positive power of love and service. The script, lyrics, and music were written by Trey Parker, Robert Lopez, and Matt Stone. Parker and Stone were best known for creating the animated comedy *South Park;* Lopez had co-written the music for the musical *Avenue Q.*

The Book of Mormon follows two Mormon missionaries as they attempt to preach the Mormon religion to the inhabitants of a remote Ugandan village. The earnest young men are challenged by the lack of interest from the locals, who are distracted by more pressing issues such as AIDS, famine, female genital mutilation, and oppression from the village warlords.

Chapter 32
Quaker Oats Come From Pepsi, Not From Quakers

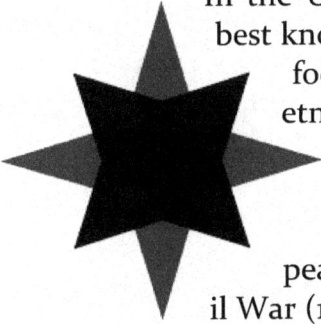

In the United States, **Quakers** are probably best known as a brand of oat-based breakfast foods, and opposition to the war in Vietnam. Officially, the **Religious Society of Friends**, the group dates back to mid-17th century England.

Many religious dissenters appeared during and after the English Civil War (1642–1651). George Fox was dissatisfied with both the Church of England and its opposition. He became convinced that it was possible to have a direct experience of Christ without ordained clergy.

After a vision in 1652, Fox travelled around England, the Netherlands and Barbados, preaching and teaching to gain adherents to his faith. His central theme was that Christ will teach his people himself. Fox considered himself to be restoring a true, "pure" Christian church.

Fox was put before magistrates for religious blasphemy. According to Fox, magistrate, Gervase Bennet "was the first that called us Quakers, because I bade them tremble at the word of the Lord." The name *Quaker* began as a way of ridiculing Fox's admonition but became widely accepted. Quakers also described themselves with terms used by the early Christian church such as *true Christianity, Saints, Children of the Light* and *Friends of the Truth*.

Quakerism gained a considerable following in England and Wales, and the numbers increased to a peak of 60,000 in 1680 (1.15% of the population). But the dominant Protestant view was that Quakers were a blasphemous challenge to social and political order. This led to official persecution in the 1660s—but was relaxed by the late 1680s.

Together with Margaret Fell, the wife of Thomas Fell (vice-chancellor of the Duchy of Lancaster and an eminent judge), Fox developed new conceptions of family and community that emphasized *holy conversation*: speech and behavior that reflected piety, faith and love. With the restructuring of the family and household came new roles for women; Fox and Fell viewed the Quaker mother as essential to developing holy conversation in her children and husband. Quaker women were also responsible for the spirituality of the larger community, coming together in "meetings" that regulated marriage and domestic behavior.

Despite growing tolerance in England and Wales, persecution of Quakers in North America began in 1656 when missionaries Mary Fisher and Ann Austin preached in Boston. They were considered heretics because of their insistence on individual obedience to the *Inner Light* (direct awareness of God that allows a person to know God's will). They were imprisoned and banished by the Massachusetts Bay Colony, their books were burned, their property was confiscated, they were imprisoned, and then deported.

In 1660, English Quaker Mary Dyer was hanged in Boston for repeatedly defying a Puritan law banning Quakers. She was one of the four executed Quakers known as the "Boston martyrs." In 1661, King Charles II forbade Massachusetts from executing anyone for professing Quakerism. Three years later England revoked the Massachusetts charter, sent over a royal governor to enforce English laws in 1686 and in 1689 passed a broad Toleration Act.

Some Quakers in North America and Great Britain became well known for their involvement in the abolition of slavery. But until the American Revolution, it was fairly common for Quakers in British America to own slaves.

Quakers embody diverse theological views. There are Quaker atheists, agnostics and humanists.

According to Professor Teresa M. Bejan: "The Quakers thus declared themselves to be, like God, 'no respecter of persons.' So they *thee*-ed and *thou*-ed their fellow human beings without distinction as a form of egalitarian social protest. And like today's proponents of gender-inclusive pronouns, they faced ridicule and persecution as a result."

During World Wars I and II, many American and English Quakers were conscientious objectors and some formed the Friends Ambulance Unit. A large number of British Quakers were conscripted into the Non-Combatant Corps during both World Wars.

Quaker action during the 1954-75 Vietnam War focused on three different areas: peaceful protest against the conduct of the war itself, counseling American conscientious objectors of all faiths, and humanitarian aid to both North and South Vietnam. Quakers were also involved in diplomats' conferences aimed at ending the war.

The **American Friends Service Committee (AFSC)** describes itself as a 'practical expression' of Quaker principles of nonviolence and justice. It works on conflict resolution and peace building alongside issues of economic, social and criminal justice.

AFSC was founded in 1917, soon after the USA entered World War I. Its initial aim was to help conscientious objectors help the war effort in nonviolent ways. Many American and British Quakers drove ambulances in France.

Between the wars AFSC helped rebuild Europe, notably with Quakerspeisung—which fed children in Germany and Austria after WW I. Later, Quakers helped Jewish refugees leave Germany before the Second World War. In the U.S. Quakers ran several relief operations such as helping Appalachian miners find alternative employment during the Depression. After Pearl Harbor, Japanese Americans were interned in large numbers and AFSC supported them, even helping them to enroll at universities. AFSC helped many refugees after WW II and later in Vietnam.

In 1947, with the Friends Service Council (their British equivalent), AFSC was awarded the **Nobel Peace Prize**. In the U.S. they became participants in the civil rights movement and the criminal justice system and aided Native Americans and immigrant workers. AFSC sponsored a series of conferences for diplomats in Switzerland and has run development projects and engaged in international mediation and community peace building initiatives.

My nearby *New Haven Friends Meeting* welcomes "all seekers of God who can accept the ways of Friends. We continually seek God and Truth with humility and, sometimes, even doubt. Friends find God's message in the teachings of many religions, and through different sources, including writings and verbal communications, as well as by direct personal experience.

We find great joy in the diversity of members and attenders of New Haven Friends Meeting. For some, Jesus is a living presence in their daily lives; for others, the life and teachings of Jesus are important as examples with a range of interpretations. Differences among our members in theological traditions and beliefs are respected and valued.

We believe that there is that of God in everyone, that God is present and still speaking to us today, and that each of us is capable of making direct contact with the living God.

We do not have an individual pastor. All Friends minister to and care for one another. We have a Ministry and Counsel

(M&C) Committee with the responsibility to identify Friends who may need special care and or support in reaching clearness about important life decisions. M&C assists in organizing Friends to provide pastoral care to any in our community who are in need.

Quakerism is a dual commitment to spiritual awareness and social action as a form of ministry. God still speaks to us and we must respond. We work towards peace, justice and reconciliation because we believe they are necessary to uphold our spiritual truths. We are led to implement our concern for equal rights for all. We have a ministry of service to humankind and nature. Carrying out our beliefs through action in our daily lives is a spiritual process through which we find commitment and strength.

Among our most treasured spiritual values are truthfulness, simplicity, a simple lifestyle, non-violence and a reverence for all life."

From "A Declaration to Charles II" (1661)

We utterly deny all outward wars and strife and fightings with outward weapons, for any end or under any pretense whatsoever. And this is our testimony to the whole world.

Quaker Oats was founded in 1901 by the merger of four Midwestern oat mills (It has been owned by Pepsico since 2001). The company states that the *Quaker Man* logo was chosen because the Quaker faith projected the values of honesty, integrity, purity and strength. Quaker Oats has never had any ties with actual Quakers. Besides oats, the company produces rice cakes, granola bars, cookies and other munchies.

The Quaker Man is apparently America's oldest registered trademark for a breakfast cereal, dating to 1877. In

1990, some Quakers complained after a Quaker Oats ad depicted Popeye as a "Quakerman" who used violence against aliens, sharks and Popeye's nemesis, Bluto.

Starting back in 1902, the company's oatmeal boxes came with coupons redeemable for free deeds to tiny lots in Milford, Connecticut (where I live!!!). The lots, some as small as 10 feet by 10 feet, were carved out of a 15-acre, never-built, subdivision called "Liberty Park."

A few children and parents redeemed coupons for deeds and started paying extremely small property taxes on their "oatmeal lots." The developer of the prospective subdivision hoped that the new landowners would hire him to build homes on the lots, although multiple tracts would need to be combined to permit building a home. The deeds created a lot of work for employees of Milford, which received almost no tax revenue from the oat deeds. In the mid-1970s, Milford put an end to the oatmeal lots with a *general foreclosure* condemning nearly all of the property, which is now part of a Bic Corporation plant.

In 1955, Quaker Oats again gave away land as part of a promotion, this one tied to the *Sergeant Preston of the Yukon* television show. The company offered deeds to land in the Klondike in Puffed Wheat and Puffed Rice cereal boxes.

The **Quaker State Motor Oil** brand name is derived from the nickname for Pennsylvania—the state founded by William Penn, a Quaker. Titusville, Pennsylvania is con-sidered to be the birthplace of the American oil industry.

Quaker State Motor Oil is produced by SOPUS Products, a division of Royal Dutch Shell, and the successor of the Pennzoil-Quaker State Company. It has nothing to do with Quakers—or oats.

Chapter 33

Evolution

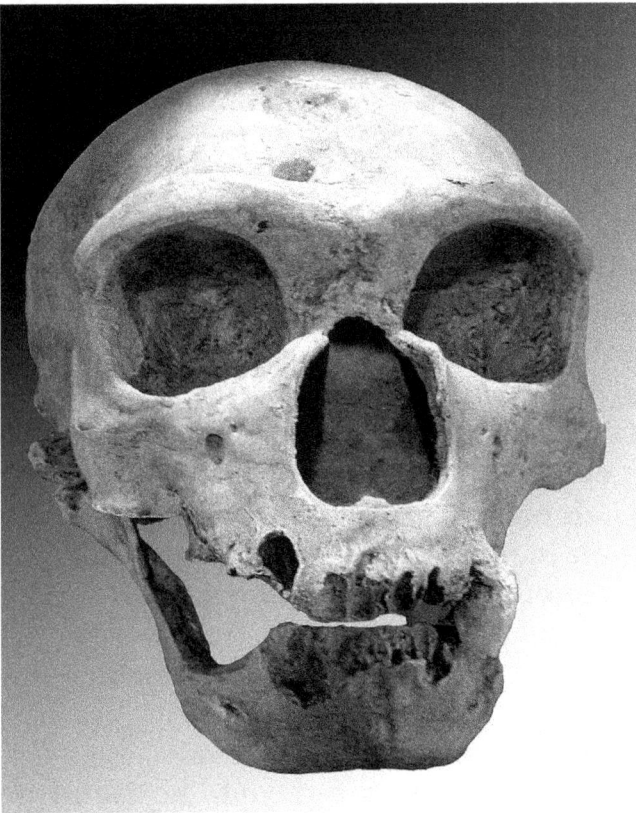

I *definitely believe in evolution*. I don't believe that God created heaven and earth in just six days and then relaxed, and that earth included a garden with a talking snake and pair of horny homo sapiens who mated and reproduced. (Hmm, did

Cain and Abel mate with their mother, or with u-named sisters, or with lesser primates? Did Adam really live 930 years? Why not just 817 years?)

My main problem with human evolution is that it just has not happened fast enough. The homo sapiens line has been evolving for hundreds of thousands of years (and it built upon earlier varieties going back many more years).

Many aspects of human anatomy that should have changed, have *not*. I have some questions for whoever is in charge of evolution:

- **Why do I have tonsils?**
- **Why do I have adenoids?**
- **Why do I have nipples?**
- **Why do I have little toes?**
- **Why do most people in 'developed' countries need eyeglasses?**
- **Why was I born with a foreskin on my penis?**
- **Why do broken bones take so long to heal?**
- **Long ago, our ancestors were often gored to death by saber-tooth tigers when teenagers. Now we live long enough to develop horrible diseases. Why?**
- **The hair on my chin and head will grow forever, yet the hair in my eyebrows, armpits and crotch is smart enough to stop growing when it reaches the proper length. Why?**
- **Why are yawns contagious from human-to-human, but not from dog to human?**
- **Why don't human beings have tails? It would complicate wearing pants, but could be useful and fun.**

Some religious Christians and Jews think that the earth is less than 6,000 years old. However, according to Carl Zimmer in the *New York Times*: "The ancestry of all living humans can be traced to Africa. Studies of DNA indicate our common ancestors lived somewhere on the continent between 260,000 and 350,000 years ago.

But how those early humans evolved is an enduring puzzle. The fossil record in Africa from that period doesn't offer easy answers. Over the decades, researchers have found just a few remains, with a strange mixture of traits.

In 1986, for example, paleoanthropologists discovered a fossil in Kenya between 270,000 and 300,000 years old. They called it "archaic Homo sapiens." Other experts argued it belonged to another species altogether. And others have simply thrown up their hands.

Two years ago, a team of scientists working in Morocco offered a major new clue. They discovered a set of fossil remains, about 315,000 years old, that belonged to Homo sapiens—the oldest remains of our species yet found."

Jericho is a Palestinian city in the West Bank. Archaeologists have unearthed the remains of more than 20 successive settlements in Jericho, the first of which dates back 11,000 years.

While completing this book I leaned that scientists say a coral reef off the coast of **Florida** is 300,000 years old.

Chapter 34

Where Did The Holy Ghost go?

When I was a child and teenager, I frequently heard Catholics discussing and praying to "the Father, the Son and the Holy Ghost."

At some time, maybe in the 1980s, "ghost" was replaced with "spirit." (However, some preachers, such as Kenneth Copeland, still say "Ghost." He also speaks in indecipherable babble.)

Billy Graham's website says, "The terms "Holy Spirit" and "Holy Ghost" mean exactly the same thing; both refer to the third Person of the Trinity (the Father, the Son and the Holy Spirit). The phrase "Holy Ghost" is simply an older term that dates back several hundred years, and is found in some old versions of the English Bible (such as the King James Version). Because the word "ghost" has a different meaning today than it did several hundred years ago, modern translations of the Bible always use "Holy Spirit."

Remember that the Holy Spirit is God Himself, and He is at work both in the world and in our hearts. When we come to Christ, the Holy Spirit comes to live within us; in fact, we can't even come to Him until He convicts us of our sins and convinces us of our need to commit our lives to Christ. Jesus said, "When he comes, he will convict the world of guilt in regard to sin and righteousness and judgment" (John 16:8).

But God has given His Spirit to us for another reason: to teach us and open our eyes to God's truth as it is found in the Bible. Is this happening in your life?"

The German term *Heiliger Geist* can be translated as either "holy ghost" or "holy spirit." The photo on the first page of this chapter shows NBC's Willie Geist, son of CBS's Bill Geist. Are they related to Casper the Friendly Ghost?

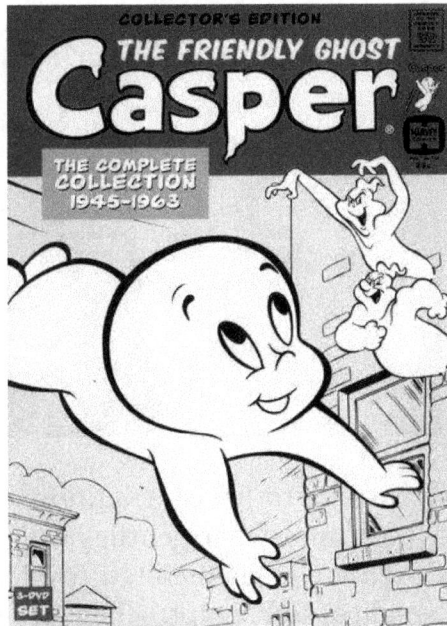

Chapter 35
Moses & The Time Warp:
A Cynical Question

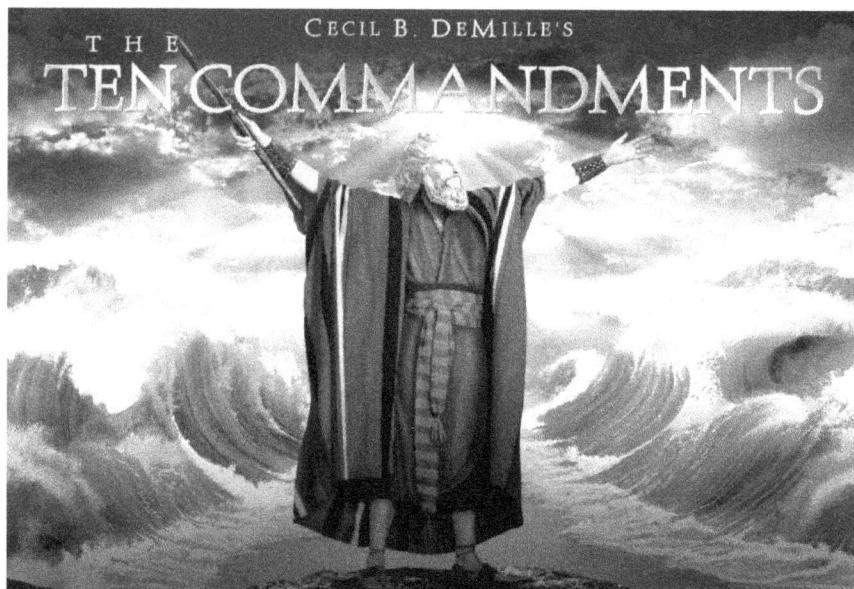

According to Jewish tradition, the Torah (the "Five Books of Moses" and what gentiles call the "Old Testament" or "Old Covenant") was dictated to Moses on Mount Sinai after the Israelites left Egypt. Allegedly the text remained in Moses' head and he taught it to others who taught it to others and it was eventually written down. **If God dictated the Torah to Moses on Mount Sinai during the Exodus, how could the Torah report on events that happened later?**

Chapter 36
Splitting Hairs: Jews & The Law

There are *many* Jewish lawyers and judges. Like medicine, writing and teaching, the legal profession is one that is *over-represented* by Jewish people, from a local courthouse to the U.S. Supreme Court. As I write this in the summer of 2019, ONE THIRD of the Supreme Justices (Breyer, Ginsburg and Kagan) are members of my tribe. Mitch McConnell blocked Obama's nomination of Jewish Merrick Garland who would have boosted the Jewish population of the SCOTUS even higher.

The first Jew on the Court was Louis Brandeis, who was nominated by President Woodrow Wilson in 1916, and his nomination was opposed by antisemites. When Brandeis joined the Court, Justice James McReynolds refused to sit next to him for an official photo. While still on the Court, Brandeis was joined by another Jew, Benjamin Cardozo, who was named by President Herbert Hoover in 1932.

Cardozo was succeeded by Jewish Felix Frankfurter in 1939. When Frankfurter retired in 1962, President John F. Kennedy named another Jew, Arthur Goldberg, to succeed him. That's when "Jewish seat" began to be widely used.

The tradition continued when Abe Fortas, nominated by President Lyndon Johnson, succeeded Goldberg in 1965. Fortas resigned in 1969. In seeking a nominee to succeed Fortas, alleged antisemite Richard Nixon had no desire to continue the "Jewish seat" tradition. After the Senate rejected his first two choices (Clement Haynsworth and G. Harrold Carswell), Nixon settled on Harry Blackmun, a Methodist and longtime friend of Chief Justice Warren Burger. That ended the decades-long tradition of having a Jew on the Court. It lasted until President Bill Clinton named Ruth Bader Ginsburg to the Court in 1993 and Stephen Breyer the following year. As I write this, both still serve, as does Elena Kagan, who joined in 2010.

Anyway, with a huge supply of Jewish lawyers educated at Harvard, Yale and elsewhere, and a whopping 613 laws in the Torah, it's no wonder that a lot of legal talent has been devoted to analyzing (and getting around) those laws when they become inconvenient.

To me, the most blatant law evasion involves the "**eruv**"(pronounced ay-roov). Under strict Jewish law, no work may be done on the Sabbath. This is understood to include carrying things or live beings, including a baby, or pushing a baby carriage—and Orthodox mommies usually have *lots* of babies. It is considered OK to transport a baby at home, but not elsewhere, which would mean that the mommies could not attend Sabbath services.

Jewish legal experts devised a workaround. The eruv is an artificial (some say "phony") extension of a home's walls, consisting of specially installed nylon fishing line, or sometimes the designation of pre-existing utility cables, that goes from pole to pole, or maybe pole to wall to pole to wall, and allegedly forms the boundary of one huge house that includes many individual homes and one or more synagogues. (The concept is actually more complex than this, but I am not writing a book about eruvs.)

Chabad says: The literal meaning of the word eruv is *blending* or *intermingling*. Under Jewish law, on Shabbat it is forbidden to carry anything—regardless of its weight, size or purpose—from a "private" domain into a "public" one or vice versa, or more than four cubits (approximately 6 feet) within a public domain. Private and public do not refer to ownership, rather to the nature of the area. An enclosed area is considered a private domain, whereas an open area is considered public for the purposes of these laws.

Practically, it is forbidden to carry something, such as a *tallit* [prayer shawl] bag or a prayer book from one's home along the street and to a synagogue or to push a baby carriage from home to a synagogue, or to another home.

It became obvious even in ancient times, that on Shabbat, as on other days, there are certain things people wish to carry. People also want to get together with their friends after synagogue and take things with them, including their babies.

Because of the design of communities in the past, many neighborhoods or even cities were walled. As such, the whole area was regarded as "private," and carrying allowed. That, however, wasn't always the case. And today, it is an obvious impracticality to build walls throughout portions of cities, crossing over or through streets and walkways, in order to place one's home and synagogue within the same "private" domain.

The answer is a *technical enclosure* which surrounds private and previously public domains and thus creates a large private domain in which carrying is permitted.

Part of the fascination in the erection and study of eruvs lies in the secular world of law and lawsuits. Numerous lawsuits have arisen in various parts of the world involving eruvs. These cases usually involve municipal regulations.

In the city of Outremont in the Canadian Province of Quebec, a number of Orthodox Jews asked the city council for permission to build an eruv. The council, led by its Jewish mayor, refused even though about one quarter of the city's population was Jewish. A non-Jewish judge overruled the city, noting that the Canadian Charter of Rights and Freedoms guarantees that religion can be practiced openly.

In the United States, legal controversies about an eruv in a community often focus on provisions of the First Amendment of the Constitution. Opponents of an eruv typically take the view that the government participation in the eruv process necessary to approve its construction violates the First Amendment's prohibition of governmental establishment of religion. Proponents take the view that it is a constitutionally permissible *accommodation* of religion rather than a forbidden *establishment*. Proponents have also argued that the Free Exercise Clause affirmatively requires government acceptance, on the grounds that government interference with or failure to accommodate an eruv constitutes discrimination against or inhibition of the constitutional right of free exercise of religion.

In the 2002 decision on *Tenafly Eruv Association v. Borough of Tenafly*, Judge Thomas L. Ambro held that Eruv Association members had no intrinsic right to add attachments to telephone poles on borough property and that the borough, if it wished, could enact a general, neutral ordinance against all attachments to utility poles that could be enforced against the eruv. However, Judge Ambro held that in this case, the borough had not enacted a genuinely general or neutral ordinance because it permitted a wide variety of attachments to utility poles for non-religious purposes. Because Tenafly permitted attachments for secular purposes, the court held, it could not selectively exclude attachments for religious purposes. The Supreme Court declined to hear the case. It was subsequently cited as precedent by a number of other federal courts."

Despite these problems, the construction of eruvs continues in many parts of the world. The Washington D.C. eruv includes the White House. The Strasbourg, France eruv includes the European Court of Human Rights.

To me, it seems like the eruv is a **con job**, intended to fool God into believing that some polypropylene fiber or copper wire is really the wall of a house or a community. Shouldn't a "great, mighty and awesome" entity with infinite wisdom be able to see through the attempted subterfuge? I suppose it's no weirder than Catholics believing that a cracker is the body of Jesus and wine is his blood.

Although religion often 'cares' little about logic, early Jewish history from about 200 to 400 CE—before the appearance of lawyers—had a powerful precursor of the modern legal profession. Rabbis devoted their lives to deep analysis of Jewish law.

Sarah Hurwitz wrote: "Hundreds of pages of the Talmud are devoted to the do's and don'ts of observing Shabbat. And to say that the Rabbis got into the weeds would be quite the understatement. Questions they pondered include: If you poke holes in an eggshell placed over a lamp and fill it with oil such that the oil drips down and keeps the lamp lit after Shabbat has started, does that constitute kindling fire? If a deer happens to enter your home and you lock it inside, does that count as doing the work of animal trapping on Shabbat? What about a lion? What should you do if a bird flies under your clothing on Shabbat and cannot get out? Would keeping the bird there count as the work of trapping an animal? These debates led to numerous laws, and plenty of additional rules and customs have been layered on since Talmudic times."

More from Chabad: "Even without an eruv, there is no problem with wearing clothing outside, provided that it is normal clothing and being worn in its normal manner, as it is considered secondary to, and "part of," the person himself. The same is true for most medical items that are attached to the body and can be considered secondary to it, such as a cast, bandage or glasses.

Rabbinic authorities historically have differed about the use of a cane, wheelchair or other similar devices by the less-able-bodied. Some have allowed their use even without an eruv and others have not. In recent years, the majority of scholars have leaned toward allowing these devices, since, if prohibited, disabled individuals might attempt to leave home on Shabbat without the device(s) and risk injury.

Loose medicines may not be carried; most authorities have agreed that it is preferable that one who constantly needs medication remain at home rather than transgressing Shabbat by carrying medication. But, if such a person leaves home, then comes in need of medication, it is permissible to break Shabbat and take the medication to the person. A small number of authorities in recent years have been permitting carrying the medication, however, since such a person may be tempted to leave home without it, and then a life may be endangered.

Many authorities allow the wearing of jewelry. As for a watch, it could be seen either as an adornment (permitted to wear) or as a tool (forbidden to carry); therefore, opinions are divided on whether people may wear wristwatches.

In communities without an eruv, it is customary to create belts, bracelets, necklaces, or similar wearable objects incorporating house keys so that the keys can be worn rather than carried when going outdoors. [Conning God again?] To be validly "worn" rather than "carried," the key needs to be an integral part of the belt, bracelet, or other item rather than simply attached to it. It may be either an adornment if worn in a manner visible to others or a component needed to keep the wearable object fastened. Special "shabbos belts" and similar items that incorporate this property are sold in religious stores.

A tallit (prayer shawl) may be worn while walking to/from the synagogue, as it is considered clothing. Prayer books and other books may not be carried. They must be taken to the synagogue prior to Shabbat or else the synagogue's prayer books must be used."

If an eruv includes multiple residences, in addition to the physical (or theoretical) enclosure containing the area, the residents must also be "conjoined" into one entity [a big happy family?] through the joint ownership of some food. This may have started long ago when multiple Jewish families lived around a central courtyard, so it was easy to have a pot of communal food in the center. I don't know how this is done today, how much food is involved, where it is stored or how many shareholders are required or allowed. Does the American president add food to the Washington eruv?

This dubious communal food ownership reminds me of what a cynical rabbi described to me as **legal fiction**: the temporary sale of food to gentiles. Before Passover ("Pesach"), observant Jews carefully clean their homes to detect and dispose of any *chametz* (or *chometz*). It's any food containing grain and water that were allowed to ferment and rise.

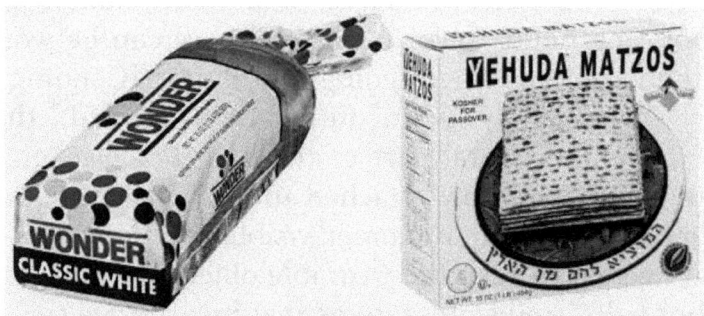

Bread is the obvious example, and *matzo* (one of several spellings) is the Pesach alternative. Other examples of chametz are cereal, cake, cookies, macaroni, pizza and beer. Any food that contains grain or grain derivatives can be chametz. Any food that is not labeled "Kosher for Passover" may potentially include chametz ingredients.

Traditionally the search is done by candlelight, with a feather, but I suppose an LED flashlight and Dustbuster could be used now.

Preparing a home for Passover, especially the kitchen, can be an arduous task, often started weeks in advance and involving little children. Prayers are said and chametz is traditionally burned. Observant Jews reserve special plates and bowls, cookware and utensils for Passover, with separate sets for meat and dairy (assuming the home is kosher).

Little crumbs and near-stale bread are easily disposed of with little regard for their financial value, but some homes may have freezers full of bagels, or perhaps breakfast cereals or pancake batter in a pantry cabinet that do not meet Pesach standards. There is a solution: the **temporary sale of the forbidden foods**. A Jewish person who owns a large quantity of chametz which she or he is reluctant to dispose

Bill of Sale Authorization

1) I, _____, the undersigned, do hereby sell any and all types of *chametz*, mixtures of *chametz*, and items that possibly contain *chametz* and *chametz noksho*, presently located at (but not limited to) the following address(es) _____

in (specific locations of *chametz* within the dwellings)

and any other location that may be found in any area of my house, home, office, vehicles, or any other place that is in my control, consisting of, but not limited to (delete those that are not applicable) foodstuffs, pet foods, medications, cosmetics, beer, liquor, "benshers", baking equipment, toys,_____, that are in my possession, including all goods in transit that are delivered to me during the period of April 10th, 2017 through April 18th, 2017 to Mr. Ron Gatz who resides at 401 S. Chester Street, Park Ridge IL, or to whomever Rabbi Efraim Twerski, acting as my agent, shall wish to sell my *chametz*.

2) I also hereby rent or sell the places where the *chametz* is present, and with regard to the *chametz* utensils, those utensils that may be sold without requiring *tvilah* upon repurchase are to be sold and those that do require *tvilah* are to be rented.

3) In the event that I shall not be in the Chicago area during the festival of *Pesach*, I grant the right to Rabbi Efraim Twerski to be my agent to rent out my entire home/apartment to Mr. Ron Gatz or to anyone else who he may contract to rent my home/apartment, for a duration beginning at the afternoon of April 9th, 2017 at 6:00 PM until and including April 18th, 2017, except those rooms that are indicated below, and retaining for myself access rights to my personal possessions, such as clothing and the like.

(Room(s) excluded from rental of dwelling: _____).

4) Buyer shall have free access to the *chametz* and/or mixtures containing *chametz*, acquired by him.

5) The key to the premises where the above mentioned goods are located can be found at the above location(s) or at _____, and will be freely provided to the buyer at his request.

6) The goods mentioned above have an approximate value of $_____. The exact assessment of the quantity and value of the goods mentioned above will take place after Pesach.

7) I hereby authorize Rabbi Efraim Twerski, or anyone else he may designate to take his place, as my agent to execute this transaction.

8) The transaction shall be executed with this document and other acts of acquisition that are effective according to Jewish and civil law, for a final sale according to the details described in the lengthy legal bill of sale.

9) The buyer's deposit is to be paid to Rabbi Efraim Twerski, or whomever he may designate.

10) This authorization is further legalized with the taking hold of the "handkerchief". *(kinyan suder)*

of, because doing so may cause considerable financial loss, may sell the chametz to a non-Jew. Sometimes the transaction is carried out directly between seller and buyer. Sometimes a rabbi (ahead) intercedes. It's also possible to use a rabbinical court or *make the sale online.*

Delegation of Power to Sell Chometz

I the undersigned, fully empower and permit Rabbi Aaron Slonim to act in my place and stead, and on my behalf to sell all chametz possessed by me, knowingly or unknowingly as defined by the Torah and Rabbinic Law (e.g. chametz, possible chametz, and all kind of chametz mixtures).

Also chametz that tends to harden and adhere to inside surfaces of pans, pots, or cooking utensils, the utensils themselves.

Rabbi Aaron Slonim is also empowered to lease all places wherein the chametz owned by me may be found, particularly at the address/es listed below, and elsewhere.

Rabbi Aaron Slonim has full right to appoint any agent or substitute in his stead and said substitute shall have full right to sell and lease as provided herein.

Rabbi Aaron Slonim also has the full power and right to act as he deems fit and proper in accordance with all the details of the Bill of Sale used in the transaction to sell all my chametz, chametz mixtures, etc., as provided herein. This power is in conformity with all Torah, Rabbinic and Civil laws.

After writing a bill of sale, the seller may keep the chametz at home without breaking the rules, since the chametz no longer belongs to those living in the home.

However, it should be put in a special place which is *rented* to the non-Jew who has purchased it. The place where this sold chametz is stored should be inconvenient, perhaps locked or taped, so that no members of the Jewish family will eat any chametz accidentally.

The bill of sale for the chametz states that it is being sold for a specific price. The non-Jewish purchaser gives the seller a down payment to acquire ownership. A stipulation on the bill of sale states that if the purchaser does not pay the balance due by the end of Passover, the chametz will revert to the original owner.

One Jewish food merchant (with 10 children) who sells via Amazon suffered a drop in his seller's rank because he did not stock bread and cookies during Passover. To restore his company's ratings, he began to sell directly to Amazon so Amazon could ship the items, and his own company never owned the forbidden items during the holiday period.

Chametz is not the only Jewish legalistic workaround that involves food. **Cholent** (with the "ch" pronounced as in "cheese") is a Jewish stew. It is usually simmered overnight for 12 hours or more and eaten for lunch on Saturday (the Sabbath) when work, including cooking, is prohibited. There are 39 general labor categories forbidden on the Sabbath.

A pot of meat and veggies and perhaps eggs is brought to a boil on Friday before the Sabbath begins, and kept warm until mealtime. Slow overnight cooking allows the flavors of the ingredients to mix.

There are many variations of the dish in various Jewish cuisines, often using leftovers. The dish is unglamorous "peasant" food, but has recently become sort of a cult favorite among young Jews and is available in some restaurants.

Before gas and electric residential stoves became common, Jews often took pots of uncooked ingredients to bakers before sunset on Fridays. The baker would put the pots in his oven, which was always kept hot, and families would pick up their cooked cholent on Saturday mornings.

The cooking style of cholent may have led to the invention of the slow cooker. Sadly, there has been at least one devastating fire caused by cholent being warmed on a malfunctioning hotplate. A fire in Brooklyn killed seven children in 2015.

Jewish people make up a *tiny* percentage of the people on the planet, but a *huge* percentage of lawyers (an estimated 25% of the partners in Manhattan's top law firms).

Jewish lawyers have been at the forefront of the fight for civil rights and labor rights, have represented famous and infamous defendants, such as O. J. Simpson; and are fixtures in politics, literature drama, comedy, and even music.

The USA's 71st Attorney General was Jewish (at right: Edward H. Levi, in office 1968–1975). Other presidential cabinet members were Jewish attorneys, including Robert Reich, Robert Rubin, Neil Goldschmidt and Philip Klutznick. So far no Jewish at-

torney has become the American president, but I recommend my senator Richard Blumenthal.

When a criminal proclaims "Get my Jew," he means he wants an appointment with his defense attorney.

The main character in TV's *Harry's Law* was Jewish lawyer Harriet Korn. On *Law & Order,* Jewish actor Steven Hill portrayed Jewish District Attorney Adam Schiff, patterned on the real Manhattan Jewish D.A. Robert Morgenthau. In *L.A. Law,* Jewish actor Michael Tucker played Jewish attorney Stuart Markowitz and Jewish actor Alan Rosenberg played Jewish attorney Eli Levinson. One of the show's producers is Steven Bochco, who is Jewish. It figures.

There are at least three lawyers in my family and my father had an unused scholarship for law school. I've been a mostly successful amateur attorney, winning cases against several highly paid professional attorneys.

Jews can be great negotiators, even against God. In the Bible Abraham learned that God was going to kill all the people in Sodom but he convinced God to agree to destroy the city only if there were as few as fifty righteous people there—and then bargained God down to 10!

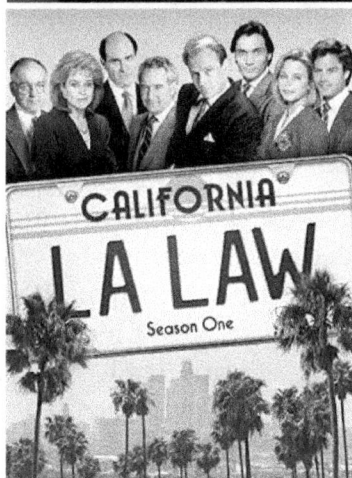

Although Donald Trump is listed as author of *The Art of the Deal*, he has employed Jewish lawyers to negotiate deals for him. Real estate lawyers Jason Greenblatt and Jared Kushner (Trump's son-in-law) were supposed to negotiate peace in the Middle East. Michael Cohen, Trump's personal "fixer," was sent to prison for three years because of campaign finance violations, tax fraud and bank fraud. Cohen is at the Otisville (New York) Federal Correctional Institution, which serves kosher food and has Sabbath services. On *Saturday Night Live*, Cohen was played by (Jewish) actor Ben Stiller.

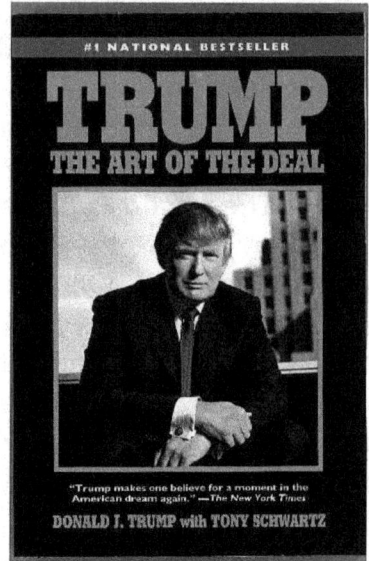

Notorious Jewish attorney Roy Cohn was both a mentor and lawyer for Trump. In 1971 Trump was accused by the Justice Department of violating the Fair Housing Act in 39 properties. Cohn filed an unsuccessful countersuit against the government for $100 million, asserting that the charges were "irresponsible and baseless." Trump settled the charges out of court in 1975.

Three years later the Trump Organization was again in court for violating the 1975 settlement. Cohn called the new charges "nothing more than a rehash of complaints by a couple of planted malcontents." "You knew when you were in Cohn's presence you were in the presence of pure evil," said another Jewish attorney, Victor A. Kovner, according to *Vanity Fair* magazine. He had been New York City's chief lawyer and he knew Cohn for years.

Chapter 37
Books & Sins

I've always had a strong (and maybe strange) reverence for books. Maybe it comes from my parents, who were avid readers. As a Jew, I am part of "the people of the book." When I was in college I sometimes spent food money on books, and I was still building bookshelves two weeks before I was due to move out of my college apartment.

When I see books in the trash, I rescue them. When a friend's older brother and his buddies gathered around a barbecue grill at the end of the junior high school year to burn their textbooks, I tried to rescue them, but was blocked by superior force. Jerks!

I seldom think of sin, but if sins do exist, book burning is certainly high on the list.

Books have always been extremely important to me. As the photo here shows, even as a little kid, I used the bathroom as a library so not a moment of potential reading time was wasted. (I don't know why I was wearing a diaper while on the toilet.)

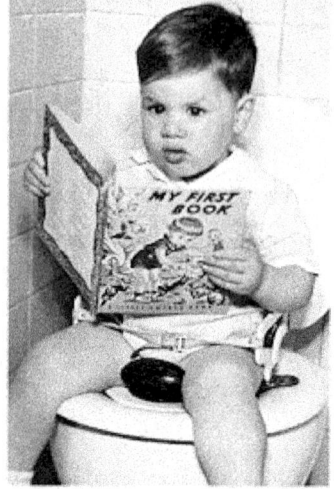

The sales brochure for the apartment my parents brought me home to in 1946 boasts of "built-in bookcases in every apartment." Now in 2019, I can visualize only two pieces of furniture from that apartment: the bunk beds I shared with my sister, Meryl, and a mahogany bookshelf that later moved with us to other homes.

As a child with an early bedtime, I read books by flashlight under the blanket. Even now, I share my bed with my wife and often a pbook or my iPad or Kindle Fire.

Before TiVo gave me the ability to fast-forward, I always read during TV commercials. I read at most meals—even at restaurants. Some people think it's rude. I think it's efficient.

After writing paperbacks since 1977 and ebooks since 2009, I decided to publish my first hardcover in 2011, a new format for my memoir. It evokes new emotions from me. The book *feels* very good. It looks beautiful, with a glossy dust jacket and the title and my name stamped in bright golden ink on the cloth that covers the binding.

A hardcover book provides a *special* experience. Perhaps ebooks will replace paperbacks, but I don't think anything can replace hardcovers.

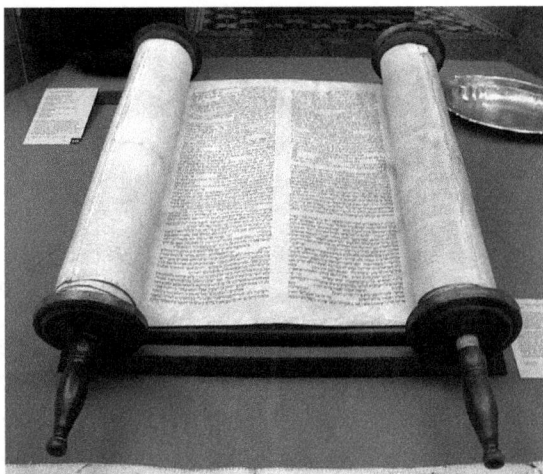

Torah scrolls are still handwritten, after thousands of years. Gravestones are still chiseled. Initials are still carved on trees. They should still be readable *long* after the last Kindle and Nook are recycled.

Even though I am the sole employee of my publishing company, my hardcover seems about 96% as "professional" as books from publishing giants. Even though I've seen my cover design and have read the title hundreds of times, I can't resist holding the book, feeling it and studying it.

My hardcover book seems so much more "real" than other formats. I'm almost in awe of it and didn't want to mark up the first proof with a red pen as I do with my paperback proofs. It would seem like defacing a library book—and *that's* a sin.

Chapter 38
Clarifying Noahide & Naugahyde

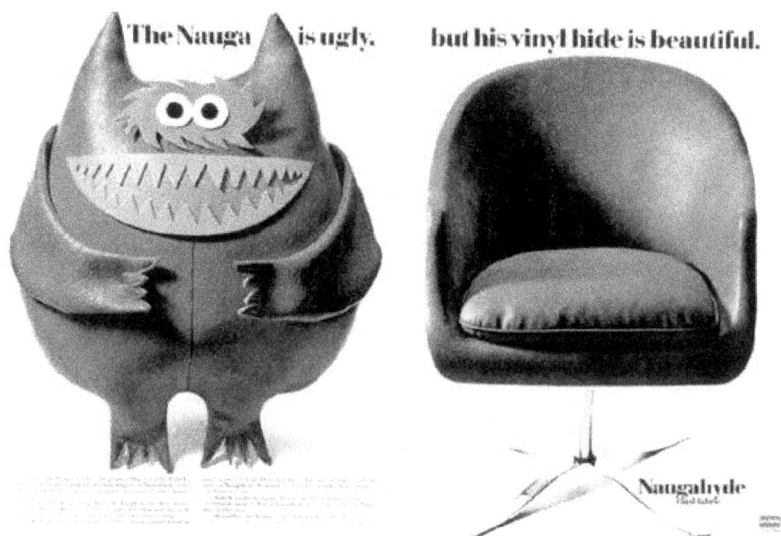

The Nauga is ugly, but his vinyl hide is beautiful.

Naugahyde

Back in the 1930s, United States Rubber Company (now Uniroyal) developed an artificial leather for upholstery. It was named Naugahyde, after Naugatuck, Connecticut, the company's hometown—which is a few miles from where I am typing this sentence. A marketing campaign in the 1960s and '70s asserted humorously that Naugahyde was obtained from the skin of an animal called a "Nauga." Unlike other animals, which are slaughtered for their hides, Naugas shed their skin without harm. The Nauga doll, a friendly monster, became popular in the 1960s and is still sold today.

Although Uniroyal no longer makes Naugahyde, tires or sneakers in Naugatuck, the town has achieved some immortality because of television. On *Maude*, housekeeper Florida Evans was replaced in 1974 by Mrs. Nell Naugatuck, an elderly (and vulgar) British woman who drinks excessively and lies compulsively.

The show's creator, Norman Lear, said her last name comes from the town. Due to the popularity of the program, actress Hermione Baddeley visited Naugatuck and was given an official ceremony at the town green.

Noahide, in contrast, is not skin removed from Noah. The term refers to both Jews and non-Jews who observe the Seven Laws of Noah. There have been groups that call themselves Noahides (and variations of the term), but they are beyond the scope of this book.

The seven Noahide laws are:

1. Do not worship idols.
2. Do not blaspheme God.
3. Do not murder.
4. Do not practice sexual immorality.
5. Do not steal.
6. Do not eat flesh from a living animal.
7. Establish Courts of Justice to build upon these laws.

The sixth law does not seem necessary, at least to Westerners living in the 21st century. However, human beings have a long, bloody history of abusing 'lower' animals for both amusement and food.

Islam and Judaism permit eating animals, but their slaughter must employ the same compassion (*rahman* in Arabic, *rahamanut* in Hebrew, and *rachmones* in Yiddish) that should be provided for people.

Causing unnecessary pain to animals is forbidden by Jewish law. There is a Talmudic rule that before sitting down to a meal one must first see that the domestic animals are fed. As a child I was taught to feed our cocker spaniel, Sniffy, before I ate because he might see me eat and not realize that I'd eventually feed him.

However, not only were Sniffy, and later, Hunter, fed first, they were also fed *during* and *after* my meal.

If reincarnation is real, I'd love to come back as my dog. It would be a great second life.

Chapter 39
The Secret of Life

If I told you the secret of life, it would no longer be the secret of life.

However, here's something I figured our long ago: *Morality does not come from religion.*

Many people brought up in religious homes turn out to be evil. Others raised as atheists innately know the difference between right and wrong and choose to do the right thing without fear of Divine damnation if they do the wrong thing.

The "golden rule" is built into people and even so-called lower animals. **Dogs and dolphins can be kind to human beings;** and lions, chimps, bees and even ants cooperate with each other.

Chapter 40
Spelling "God"

G-d?

Unlike some other cynics and nonbelievers, I am not reluctant to type "God" with an uppercase "G." This policy may shield me from the slings and arrows of fervent theists, but it really is an effort to prevent ambiguity with deities other than the traditional Biblical God.

Zeus and Apollo were gods, but not *the* God.

TV Canine Theology Break

On both the original and remakes of *Magnum, P.I.*, the Doberman Pincher dogs owned by Higgins are named "Zeus" and "Apollo." In Greek mythology, Zeus was the king of the gods and Apollo was his son.

Some religious Jews will not type or write "God," but instead use a hyphenated "G-d." This strange practice is due to a belief that all labels for the deity are holy and must be treated with great respect. If a paper has "God" on it, then it is not supposed to be destroyed or thrown away, but must be buried in a Jewish cemetery (This is done with old prayer books,

Bibles and Torahs, too.) Computers and the Internet have broadened the custom to avoid typing "God" out of fear that the name would be accidentally deleted.

Computer spell checkers, however, are not Orthodox, and typing "G-d" may result in an automatic correction to "God."

According to Jewish educator and writer Ariela Pelaia in LearnReligions.com, "Over the centuries the Hebrew name for God has accumulated many layers of tradition in Judaism. The Hebrew name for God, YHWH (in Hebrew spelled yud-hay-vav-hay or יהוה) and known as the Tetragrammaton, is never pronounced out loud in Judaism and is one of the ancient names of God. This name is also written as JHWH, which is where the word "JeHoVaH" in Christianity comes from. In *History of the World: Part I,* Mel Brooks as Moses says "Jehovah."

Other sacred names for God include:

Elohim (אלה ם) and variations, including El (אל), Eloha, Elohai ("my God") and Elohaynu ("our God")

El Shaddai (שד י אל): God Almighty

Tzevaot (צבא ת): Lord of Hosts

According to Maimonides, any book that contains these names written in Hebrew is treated with reverence, and the name cannot be destroyed, erased, or effaced, and any books or writings containing the name cannot be thrown away. Instead, these books are stored in a *genizah,* which is a special storage space sometimes found in a synagogue or other Jewish facility until they can be given a proper burial in a Jewish cemetery. This law applies to all seven of the ancient names of God.

Among many traditional Jews even the word "Adonai," meaning "My Lord" or "My God," is not spoken outside of prayer services. Because "Adonai" is so closely linked to the name of God, over time it has been accorded more and more reverence as well. Outside of prayer services, traditional Jews will replace "Adonai" with "HaShem" meaning "the Name" or some other way of referring to God without using "Adonai."

Furthermore, because YHWH and "Adonai" are not used casually, literally dozens of different ways to refer to God have developed in Judaism. Each name is linked to different conceptions of God's nature and aspects of the Divine. For example, God can be referred to in Hebrew as "the Merciful One," "Master of the Universe," "the Creator," and "our King," among many other names.

Alternatively, there have been some Jews also use G!d in the same way, utilizing the exclamation point to convey their enthusiasm for Judaism and God.

In Sun-Sentinel.com, Rabbi Marc Gelman wrote, "In Judaism, God's actual name is writable but unpronounceable. That name is made up of four Hebrew letters that roughly translate into the English letters YHWH. Some scholars try to translate it as Yahweh, though no religious Jew would use that word. Jehovah's Witnesses call God Jehovah because they think it's the closest English word for God.

The issue about writing the name of God is all about what constitutes a violation of the second of the Ten Commandments, which prohibits us from taking the name of God in vain. Obviously, using God's name in a curse, or speaking or writing of God in a disrespectful manner are clear violations of this sacred commandment.

But what if you are just writing the name of God? Must you take out the "o" so you're not taking the name in vain or so that, as your teachers told you, you never have to throw God's name into the wastebasket? For some people, this is a comforting ritual that reminds them that God is holy and the name of God is also holy. Writing "G-d" is not a law but just a custom that helps make life more reverent for some observant Jews."

In the "Philologos" column in Forward.com I read, "And what about all the places where gentiles have written the word "God"? Are Jews also commanded to rescue, to the best of their abilities, these millions and billions of pages from destruction? Should an observant Jew buy every book on a used-book stand that might have the word "God" in it to prevent these books from being junked? And if not, is he not an accomplice in the desecration of God's name, no matter how many times he says or writes "Hashem"? By what logic can the English word "God" be considered holy when written by a Jew but not when written by a non-Jew?"

Yahweh ben Yahweh (1935–2007) was born as Hulon Mitchell Jr., a black nationalist and separatist who created the Nation of Yahweh in 1979 in Florida. His self-proclaimed name means "God, Son of God." He could have only been deeming himself to be "son of God, not God," but many of his followers considered him to be God Incarnate. In 1992 he was convicted of conspiracy to commit murder and sentenced to 18 years in prison.

Copycats! Just as Jewish bagels are now sold in thousands of non-Jewish supermarkets and served at McDonald's, and the Jewish tradition of smashing wine glasses at weddings has been mimicked at gentile marriage ceremonies, the hyphenated G-d has recently been used by Mormons and perhaps other Christians. While writing this book I encountered "J-s" for "Jesus."

Chapter 41

Is Christian Science Scientific?

Christian Science—like Mormonism, Messianic Judaism and Jehovah's Witnesses—is a religion that was **Made in the USA,** but it's called a "worldwide movement of spiritual healers." It was developed in New England by Mary Baker Eddy (1821–1910). She argued in her 1875 book *Science and Health* that **sickness is an illusion that can be corrected by prayer alone.** The book became Christian Science's primary reference, along with the Bible, and many millions of copies have been published.

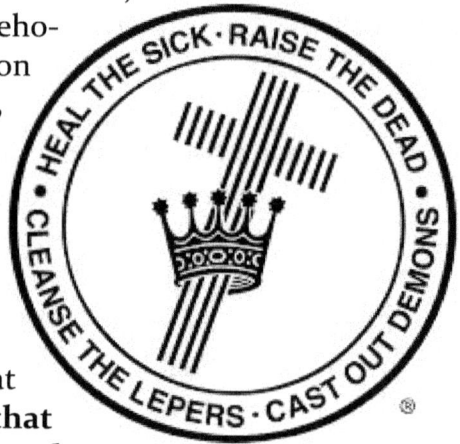

Tenets of Christian Science:

1. As adherents of Truth, we take the inspired Word of the Bible as our sufficient guide to eternal Life.
2. We acknowledge and adore one supreme and infinite God. We acknowledge His Son, one Christ; the Holy Ghost or divine Comforter; and man in God's image and likeness.

3. We acknowledge God's forgiveness of sin in the destruction of sin and the spiritual understanding that casts out evil as unreal. But the belief in sin is punished so long as the belief lasts.
4. We acknowledge Jesus's atonement as the evidence of divine, efficacious Love, unfolding man's unity with God through Christ Jesus the Way-shower; and we acknowledge that man is saved through Christ, through Truth, Life, and Love as demonstrated by the Galilean Prophet in healing the sick and overcoming sin and death.
5. We acknowledge that the crucifixion of Jesus and his resurrection served to uplift faith to understand eternal Life, even the allness of Soul, Spirit, and the nothingness of matter.
6. And we solemnly promise to watch, and pray for that Mind to be in us which was also in Christ Jesus; to do unto others as we would have them do unto us; and to be merciful, just, and pure.

The church says: "God's love is at the core of Christian Science. Mary Baker Eddy wrote that 'Divine Love is the substance of Christian Science, the basis of its demonstration, yea, its foundation and superstructure.' Those who practice Christian Science do their best to live the bold, generous, and compassionate love that Christ Jesus laid out in his Sermon on the Mount. This is the heart of its Christianity.

Christian Science is also a science because it's based on God as infinite Principle as well as unchanging Love. God loves all of us unconditionally and is the only true power and source of all good. Christian Science explains the spiritual laws of Love that Jesus relied on to heal sickness and sin. These laws are reliable and can be proven. People are doing the same kind of healing today as they learn more about what God really is."

Eddy and 26 followers were granted a charter in 1879 to found the **Church of Christ, Scientist**, and in 1894 the "Mother Church," "The First Church of Christ, Scientist," was built in Boston (shown on previous page with huge addition from 1906).

Christian Science became the fastest growing religion in the United States, with nearly 270,000 American members by 1936. That total declined to just over 100,000 in 1990 and under 50,000 by 2009. In 2015, the total may have been as low as 15,000. "The Christian Science Church's decline is not surprising because its doctrines have little appeal to modern youth," according to Quackwatch.org.

The church is known for its public "Reading Rooms" in various countries and its newspaper, the superb *Christian Science Monitor*—which won multiple Pulitzer Prizes. It's "a global newspaper that provides balanced, humane coverage of world news. It is alert to progress and promise as well as to humanity's need to address suffering and conflict. It was established to "injure no man, but to bless all mankind." The last daily print edition was published in 2009 but there is a daily online edition and a weekly print magazine.

After *Science and Health* Eddy wrote 15 more books and started weekly and monthly magazines with articles on Christian Science practice and testimonies of healing.

Eddy described Christian Science as a return to "primitive Christianity and its lost element of healing." Christian Scientists believe that **reality is purely spiritual and the material world an illusion. They view disease as mental error rather than physical disorder, and that the sick should be treated not by medicine but by prayer that seeks to correct the beliefs responsible for the illusion of ill health.**

Contrary to common belief, the church does not require that members avoid all medical care—they use dentists, optometrists, obstetricians and orthopedists; and get vaccinations when required by law.

However, the church maintains that prayer is most effective when *not* combined with medicine. Between the 1880s and 1990s, the avoidance of medical treatment led to the deaths of several Christian Science adherents and their children. Parents and others were prosecuted for, and in a few cases convicted of, manslaughter or neglect.

Born on a New Hampshire farm, Eddy was the youngest of six children in a family of Congregationalists. Her father was a deeply religious man, but according to one account, "Christianity to him was warfare against sin, not a religion of human brotherhood."

As was common with most women at the time, Eddy had little formal education, but she read widely at home. From childhood she had chronic ill health, including indigestion, spinal inflammation and fainting spells.

Eddy's first husband died just before her 23rd birthday, six months after they married and three months before their son was born, leaving her penniless. Because of her poor health she lost custody of the boy when he was four, although sources differ as to whether she could have prevented this.

Her second husband left her after 13 years of marriage; Eddy said that he had promised to become her child's legal guardian, but it is unclear whether he did, and Eddy lost contact with her son until he was in his thirties. Her third husband, Asa Gilbert Eddy, died five years after they married; she believed he had been killed by *malicious animal magnetism*. Six years later, when she was 67 and apparently in need of loyalty and affection, she adopted a 41-year-old homeopath as her second son.

Mark Twain, a prominent critic of hers, described her in 1907 as "vain, untruthful [and] jealous," but **"the most interesting woman that ever lived, and the most extraordinary."**

Eddy studied the Bible her whole life. In 1866, she had a dramatic recovery from a life-threatening accident after reading about one of Jesus's alleged healings. From that moment she wanted to know how she had been healed. She read the Bible, prayed for answers and deduced that spiritual healing was based on "Divine Laws of God." According to the church, she proved that these laws could be applied by anyone to heal every form of human suffering and sin.

The church says: "Spiritual healing isn't miraculous, but an effect of understanding God's all-power and love. It's as provable today as it was in biblical times. For the next 40 years, Mary Baker Eddy practiced, taught and shared this healing Science of Christianity.

As Mary Baker Eddy became known as a Christian healer, she was often asked to cure cases that had been given up by doctors. Once she went to see a woman who'd been given up as dying by a well-known physician. She wrote about this experience, 'On seeing her immediately restored by me without material aid, he asked earnestly if I had a work describing my system of healing... he urged me immediately to write a book which should explain to the world my curative system of metaphysics.'

At the time, she was already writing notes that would expand into her textbook, *Science and Health with Key to the Scriptures*. This book contains the full explanation of Christian Science and its biblical foundation of spiritual healing. For over a century, readers have shared how reading and studying Science and Health has given them a new spiritual sense of the Bible and of their unchangeable relationship to God. These new insights result in physical healing and moral regeneration, according to the church.

Science and Health expanded on Eddy's view that sickness was a mental error. People said that simply reading it had healed them; cures were claimed for everything from cancer to blindness. Eddy wrote in the *New York Sun* in December 1898, in an article called 'To the Christian World,' that she had personally healed tuberculosis, diphtheria and 'at one visit a cancer that had eaten the flesh of the neck and exposed the jugular vein so that it stood out like a cord. I have physically restored sight to the blind, hearing to the deaf, speech to the dumb, and have made the lame walk.'"

Eddy wrote that her views had derived, in part, from having witnessed the apparent recovery of patients she had treated with homeopathic remedies so diluted they were drinking plain water. She concluded that "Divine Mind" was the healer.

She argued that even naming and reading about disease could turn thoughts into physical symptoms, and that the **recording of ages might reduce the human lifespan.** To explain how individuals could be harmed by poison without holding beliefs about it, she referred to the power of majority opinion.

Eddy allowed exceptions from Christian Science prayer, including for dentistry, optometry and broken limbs. She said she had healed broken bones using "mental surgery," but that this skill would be the last to be learned. For the most part then and now, Christian Scientists believe that medicine and Christian Science are incompatible. Medicine asserts that something needs to be fixed, while Christian Science asserts that spiritual reality is perfect and beliefs to the contrary need to be corrected.

In the 1890s Richard Cabot of Harvard Medical School studied the healing testimonies published by the *Christian Science Journal* for his senior thesis. He wrote that the claims were based on self-diagnosis or secondhand reports from doctors, and attributed them to the placebo effect. In 1900 medical lecturer William Purrington called the beneficiaries "hysterical patients... the victims of obscure nervous ailments."

Sociology professor Rodney Stark wrote that a key to Christian Science's original appeal was that its success rate compared favorably with that of physicians, particularly when it came to women's health. "Most doctors," he said, "had not been to medical school, there were no antibiotics, and surgical practices were poor. By comparison the placebo effect (being treated at all, no matter what the treatment was) worked well." Stark argued that the "very elaborate and intensely psychological Christian Science 'treatments' maximize such effects, while having the advantage of not causing further harm."

Eddy believed that several students were using "malicious animal magnetism," or evil thought, against her. When her husband died in 1882 she told the *Boston Globe* that malicious animal magnetism killed him.

Eddy set up what she called a secret society of her students to deal with malicious animal magnetism. Adam H. Dickey, Eddy's private secretary for the last three years of her life, wrote that hour-long watches were held in her home three times a day to protect her against it. The *Manual of the Mother Church* forbids members from practicing it and requires that Christian Science teachers instruct students "how to defend themselves against mental malpractice, and never to return evil for evil."

In 1878 Eddy brought a case against Daniel Spofford, in Salem, Massachusetts, for what came to be known as the "second Salem witchcraft trial." The case was filed in the name of one of Spofford's patients, Lucretia Brown, who said that he had bewitched her, though Eddy appeared in court on Brown's behalf. In preparation for the hearing, Eddy organized a 24-hour watch, during which she asked 12 students to think about Spofford for two hours each and block malicious mesmerism from him. She arrived at the court with 20 supporters, but Judge Horace Gray dismissed the case.

In October 1878 Eddy's husband and another student, Edward Arens, were charged with conspiring to murder Spofford. A barman said they had offered him $500 to do it. After a complex series of claims and counterclaims, the charges were dropped when a witness retracted his statement. Eddy attributed the allegation to a plot by former students to weaken sales of the second edition of her book.

Some Healing Claims...
(reported by ChristianScience.com)

1. Dyan had a medically diagnosed astigmatism and wore eyeglasses. She prayed about the vision problem and the defect cleared up.
2. A growth appeared on Rick's body, and he decided to pray about it. Within days it completely disappeared.
3. While dealing with a throat infection, a spiritual insight led to Brian's quick recovery.
4. Emily had an eating disorder and called a Christian Science practitioner for help. Through the course of a year, not only was she healed of the eating disorder, but she no longer needed prescription eyeglasses.

...And Challenges
(reported by Quackwatch.org)

1. Rita Swan's 16-month-old son Matthew died of meningitis in 1977 under the care of two Christian Science practitioners. She quickly collected allegations of 75 deaths and 95 serious injuries to children of Christian Scien-

tists. In a trial, church officials testified that there were no training, workshops or meetings for practitioners that included any discussion on how to evaluate the seriousness of a child's condition. During an appearance on the *Donahue* show the Swans were asked why Matthew's illness had not been reported to state health authorities as required by law. They said that no one made the diagnosis. Also, as devout believers, they did not want to face possible abandonment by the church for seeking a medical opinion.

2. A 1993 lawsuit following the death of an 11-year-old boy resulted in a $1.5 million judgment against the boy's mother and stepfather and two Christian Science practitioners. Reportedly, the boy died after passing into a diabetic coma while the mother prayed at his bedside and the practitioner took notes about his condition.

3. C.S. nurses cannot take a pulse, use a fever thermometer, give an enema or even a backrub. They have no training in recognizing contagious diseases. They have been retained to attend sick children and took notes as the children suffered and died—but have not called for medical care nor recommended that parents obtain it. They observed children having "heavy convulsions," vomiting repeatedly, and urinating uncontrollably. They saw children moaning in pain and too weak to get out of bed. They have seen their eyes roll upward and fix in a glassy stare. One Christian Science nurse force-fed a toddler as he was dying of a bowel obstruction.

Although I am skeptical and cynical about all religions, Christian Science seems suitable for *extra doses* of skepticism and cynicism. I can't help thinking of this line I first heard back in the 1960s: "**There is nothing more pathetic than a Christian Scientist with cancer.**"

Chapter 42
Creator & Creation

According to the *Christian Post*, The Lutheran Church—Missouri Synod passed a resolution at their convention in Tampa in 2019 affirming the belief that God created the Earth "in six natural days."

Resolution 5-09A, titled "To Confess the Biblical Six-Day Creation" states: "We confess that the duration of those natural days is proclaimed in God's Word: 'there was evening and there was morning, the first day."

The resolution also declared that the creation of Adam as the first human being was a "historical event" and *rejected the claims of the theory of evolution.*

Resolution 5-09A also called on pastors to equip congregations with resources on faith and science and drew from previous resolutions on the origins debate, including one adopted in 1932.

"We teach that God has created heaven and earth, and that in the manner and in the space of time recorded in the Holy Scriptures, especially Gen. 1 and 2, namely, by His almighty creative word, and in six days. We reject every doctrine which denies or limits the work of creation as taught in Scripture," stated the 1932 resolution.

"Since no man was present when it pleased God to create the world, we must look for a reliable account of creation to God's own record, found in God's own book, the Bible. We accept God's own record with full confidence and confess with Luther's Catechism: 'I believe that God has made me and all creatures.'"

Pastors are split on the age of the Earth. A 2011 LifeWay Research survey showed that 46 percent of pastors agree that the Earth is 6,000 years old while 43 percent disagree (the survey has a sampling error of +/-3.2%). Those with graduate degrees are less likely to agree with Young Earth Creationism.

Young Earth creationists arrive at 6,000 years (for both the Earth and the universe) by adding five days of creation (since Adam was said to have been created on the sixth day in the Bible), around 2,000 years between Adam and Abraham, and around 4,000 years between Abraham and the present (scholars say Abraham lived about 2,000 B.C.)

A film—titled *Is Genesis History?*—was released in 2017 to support the Young Earth view and debunk the notion that those who hold such a position are "unscientific" or "stupid."

Creationist Ken Ham says there's a civil war happening in America against young earth creationism and that an atheistic view of evolution is permeating the world. The film makes the case for creation in six literal days and presents evidence that support the accounts in the book of Genesis.

Ham, president of Answers in Genesis and Ark Encounter, argued that despite what the current popular scientific paradigm promotes, the Bible is a record of history that God has revealed to His creation, which says that all are sinners that rebelled against God like Adam and are in need of salvation.

Chabad Rabbi Schneuer Wilhelm told me that there is scientific proof that creation took a literal six days, fewer than 6,000 years ago, and that Adam was created as an adult. I respect and like this rabbi a lot, but I believe that the planet took a *long time* to come together, is ancient, that we homo sapiens evolved from simpler creatures, and that the first one was *not* named "Adam."

In 2019 researchers at the Universities of Utrecht, Oslo and Zürich announced an ancient continent, now buried under the Mediterranean and called "Greater Adria." They analyzed the region as far back as the Triassic period, approximately 240 million years ago.

In *rabbiwithanswers.com*, Rabbi Tully Bryks rsponded to the question, "Was the world really created in just six days or are scientists correct that it took 13.8 billion years?" [Slightly edited, with my comments within brackets.]

Since G-d is the one who created the world, a world which contains all the laws of science and nature, there can never be a conflict between science and the *Torah*. If there does appear to be a conflict, it means that we either need to get a better understanding of the *Torah*, a better understanding of the science, or perhaps we need a better understanding of both. Biblical commentators disagree as to whether the first six days of creation were literally 24 hours each or if they were actually much longer than 24 hours. It is important to note that those commentators who maintain that each "day" actually represented a much longer period of time espoused their positions hundreds of years ago, well before scientists postulated that the world is 13+ billion years old. As such, they are not reinventing/reinterpreting the Torah in response to recent scientific discovery. With regard to the seventh day of creation (the Sabbath), the general consensus [BY WHOM?] is that time functioned normally once Adam was created on the sixth day, which would make the world 5773 years old [when this was written], plus six "days."

Here are some of the many possibilities:

- Since the sun wasn't created until the fourth day, it would make sense that at least the first 3-4 days were not 24-hour days. Days 5-7 could still be 24-hour days, but the first four days could represent billions of years.

- Each "day" of creation could really represent an equal number of thousands, millions or billions of years. So if the world is 13.8 billion years old, each "day" would really be 2.3 billion years.

- According to scientists, most of the 13.8 billion years since the "Big Bang" involve development well before the existence of planet earth, which is part of a relatively young solar system. Assuming that G-d's "clock" co-existed and tracked the mass/energy that would eventually form our planet, and since time passes more slowly when moving more quickly, then when His "clock" was surrounded by mostly energy in the earlier stages, time would have passed more slowly. Going with the literal approach, in which each of the seven days were 24-hour days as we know them, it could be that some of the miraculous events since the beginning of creation, such as the intense water pressure during the flood of Noah or the intense heat during the fiery destruction of Sodom, could have somehow corrupted our scientific methods for dating things. According to this approach, the entire universe is really under 6,000 years old. [Hard To Believe]

- Another literal approach maintains that our world was preceded by other worlds. As such, all of the billions of years' worth of history, possibly even including dinosaurs, can be accounted for in these previous worlds. [No Evidence]

- Another approach that maintains that the world is less than 6,000 years old is that G-d created the world in six days, but did billions of years' worth of work each day. The Garden of Eden was created with lots of vegetation, including fully-grown trees, which would have been seen as hundreds of years old. Adam and Eve were created as fully grown adults.

Unlike the Torah, which we believe to be absolute, scientific knowledge is a fluid process. Scientific "facts" change multiple times, as new discoveries yield new and changing theories and "facts." One great example of what was once accepted as a scientific fact was the universal belief that the earth is flat. [Few people believe that now.]

The year number on the Jewish calendar represents the number of years since creation, calculated by adding up the ages of people in the Bible, back to the beginning. This does not necessarily mean that the universe has existed for fewer than 6,000 years of about 365 days each. Even many religious people readily acknowledge that the first six "days" of creation are not necessarily 24-hour days. A 24-hour day would be meaningless until the creation of the sun on the fourth "day."

HUMOR BREAK: The **Jewish** calendar started at creation and the new year **5780** began in the fall of 2019 CE as I was finishing this book.

But, according to the **Chinese** calendar, the year is **4717**.

So, what did Jewish people eat for the first 1063 years until the appearance of Chinese restaurants?

Human civilization has many creation stories, myths, legends and theories. Obviously, no human being witnessed creation. We're not even sure when the universe was created (14 billion years or 6 thousand years or another number) and what existed before the universe.

Just as young children ask their parents where they came from, and ultimately reject the explanation that they were found under a toadstool or delivered by a stork, many adult humans reject the creation stories. Ahead are a few, in no particular order, for your consideration (with BIG thanks to the Wikipedia God):

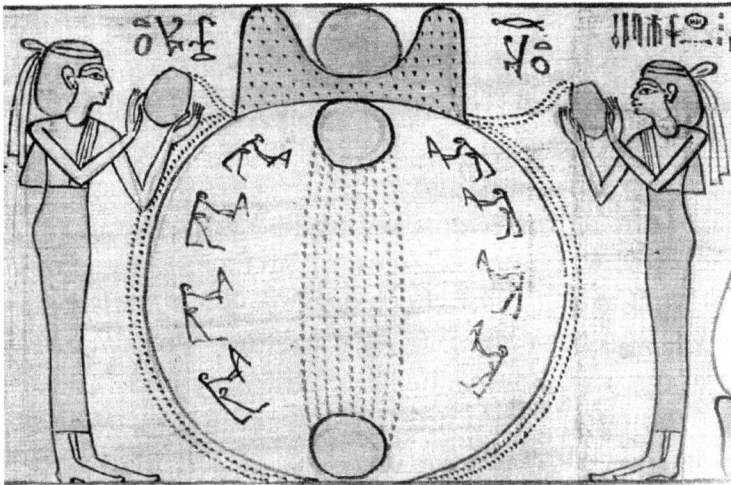

The **ancient Egyptians** had multiple creation legends from different parts of the country. In all of these myths, the world was said to have emerged from an infinite, lifeless sea when the sun rose for the first time, in a distant period sometimes transcribed as Zep Tepi, "the first occasion." Different myths attributed the creation to different gods: the set of eight primordial deities called the Ogdoad, the self-engendered god Atum and his offspring, the contemplative deity Ptah, and the mysterious, transcendent god Amun. While these differing legends competed to some extent, in other ways they were complementary. They all held that the world had arisen out of the lifeless waters of chaos, called Nu. They also included a pyramid-shaped mound, called the *benben*, which was the first thing to emerge from the waters.

These elements were likely inspired by the flooding of the Nile River each year; the receding floodwaters left fertile soil in their wake, and the Egyptians may have equated this with the emergence of life from the primeval chaos. The imagery of the pyramidal mound derived from the highest mounds of earth emerging as the river receded.

The sun was also closely associated with creation, and it was said to have first risen from the mound, as the general sun-god Ra or as the god Khepri, who represented the newly-risen sun. There were many versions of the sun's emergence, and it was said to have emerged directly from the mound or from a lotus flower that grew from the mound, in the form of a heron, falcon, scarab beetle, or human child.

Another common element of Egyptian cosmogonies is the familiar figure of the cosmic egg, a substitute for the primeval waters or the primeval mound. One variant of the cosmic egg version teaches that the sun god, as primeval power, emerged from the primeval mound, which itself stood in the chaos of the primeval sea. The different creation accounts were each associated with the cult of a particular god in one of the major cities of Egypt: Hermopolis, Heliopolis, Memphis, and Thebes.

NOTE: the symbol used before each section ahead is Aleph, the first letter in the Hebrew alphabet. I think it's appropriate for beginnings.

א

The **Cherokee** creation belief describes the earth as a great floating island surrounded by seawater, hanging from the sky by cords attached at the four cardinal points.

The story tells that the first earth came to be when Dâyuni'sï, the little Water Beetle came from Gälûñ'lätï, the sky realm, the Water Beetle was not affected by the natural laws of cause and effect, existing outside of the causality and went to see what was below the water. He scurried over the surface of the water, but found no solid place to rest. He dived to the bottom of the water and brought up some soft mud. This mud expanded in every direction and became the earth.

The other animals in Gälûñ'lätï were eager to come down to the new earth, and first birds were sent to see if the mud was dry. A buzzard was sent ahead to make preparations for the others, but the earth was still soft. When he grew tired, his wings dipped very low and brushed the soft mud, gouging mountains and valleys in the smooth surface, and the animals were forced to wait again.

When it was finally dry they all came down. It was dark, so they took the sun and set it in a track to run east to west, at first setting it too low and the red crawfish was scorched. They elevated the sun several times in order to reduce its heat. The story also tells how plants and animals acquired certain characteristics, and is related to one of their medicine rituals. They all were told to stay awake for seven nights, but only a few animals, such as owl and panther, succeeded and they were given the power to see and prey upon the others at night.

Only a few trees succeeded as well, namely cedar, pine, spruce and laurel, so the rest were forced to shed their leaves in the winter. The first people were a brother and sister. Once the brother hit his sister with a fish and told her to multiply. Following this, she gave birth to a child every seven days and soon there were too many people, so women were forced to have just one child every year.

א

There are many **Mongol** creation myths. In the most ancient one, the creation of the world is attributed to a Buddhist deity. At the start of time there was only water, and from the heavens Lama came down to it holding an iron rod from which he began to stir. As he began to stir the water, the stirring brought about a wind and fire which caused a thickening at the center of the waters to form the earth.

Another narrative also attributes the creation of heaven and earth to a lama called Udan. Udan began by separating earth from heaven, and then dividing heaven and earth both into nine stories, and creating nine rivers. After the creation of the earth itself, the first male and female couple were created out of clay and they became the progenitors of all humanity.

In another example the world began as an agitating gas which grew increasingly warm and damp, precipitating a heavy rain that created the oceans. Dust and sand emerged to the surface and became earth. Yet another account tells of the Buddha Sakyamuni searching the surface of the sea for a means to create the earth and spotted a golden frog. From its east side, Buddha pierced the frog through, causing it to spin and face north. From its mouth burst fire and from its rump streamed water. Buddha tossed golden sand on his back which became land. And this was the origin of the five earthly elements, wood and metal from the arrow, and fire, water and sand.

For **ancient Greeks** an account of the beginning of things is reported by Hesiod in his *Theogony*. He begins with Chaos, a yawning nothingness. Out of the void emerged Gaia (the Earth) and other Divine beings: Eros (Love), the Abyss (the Tartarus), and the Erebus. Without male assistance, Gaia gave birth to Uranus (the Sky) who then fertilized her. From that union were born first the Titans—six males and six females. After Cronus was born, Gaia and Uranus decreed no more Titans were to be born. They were followed by the one-eyed Cyclopes and the Hecatonchires or Hundred-Handed Ones, who were both thrown into Tartarus by Uranus. This made Gaia furious. Cronus was convinced by Gaia to castrate his father. He did this, and became the ruler of the Titans with his sister-wife Rhea as his consort, and the other Titans became his court.

A motif of father-against-son conflict was repeated when Cronus was confronted by his son, Zeus. Because Cronus had betrayed his father, he feared that his offspring would do the same, and so each time Rhea gave birth, he snatched up the child and ate it. Rhea hated this and tricked him by hiding Zeus and wrapping a stone in a baby's blanket, which Cronus ate. When Zeus was full grown, he fed Cronus a drugged drink which caused him to vomit, throwing up Rhea's other children and the stone, which had been sitting in Cronus's stomach all this time. Zeus then challenged Cronus to war for the kingship of the gods. At last, with the help of the Cyclopes (whom Zeus freed from Tartarus), Zeus and his siblings were victorious, while Cronus and the Titans were hurled down to imprisonment in Tartarus.

Zeus was plagued by the same concern, and after a prophecy that the offspring of his first wife, Metis, would give birth to a god "greater than he," Zeus swallowed her. She was already pregnant with Athena, however, and she burst forth from his head—fully-grown and dressed for war.

The Yoruba regard Olodumare as the principal agent of creation. According to a Yoruba account of creation, during a certain stage in this process, the "truth" was sent to confirm the habitability of the newly formed planets. The earth being one of these was visited but deemed too wet for conventional life.

After a successful period of time, a number of divinities led by Obatala were sent to accomplish the task of helping earth develop its crust. On one of their visits to the realm, the arch-divinity Obatala took to the stage equipped with a mollusk that concealed some form of soil; winged beasts and some cloth like material. The contents were emptied onto what soon became a large mound on the surface of the water and soon after, the winged-beasts began to scatter this around until the point where it gradually made into a large patch of dry land; the various indentations they created eventually becoming hills and valleys.

Obatala leaped onto a high-ground and named the place Ife. The land became fertile and plant life began to flourish. From handfuls of earth he began to mold figurines. Meanwhile, as this was happening on earth, Olodumare gathered the gases from the far reaches of space and sparked an explosion that shaped into a fireball. He subsequently sent it to Ife, where it dried much of the land and simultaneously began to bake the motionless figurines. It was at this point that Olodumare released the "breath of life" to blow across the land, and the figurines slowly came into being as the first people of Ife. For this reason, Ife is locally referred to as "Ife Oodaye" ("cradle of existence").

א

In the **pre-Inca** and **Inca** mythology in the Andes region of South America Viracocha is the great creator deity. Its full name (and some spelling alternatives) are Wiracocha, Apu Qun Tiqsi Wiraqutra, and Kon-Tiki—the source of the name of Thor Heyerdahl's raft.

Viracocha was one of the most important deities in the Inca pantheon and seen as the creator of all things, or the substance from which all things are created, and intimately associated with the sea. Viracocha created the universe, sun, moon, and stars, time (by commanding the sun to move over the sky) and civilization itself. Viracocha was worshipped as god of the sun and of storms. He was represented as wearing the sun for a crown, with thunderbolts in his hands, and tears descending from his eyes as rain.

According to a myth Viracocha rose from Lake Titicaca (or sometimes the cave of Paqariq Tampu) during the time of darkness to bring forth light. He made the sun, moon, and the stars. He made mankind by breathing into stones, but his first creation were brainless giants that displeased him. So he destroyed it with a flood and made a new, better one from smaller stones. Viracocha eventually disappeared across the Pacific Ocean (by walking on the water), and never returned. He wandered the earth disguised as a beggar, teaching his new creations the basics of civilization, as well as working numerous miracles. He wept when he saw the plight of the creatures he had created It was thought that Viracocha would re-appear in times of trouble.

In one legend he had one son, Inti, and two daughters, Mama Killa and Pachamama. In this legend, he destroyed the people around Lake Titicaca with a Great Flood called Unu Pachakuti lasting 60 days and 60 nights, saving two to bring civilization to the rest of the world, these two beings are Manco Cápac, the son of Inti (sometimes taken as the son of Viracocha), which name means "splendid foundation," and Mama Uqllu, which means "mother fertility." These two founded the Inca civilization carrying a golden staff, called 'tapac-yauri'. In another legend, he fathered the first eight civilized human beings. In some stories, he has a wife called Mama Qucha.

In another legend, Viracocha had two sons, Imahmana Viracocha and Tocapo Viracocha. After the Great Flood and the Creation, Viracocha sent his sons to visit the tribes to the northeast and northwest to determine if they still obeyed his commandments. Viracocha himself traveled North. During their journey, Imaymana and Tocapo gave names to all the trees, flowers, fruits, and herbs. They also taught the tribes which of these were edible, which had medicinal properties, and which were poisonous. Eventually, Viracocha, Tocapo and Imahmana arrived at Cusco (in modern-day Peru) and the Pacific seacoast where they walked across the water until they disappeared. The word "Viracocha" literally means "Sea Foam."

א

Scandanavian creation stories (and even news reports) are often difficult for Americans to follow because of the unfamiliar spellings, like "Häagen-Dazs." *Völuspá* is a poem that tells the story of the creation of the world and its coming end, related to the audience by a "völva" (not Volvo) seeress addressing the Norse god Odin.

The poem starts with the völva requesting silence from "the sons of Heimdallr" (human beings) and asking Odin whether he wants her to recite ancient lore. She says she remembers ancient giants who reared her.

She then relates a creation myth and mentions Ymir (a primeval being who was born from venom that dripped from the icy Élivágar rivers and lived in the grassless void of Ginnungagap. Ymir birthed a male and female from his armpits, and his legs begat a six-headed being).

The world was empty until the sons of Burr lifted the earth out of the sea. The Æsir then established order in the cosmos by finding places for the sun, the moon and the stars, thereby starting the cycle of day and night. A golden age ensued where the Æsir had plenty of gold and happily constructed temples and made tools. But then three mighty giant maidens came from Jötunheimr and the golden age came to an end. The Æsir then created the dwarves, of whom Mótsognir and Durinn are the mightiest.

At this point, 10 of the poem's stanzas are over and six stanzas begin which contain names of dwarves. This section, sometimes called "Dvergatal" ("Catalogue of Dwarves"), is sometimes omitted by editors and translators.

After the "Dvergatal," the creation of the first man and woman are recounted and Yggdrasil, the world-tree, is described. The seer recalls the burning of Gullveig that led to the first "folk" war, and what occurred in the struggle between the Æsir and Vanir. She then recalls the time Freyja was given to the giants, which is commonly interpreted as a reference to the myth of the giant builder, as told in Gylfaginning.

The seeress then reveals to Odin that she knows some of his own secrets, and that he sacrificed an eye in pursuit of knowledge. She tells him she knows where his eye is hidden and how he gave it up in exchange for knowledge. She asks him in several refrains if he understands, or if he would like to hear more.

In one version, the seeress goes on to describe the slaying of Baldr, best and fairest of the gods and the enmity of Loki, and of others. She then predicts the destruction of the gods when fire and flood overwhelm heaven and earth as the gods fight their final battles with their enemies. This is the "fate of the gods"—Ragnarök. She describes the summons to battle, the deaths of many of the gods and how Odin, himself, is slain by Fenrir, the great wolf.

Thor, the god of thunder and sworn protector of the earth, faces Jörmungandr, the world serpent, and wins but Thor is only able to take nine steps afterward before collapsing due to the serpent's venom. Víðarr faces Fenrir and kicks his jaw open before stabbing the wolf in the heart with his spear. The god Freyr fights the giant Surtr, who wields a fiery sword that shines brighter than the sun, and Freyr falls.

Finally a beautiful reborn world will rise from the ashes of death and destruction where Baldr and Höðr will live again in a new world where the earth sprouts abundance without sowing seed. The surviving Æsir reunite with Hœnir and meet together at the field of Iðavöllr, discussing Jörmungandr, great events of the past, and the runic alphabet. A final stanza describes the sudden appearance of Nidhogg the dragon, bearing corpses in his wings, before the seeress emerges from her trance.

א

The **Genesis** creation narrative is the creation myth of both Judaism and Christianity, and has similarities to the Muslim story in the Quran. The narrative is made up of two stories, roughly equivalent to the first two chapters of the Book of Genesis. In the first, Elohim (the Hebrew generic word for God or Gods) creates the heavens and the Earth in six days, then rests on, blesses and sanctifies the seventh. In the second story, God, now referred to by the personal name Yahweh, creates Adam, the first man, from dust and places him in the Garden of Eden, where he is given dominion over the animals. Eve, the first woman, is created from Adam and as his companion.

Borrowing themes from Mesopotamian mythology, but adapting them to the Israelite people's belief in one God, the first major comprehensive draft of the Pentateuch (the series of five books which begins with Genesis and ends with Deuteronomy) was composed in the late 7th or the 6th century BCE (the Jahwist source) and was later expanded by other authors (the Priestly source) into a work very much like the one we have today. The combined narrative is a critique of the Mesopotamian theology of creation: Genesis affirms monotheism and denies polytheism.

How much history lies behind the story of Genesis? Because the action of the primeval story is not represented as taking place on the plane of ordinary human history and has so many affinities with ancient mythology, it is very far-fetched to speak of its narratives as historical at all. There is much debate, even among believers, about the actual timing of creation: Did the process take six days of 24 hours each, or millions or billions of years?

אָ

The **Muslim** Quran states that "the heavens and the earth were of one piece" before being parted. God then created the landscape of the earth, placed the sky above it as a roof, and created the day and night cycles by appointing an orbit for both the sun and moon. Some modern Muslims interpret the Quran's story of creation in the context of science, and believe that the scientific theory of an expanding universe is described in the Quran.

Sūrat al-Aʿrāf states that the "heavens and the earth" were created in the equivalent of six *yawm*. The Arabic word *yawm* (similar to the nearly identical Hebrew word) means "day," and so some Muslims believe the universe was created in six days, akin to the story of creation in the Genesis. However, other scholars interpret the term *yawm* to mean a unit of time much longer than a day, as the Quran states that in the afterlife, one day is equivalent to 50,000 years or 1,000 years. After completing the Creation, God "settled Himself upon the Throne." A "day of rest" does not appear in the Quran.

Sunni theologian Said Nursî stated the Earth was already inhabited by intelligent species before humankind. He considered, supported by the hadiths from Ibn Abbas and Tabari, the Jinn lived here before but were almost wiped out by fire. A few interpreters of the Quran believed that even before Jinn, other creatures like Hinn lived on the Earth.

The characters of Adam and his wife (in Islamic tradition called Ḥawwāh) appear in the Quran as the first man and woman. The Quran states that they were created from clay, and were brought to life by the Divine breath of God entering their bodies. While verses in the Quran and some ahadith indicate that God created Adam first and that Eve was created from Adam, some scholars proposed that the verses could have multiple interpretations.

The majority of Islamic scholars believe that Adam and Eve were supernaturally created through a miracle by God, though some modern scholars have instead asserted that they evolved naturally from a common ancestor.

A story is told that **Isaac Newton's apprentice**, a professed atheist, walked into a room to find Newton standing in front of a model of our solar system, suspended in the air from the ceiling. This model was an impressive replica of our solar system. Every planet resembled the ones in real life and even rotated around the model sun. The apprentice told Newton how impressed he was with Newton's creation. But the apprentice was quite incredulous when Newton told him that he had not created the model. Newton explained that when he walked into the room, he found a large pile of materials on the floor, which included paper, string, paint and the like. He gave the pile a really big kick and the materials randomly connected with one another, forming an exact replica of our solar system. The apprentice exclaimed that it is not possible for this complex model of the solar system to have come about randomly. Newton retorted that if all the requisite materials were in that pile, it was certainly possible for his kick to have randomly caused this masterpiece of a model. While his apprentice acknowledged that it was technically possible, he explained that the odds were so low for it to have formed by chance, that only a fool would believe that this model of the solar system did not have a designer or creator. At that point, Newton pointed out the irony of this atheist's words—"If a mere model of the solar system must have had a creator, certainly the real solar system must have had a creator as well!" And the real universe is much more complex—it's not just a few balls rotating around, but millions of planets and stars. And the complexity of any life-form adds a whole new level of intricacy. —Rabbi Tully Bryks

Chapter 43
The End Of The World
(but not yet the end of the book)

Science—and science fiction—provide many suggestions about the end of our world. It could be a global war, a nuclear accident, the sun going cold, cyber-terrorism, long-term radical climate change, a giant asteroid hitting us, the Earth being pulled into the sun, the return of dinosaurs, a laser attack from Martians, or who knows what?

The **rapture** is a concept believed by some Christians, particularly American evangelicals, consisting of an **end time** event when all living Christian believers plus resurrected dead believers will rise into Heaven and join Christ.

This is a theory that grew out of the translations of the Bible that John Nelson Darby edited to fit his doctrines, which were promulgated by the cult followers of Darbyism—a doctrine that has been deemed heretical by most mainstream Christians.

Some adherents believe the rapture is predicted and described in Paul's First Epistle to the Thessalonians in the Bible, where he uses the Greek *harpazo*, meaning "to snatch away" or "seize." Though it has been used differently in the past, the term is now often used by certain believers to distinguish this particular event from the **Second Coming** of Jesus to Earth mentioned in Second Thessalonians, Gospel of Matthew, First Corinthians, and Revelation, usually viewing it as preceding the Second Coming and followed by a thousand year millennial kingdom.

Adherents of this perspective are sometimes referred to as **premillenial dispensationalists**, but among them are differing viewpoints about the timing of the event.

The term "rapture" is useful in discussing or disputing the exact timing or the scope of the event, particularly when asserting the "**pre-tribulation**" view that the rapture will occur before, not during, the Second Coming, with or without an extended Tribulation period. The term is most frequently used among Christian theologians and fundamentalist Christians in the United States. Other, older uses of "rapture" were simply as a term for any mystical union with God or for eternal life in Heaven with God.

In *The Rapture, How Will You Prepare for It?*, author Tom Bousquet warns potential rapturees that the families they leave behind need to be provided for with cash or credit cards not connected to raptures. He says that credit card companies will probably not extend credit to those left behind and life insurance companies will likely delay paying based on the disappearance of rapturees.

In his *Estate Planning for the Rapture*, Bousquet provides both advice and suggested forms to do estate planning for the coming rapture. He was president of the Law Bachelors Drinking Club at the University of Texas and chairman of the Houston Martini Society and a member of the Houston Margarita Society. He says he could not find a purpose for his life, but has now found the Lord's work as his purpose. Tom says that the Lord placed the burden on him to write and Tom believes the Rapture is getting closer each day. "This is especially true now that the Great Deceiver (Rev. 13:14) is now on the world scene and the Nation of Israel is under constant attack."

There are differing views among Christians regarding the timing of Christ's return, such as whether it will occur in one event or two, and the meaning of the aerial gathering described in 1 Thessalonians 4.

Many Christians do not subscribe to rapture-oriented theological views. Catholics, as well as Eastern Orthodox, Anglicans, Lutherans and most Reformed (Calvinist) Christians, do not generally use "rapture" as a specific theological term, nor do any of these bodies subscribe to the **premillennialist dispensationalist** theological views associated with its use, but do believe in the phenomenon—primarily in the sense of the elect gathering with Christ in heaven after his Second Coming.

These denominations do not believe that a group of people is left behind on earth for an extended Tribulation period after the events of 1 Thessalonians 4:17.

Pre-tribulation rapture theology originated in the eighteenth century, with the Puritan preachers Increase and Cotton Mather (at right), and was popularized extensively in the 1830s by John Nelson Darby and the Plymouth Brethren, and further in the United States by the wide circulation of the Scofield Reference Bible in the early 20th century.

Rapture adherents, to me, are at least a little bit nuts (and they may think I'm nuts, but that's OK). Rapture theology is complex and diverse. I have not bothered to learn the differences, between, for example, Prewrath premillennialism and Partial pretribulation premillennialism. It's tough enough to keep track of kosher and non-kosher foods.

Our beloved but abused planet Earth was supposed to end on July 29, 2016—but it and we are still here. That date is one of many rapture dates that have been announced, anticipated, and not happened. Predictions of apocalyptic events that would result in the extinction of humanity and the destruction of the planet have been made for thousands of years.

Polls conducted in 2012 across 20 countries found over 14% of people believe the world will end in their lifetime, with percentages ranging from 6% of people in France to 22% in the US and Turkey. Belief in the apocalypse is most prevalent in people with less education, less household

incomes, and those under the age of 35.

Herbert W. Armstrong, (at left) founder of the Radio Church of God, later the Worldwide Church of God, told members of his church that the Rapture would take place in 1936 and that only they would be saved. After the prophecy failed, he changed the date three more times.

Armstrong espoused *British Israelism*, a pseudo archaeological belief that the people of the British Isles are "genetically, racially, and linguistically the direct descendants" of the Ten Lost Tribes of ancient Israel.

Murder cult leader Charles Manson (at right) predicted that "Helter skelter," an apocalyptic race war, would occur in 1969.

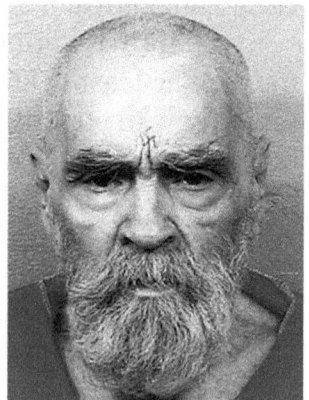

People's Temple cult leader Jim Jones predicted that a nuclear holocaust would take place in 1967. He claimed to be the reincarnation of Jesus, Akhenaten, the Buddha, Vladimir Lenin and Father Divine. Jones organized a mass suicide at Jonestown, Guyana in 1978 and shot himself after the deaths of his followers from drinking a mixture of poison and a sweet drink. The mass suicide gave us the phrase "Drink the Kool-Aid," for the action of someone who engages in a likely doomed or dangerous practice because of perceived great rewards.

Other unfulfilled end times predictions have been made by religious leaders such as Pat Robertson (at right), Sun Myung Moon and Ed Dobson, as well as the alleged psychics Jeane Dixon, George Van Tassel and The Amazing Criswell.

The satirical card shown ahead calls attention to the many missed rapture dates.

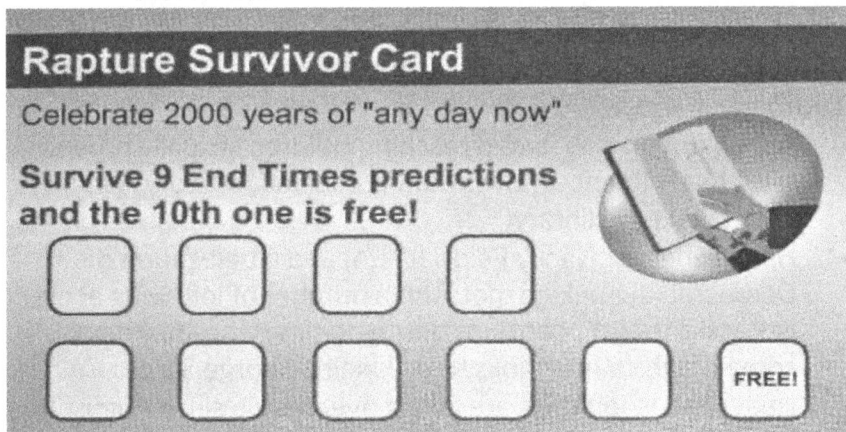

End Times Prophecies declared the second coming of Jesus Christ will occur at the same time the world would end in 2016 in a chain of events caused by the "polar flip" phenomenon. CBS reported that the group said the polar shift would trigger worldwide tremors setting off multiple earthquakes and a "rolling cloud" that would destroy the world. An End Times Prophecies video promised "a magnetic polar flip and catastrophic global earthquake." However, we are still here, the earth is not reeling, there is no catastrophic global earthquake, and Jesus Christ is nowhere to be found. Oh well.

A 17-minute **Armageddon News** video, posted on YouTube and viewed more than 6.3 million times, explains the end-of-the world theory, declaring: The polar flip will make the stars race across the sky, and the vacuum from the reeling of the Earth will pull the atmosphere along the ground, trying to catch up, creating what is known as a rolling cloud.

USA Today pointed out that the polar flip is real, but also noted: The polar reversal is a routine global phenomenon that happens gradually as a result of shifting liquid iron in the Earth's core, according to NASA. It's a slow process, though NASA does indicate some of the most intense drifting will be June 14 to Aug. 19 in 2016.

A politically and religiously conservative website called **RaptureReady.com** publishes items which its administrators think prove that the Rapture is imminent, including:

- A drag queen was filmed teaching children sexually provocative "twerk" dance moves during a so-called "story hour" event at a local library.
- House Speaker Nancy Pelosi (D-CA) and a delegation of Democrat lawmakers met with a number of left-wing activists and socialist politicians during their visit to Guatemala, some of which have links to billionaire George Soros.
- Heavy monsoon rains are falling over Kerala since August 7, increasing river levels and causing deadly floods and land-

slides. At least 28 people have been killed and 27 others are still missing. More than 64 000 people have been evacuated.

- Suspicions are growing that Russia has suffered another nuclear accident after ambulances covered in protective film were seen transporting six people with serious radiation poisoning in a mystery explosion at a military base.
- A policy-naked party that would kill a baby on its birthday, believes you can marry your cat and denounces the rule of law will hawk their moral superiority. And half of America will cheer them on. And so will the principal enemy of the people—the majority dishonest media, a media that has convinced nearly half of America that Russia elected Donald Trump—the most extraordinary hoax ever. This is the Democratic Party.

I realize this web page will be addressing two audiences: those of you who read this page before the rapture and those of you who read it after the rapture. My focus here will be on those who have found this page after the rapture of the Church. For anyone reading this material before the pre-trib rapture, I highly recommend that you ponder the negative consequences of being left behind and seriously consider committing your life to Jesus if you have not done so already.

If you are reading this after the rapture, you need to realize that you have been left behind. At this time, you may be feeling rejected by God. You might be saying to yourself, "Why didn't He take me?" or "I don't understand; I've led a good life." The problem isn't that God rejected you; the problem is that you have rejected Him. By not committing your life to Jesus and by declining to follow Him, you have left Him with no choice but to leave you behind.

"Not everyone that saith unto me, Lord, Lord, shall enter into the kingdom of heaven; but he that doeth the will of my Father which is in heaven."

"For whosoever shall do the will of my Father which is in heaven, the same is my brother, and sister, and mother."

"Come now, and let us reason together, saith the LORD: though your sins be as scarlet, they shall be as white as snow; though they be red like crimson, they shall be as wool."

Is There Hope For Me?

Depending on when you read this article, you may have heard people say, "Because we've missed the rapture, we are lost forever." That assumption is totally wrong! The only way you can find yourself eternally lost is by receiving the Mark of the Beast on your right hand or forehead. Barring that, as long as you have breath in your lungs, you can gain salvation by trusting in Jesus Christ as your Savior.

Scientists have suggested finality for hundreds of thousands or even millions or billions of years from now—so don't start packing to leave just yet.

I recently watched *The End Times*, a lengthy video produced by Questar Entertainment. I'd describe it as mediocre sci-fi: a mix of bad science, not-so-scary horror, questionable history and wacky theology. Here's what I got from it:

1. The rapture is easily the most exciting event that could be conceived by the mind of men.
2. It could occur at any moment, in the twinkling of an eye.
3. The entire planet will be shaken by a shout and a piercing trumpet blast.
4. In cemeteries around the world graves will be split open and Christians who have died will rise from the ground, not as decaying flesh and bones but as living human beings ready to meet Christ in the air.

5. An instant later millions of people from every walk of life will vanish.
6. In the hours that follow, a panic-stricken world will attempt to come to grips with the unexplainable.
7. Chaos will be rampant.
8. News media and governments will offer false explanations (e.g., people were taken by space aliens).
9. It will be a seven-day literal hell-on-earth and nobody will be spared.
10. The Antichrist coming from Europe will broker a seven-year peace between Israel and the Arabs which starts the tribulation.
11. Empowered by Satan, he will rule the world.
12. There will be a new era of unprecedented prosperity and peace.
13. The Antichrist will be hailed as a savior.
14. He will enable rebuilding of the Temple in Jerusalem.
15. The Muslim Dome of the Rock will be moved to make way for the Temple.
16. Joy is short lived.
17. The Antichrist reveals his true nature midway through treachery.
18. He unleashes a torrent of persecution against the Jews.
19. The Antichrist moves beyond military and economic domination and demands to be worshiped as a god.
20. Every person must wear 666, the mark of the beast.
21. He erects an idol of himself in the new Jewish Temple.
22. In a miracle, the idol will speak, demanding that people bow down to it.
23. Jews will hide in the wilderness south of Jerusalem, possibly in the city of Petra in Armageddon in Jordan.
24. There God will protect and sustain the Jews with water from rocks and manna from heaven, as during the Exodus.
25. The death toll will be more than 1 million per day.

26. Anger against Jews increases.
27. The Antichrist orders his army of the European Confederacy to converge on Israel, committed to the total annihilation of the Jews.
28. Another army of 200 million marches from the east.
29. The Antichrist attacks Jerusalem.
30. The Jews are defeated, suffering enormous casualties.
31. The Antichrist then sends armies into the wilderness to attack the hidden Jews.
32. Jews then pray to the long-rejected Messiah, Jesus.
33. The universe is shaken to its core.
34. There is no light from the sun or moon. Stars fall from the sky.
35. Then a brilliant light illuminates the entire globe.
36. As Jesus appears, the Antichrist and his armies are filled with rage.
37. Millions of soldiers launch an attack on Jesus.
38. Jesus says a word and the army of Antichrist is defeated.
39. Control of earth passes from Satan to God.
40. The planet is renewed.
41. Jesus rules from Jerusalem for 1,000 years.

A bit more lunacy: 'Pastor' Rick Wiles says that
1. "Judaism is anti-Christ."
2. "The Antichrist will be a homosexual Jew."
3. "If you have any item with a Jewish star on it, you have an occult image."
4. "The Jews are in rebellion against God."
5. "Christians are going to be killed by the synagogue of Satan." (not by Muslims)
6. Israel and the Jewish mafia assassinated John F. Kennedy.

Chapter 44
Conclusions

So, after 61 years of doubting and pondering, plus three months of interviewing and reading, what have I discovered and what have I decided?

I still don't care about baseball. Sure, I now understand how the game works, but it simply has little appeal to me. It seems like in 80% of the time spent playing (or watching) a game, *very little happens*. Maybe I have an abnormally limited attention span, but the only sports that can keep me stimulated are hockey and basketball—because they have *constant action*. Football interruptions are pervasive and annoying, with more "TIME OUT" than "time in."

I almost never go to movies that are longer than 90 minutes, because they turn into expensive naps. CONFESSION: I sometimes fell asleep while typing this book.

Earlier in the book I mentioned that my father often fell asleep in synagogues and I suggested that religious services should be limited to 30 minutes.

Perhaps a 60-minute limit for "the national pastime" would eliminate wasted time—and attract new fans. A lot of the time when the muscle-bound millionaires in snazzy uniforms are supposed to "PLAY BALL" they do little more than stand, stare, yawn and scratch. The fans in the stands also stare, yawn and scratch—but usually while seated.

The **seventh-inning stretch** is a tradition that takes place in the middle of the seventh inning of a ball game. The game stops, and people who *paid to watch a game* will stand up and stretch out their arms and legs—and sometimes walk around, go to the john and buy snacks.

In most ballparks the fans sing *Take Me Out to the Ball Game* or, since the September 11 terrorists' attacks, sing *God Bless America*. If a game goes into extra innings, a 14th, 21st or even 28th inning stretch would be possible. But if games took just one hour, stretches would be unnecessary.

Financial planners, the Pitney-Bowes company and at least one medical journal have said we are in an "era of specialization." Maybe baseball should accept the idea. Perhaps we could choose from *several kinds of baseball games*. Maybe there could be games just for pitching, and for hitting, and for fielding, and for running. A successful baseball team requires people who have the talents to master multiple skills. Pinch Hitters and Designated Hitters, however, are presumed to be better hitters than the players they temporarily replace at home plate. Pitchers are seldom good hitters.

I might be willing to pay 10 bucks to see a bunch of 21st-century Mickey Mantles, Babe Ruths and Ty Cobbs whack balls into the bleachers—even if they did not need to run around the bases.

The Home Run Derby is an annual home run hitting competition in Major League Baseball usually held the day before the All-Star Game, which puts the contest on a Monday in July. Maybe we should have derbies every week, or every day.

I am fascinated by the connections between baseball and religion.

(above) Here's Billy Graham preaching at a stadium.

In *Preaching Today,* Minister Nancy Becker wrote: "The world of baseball is a dramatic presentation of some of life's most important and universal lessons. I'm not saying that Abner Doubleday intended to make a theological statement about the meaning of life when he invented the game of baseball. But he did invent a game that dramatizes the very human predicament of trying to measure up to a standard of perfection and always falling short. The apostle Paul talked a lot about standards of perfection that are impossible to meet. To Paul, those standards were the Hebrew law. Paul said the law is a curse, always reminding us of how inadequate we really are. The law, he says, is set up to show us that we cannot do right; we can never be good enough because we cannot live up to its standards."

Terry Rush was a minister at Tulsa, Oklahoma's Memorial Drive Church of Christ and a multi-decade fan of the St. Louis Cardinals' fantasy baseball camp, where fans get together for play and interaction with favorite players.

He told *The Oklahoman* that he and his younger brother, John, picked up their bats and gloves with the intent of hitting a few balls any time they got a chance. The two dreamed of going to Busch Stadium to see the Cardinals play and of one day donning players' jerseys themselves.

Many years and much ministry later, Terry was reading a baseball magazine and saw an advertisement about a Cardinals mini-camp for non-pro players who longed to mingle with former professional ballplayers and be coached by them.

Knowing he was a fan of the Cardinals, a family at the church paid for Rush to attend the camp. The next year, he funded the trip himself. After that, the congregation began making the trip an annual treat for the pastor.

Twitter provides little room for biographies, but the first thing stated by Nick Ahmed, shortstop for the Arizona Diamondbacks is "Child of God." A recent tweet quotes both

Billy Graham and Isaiah. Despite his Muslim-sounding last name, Ahmed is a Christian.

Ballplayers Jesus Delgado, Jesus Guzman and Jesus Aguilar are obviously named for a more famous Jesus. Other players are named "Christian."

Tim Tebow switched from football to baseball (now the New York Mets). He is known for kneeling in prayer at games—an action that became known as "Tebowing." In the Philippines, where he was born, Tebow has preached and assisted many evangelists. In the USA he has discussed his Christian faith at prisons, schools, churches, youth groups and conferences.

Tebow stated that he has maintained his virginity and is a group leader for the Fellowship of Christian Athletes—which decrees that leaders sign a "Statement of Sexual Purity," agreeing that sex outside marriage and homosexual acts are unacceptable to God.

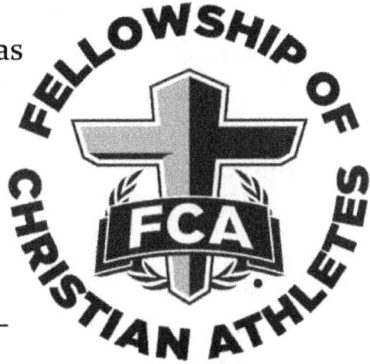

In early 2019 Tebow became engaged to Demi-Leigh Nel-Peters, a model and Miss Universe 2017. Is Tebow still a virgin? Ask them.

A 2012 Easter Sunday crowd of about 30,000 in Texas heard Tebow say: "Regardless of what happens, I still honor my Lord and Savior Jesus Christ, because at the end of the day, that's what's important—win or lose. We need to get back to one nation under God," and that he hopes one day high school athletes will feel okay getting down on one knee on the football field.

In 1965 Los Angeles Dodgers Jewish pitcher Sandy Koufax made history and provided a teaching moment for many rabbis by *not* pitching in a World Series game.

"By refusing to pitch that day, Koufax became inextricably linked with the American Jewish experience," wrote Jane Leavy in her Koufax biography in 2002. "He was the New Patriarch: Abraham, Isaac, Jacob and Sandy. A moral exemplar, and single too! (Such a catch!)"

Cooperstown's Baseball Hall of Fame acknowledges three claims for the origin of the Seventh Inning Stretch. One theory states that Manhattan College's Brother Jasper of Mary, the first athletic director and "prefect of discipline" at the school, called a timeout before the seventh inning at-bat in a muggy 1882 summer game.

Realizing that the crowd was restless, he told the students to stand up and stretch until the game resumed. The stretch caught on in the major leagues because the college team played the New York Giants into the 1890s and other teams copied the practice, which, of course, continues today.

Korean Rev. Sun Myung Moon attracted 25,000 spectators to Yankee Stadium for a rally in 1969. Preachers such as Billy Graham and Joel Osteen have also drawn huge crowds to baseball stadiums.

Thousands of members of Rev. Moon's Unification Church, known as "Moonies," got married in mass weddings in ball parks. If you're interested and have lots of friends and relatives, the rental fee for Yankee Stadium is estimated to be $100,000.

But non-Moonies with a mere handful of guests can get joined together in the stadium for less than $10,000 (hotdogs and beer cost extra).

If you'd like to propose via a scoreboard announcement, prices at various stadiums range from under $50 to $2,500. Is a match made in Chicago's Wrigley Field or Boston's Fenway Park as good as a match made in heaven? Maybe God knows.

My attitudes about 𝕲𝖔𝖉 are unchanged.

Despite intensive research, pleasant interviews and fervent tales from clergy—and even from relatives—I still am not a believer, and still think I am unlikely to undergo a deathbed conversion. If it happens, somebody else will have to write about it. It might make a good book.

However, despite my lack of fear of Divine retribution, I want to live my remaining time as a moral, caring, helpful person. I recognize the importance of *rahamanut* ("compassion" in Hebrew).

If God does exist, I think that she, he or it will approve. In an episode of *God Friended Me*, Joe Morton as Rev. Arthur Finer (father of the main character Miles Finer), said that **"Belief in God is not necessary for belief in good."** I like that.

As before I started my spiritual quest, I am still willing to acknowledge the existence of a creative force (the "Prime Catalyst"), but not a "Supreme Being" to be feared or prayed to. I simply have not detected evidence.

I can certainly appreciate the beauty of a rainbow, a ruby, a rose, a Miss Universe or a golden retriever pup—but their appearances are not enough to get me to self-flagellate, beg for forgiveness, kneel or pray.

It's not that I don't believe the reports from believers who say they have witnessed God, or that I think these people are on drugs or nuts. It's just that their experiences—even if true—are not enough motivation for me to change my life.

In my visits to nearby churches and synagogues, I met some truly wonderful people—compassionate, humorous, patient, knowledgeable, intelligent and devoted to both God and to other human beings. But their exemplary lives were inadequate to get me to change my ways and sign up.

I was particularly impressed by the righteous social efforts of the churches in my neighborhood—previously 'foreign' to me. I could easily ally myself with any of them except for one problem: Jesus. He may have been a wonderful man, and a member of *my* tribe; but to me he was a *man*—not a god or part of a godly trio.

Being a Christian seems like joining a fan club, and I've never joined a fan club. Not even for the Rolling Stones, and I *love* the Stones.

Becoming a "Jew for Jesus" would be a *bigger problem*. I am a Jew. Maybe I could become "for Jesus," but that would mean I was no longer Jewish. Being a Jew for Jesus simply makes no sense to me. It's like being a vegetarian carnivore.

I may not believe in God, but I think I'll always believe in the Jewish people.

What else?

1. I was surprised to learn that mainline Protestant congregations are more liberal than newer non-denominational churches.
2. I was surprised to learn that mainline Protestant congregations are shrinking while newer non-denominational churches are growing.
3. I was surprised to learn that Puritans were not as terrible as I thought they were (but burning suspected witches and hanging Quakers was not nice).
4. I was surprised to find out that many things I researched and wrote about turned out to have personal connections to me.
5. I was pleased to learn that snake handling and venom drinking have pretty much disappeared.
6. I was pleased to find that Jehovah's Witnesses are friendly, non-confrontational folks (but I don't like rejection of blood transfusions).
7. I found Jews for Jesus to be *even more annoying* than I had imagined them to be.
8. I found the varieties and theories of tribulationists to be incomprehensible.
9. I was greatly disappointed to learn that there are Jews (members of *my* tribe) who accept the Torah literally, including the six-day creation schedule.
10. I was pleased to find friendly Muslims who did not want to kill me.
11. I was surprised and disappointed that *no* Catholic priest or nun was willing to be interviewed.
12. I was horrified to learn of misogynist Satmar Hasidim.
13. I still don't like Evangelicals.
14. I was surprised that no clergy person I spoke to regards God to be a supreme BEING. "Spirit" is a typical label.

15. I was pleased that Christian and Muslim clergy people are quite knowledgeable about Judaism—and are not critical (at least when speaking to me).
16. I was pleased that no clergy person I spoke to tried to convert me, and none asked for a donation.
17. I am amazed to have encountered a great many nonbelievers who are not shy about revealing their status in public.
18. I don't understand such Christian concepts as salvation, revelation and grace.

I was surprised at the apparent over-representation of Google links to "Christian publishing" compared to publishing for other religions. There are about 150 Christians to every Jew on the planet, but the ratio of links for "Christian publishing" to "Jewish publishing" is only about 3.7 to one. Strangely, the ratio of "Christian self-publishing" to "Jewish self-publishing" is 4,370 to one!

- Why do the members of my tribe—who obviously do a huge amount of writing and publishing—have such a tiny need for religious self-publishing compared to Christians?
- Do Christian writers feel they are blocked by traditional secular publishing companies, or merely feel more comfortable dealing with Christian publishers?
- Why do followers of Islam ("people of the book" like Christians and Jews) who make up over one-fifth of the world's population and are strongly involved in publishing, have a tiny need for self-publishing that reflects Islam?
- Why do Hindus and Buddhists—who comprise a fifth of the planet's people and have major involvement in publishing, have no apparent need for self-publishing that reflects their faiths?
- Why do the millions of Sikhs, Baha'is, Confucians, Jains and Shintos have no need for self-publishing services that cater to followers of their faiths?
- Why do Christians have a much stronger need or desire to self-publish than do the followers of other major religions?

Chapter 45
Some Things To Think About:

"The Jews are waiting for the first coming of the Messiah, while Catholics are waiting for the Second Coming."
—U.S. Conf. of Catholic Bishops

"Miami Beach is the waiting room for heaven."
—Unknown

"But while we are all waiting, it's important to remember that we Catholics have Jewish roots. Our Mass is rooted in the Passover meal and in the synagogue liturgies of the first century. Many of our feasts and seasons, like Pentecost, are rooted in Jewish feast days. Many of our ideas about God and the world come from our Jewish roots..."
—Patheos.com

"Whoever saves a life, saves the whole world."
—Talmud

"People expect their rabbi to be a stand-in for God, who they think looks like a guy with a beard sitting on a cloud. I don't look like that. ... Being a divorced and lesbian rabbi and mom deepened my understanding of human experience. It broadened who I can relate to. ... You can't go 10 city blocks in New York without running into a lesbian rabbi."
—Rabbi Lisa Grushcow, *New York Times*

"Prayer begins where our power ends."
—Abraham Joshua Heschel (theologian, professor, author)

"The problem is, God gave me a brain and a penis and only enough blood to run one at a time."
—Robin Williams (funny guy)

"The belief that Trump is a Messiah is rampant and dangerous."
—*Psychology Today*

"Doubt is good for the human soul."
—Rabbi Emanuel Rackman

"In recent decades, we've seen millions of unborn babies murdered, young children taught to question their gender, marriage redefined, and God pushed completely off the campuses of

our public schools. Had the church at large not been so weak when these national sins surfaced, it would never have allowed them to harden into the brick and mortar laws we have today."
—Frances Swaggart (wife of evangelist Jimmy Swaggart)

"All animals are equal, but some animals are more equal than others."
—George Orwell, *Animal House*

"Cleanliness is next to godliness, and next to impossible."
—Unknown

"Belief in God is not necessary for belief in good."
—*God Friended Me*

"There have been many theories about the origin of religion. Yet it seems that creating gods is something that human beings have always done. When one religious idea ceases to work for them, it is simply replaced.

These ideas disappear quietly, like the Sky God, with no great fanfare. In our own day, many people would say that the God worshipped for centuries by Jews, Christians and Muslims has become as remote as the Sky God.

Some have actually claimed that he has died. Certainly he seems to be disappearing from the lives of an increasing number of people, especially in Western Europe.

They speak of a "God-shaped hole" in their consciousness where he used to be, because, irrelevant though he may seem in certain quarters, he has played a crucial role in our history and has been one of the greatest human ideas of all time."
—Karen Armstrong, *A History of God: The 4,000-Year Quest of Judaism, Christianity and Islam*

"He no play-a da game, he no make-a da rules."
—Former U.S. Secretary of Agriculture Earl Butz, reacting to Pope Paul VI's opposition to using artificial contraception

The pastor of a Baptist church in Alabama was arrested just days after confessing he'd molested at least one young boy from his congregation. John Martin, the lead pastor of Lighthouse Baptist Church, confessed to four counts of sexual abuse on June 23, 2019. He was arrested on felony sex abuse charges after members of his church reported him to

authorities. The 41-year-old pastor confessed to his congregation from the pulpit, after telling his wife. He called the abuse an "affair," court records say. Before being arrested, he'd checked himself into a psychiatric unit and turned over two guns.
—WAFF Television

"Roses are reddish. Violets are bluish. If it wasn't for Jesus, everyone would be Jewish."
—Unknown

"Faith is not that complicated. Religion always is."
—Timothy Egan, *New York Times*

"The best cure for Christianity is reading the Bible."
—Mark Twain (author)

"In Ireland 95% of the population is Catholic, 5% is Protestant, and I am chief rabbi of the rest."
—Lord Immanuel Jakobovits

"Man plans and God laughs."
—Unknown Jew

"The Torah, the New Testament and the Koran all have the interest of humankind at their core. Therefore, it is our obligation to work together for the betterment of humanity."
—Abdullah bin Abdul Aziz (king of Saudi Arabia)

"God has a very big heart, but there is one sin he will not forgive: if a woman calls a man to her bed and he will not go."
—Nikos Kazantzakis, *Zorba the Greek*

"We're not a speck of dust floating in this vast space, but the Earth is the center of things. We're not moving. We're not a planet. This is it. Heaven is above the Earth, hell is below the Earth."
—Asheley Landrum (hoax investigator)

"Does anyone have any suggestions for how to pray at the right times and deal with sleep disorders at the same time? I have insomnia which often makes it hard for me to get to sleep. I need to get tested for sleep apnea because I keep waking up, unable to breathe. But, regardless of what I have, I wake up exhausted."
—Orthodox Jewish woman on Facebook

"God is without beginning or end, Satan has a starting point. God is eternal, Satan is temporal. God is all powerful, Satan's power is severely limited.

God speaks life into existence. Satan the murderer is not always allowed to speak at all. God owns heaven; Satan is sometimes allowed to visit."
—Precept.org

"We are as nothing. The fragility of man, in respect to God. We are nothing but creatures."
—Monsignor Chauvet (rector of Notre-Dame Cathedral in Paris)

"My dad was raised as an Orthodox Jew and lost his faith completely after the Holocaust. My mother was raised in a kosher home, but only the boys (her two brothers) had religious training. Mom and four sisters had none. I once asked my mother if she believed in God, and she shrugged and said, 'If there is a God, I can't imagine that he'd want more than for all of us to be kind to each other.' That works for me. To be honest, that's all the religion I need."
—Linda Fields, Facebook

Almost no forms of **Judaism** share the traditional majority Christian belief in the immortality of the soul, therefore Sheol (Hades in the Septuagint, "the grave" in many instances in the *King James Bible*) is simply the destination for all the dead, and no "problem of Sheol" exists. Gehenna, found in the Mishnah, is the Lake of Fire or destination of the living sinners and raised wicked at Judgment Day, and the place of either destruction, in the Mishnah or, in some rabbinical texts, eternal torment, which would potentially create a "problem of Gehenna."

In **Christianity**, hell has traditionally been regarded as a place of punishment for wrongdoing or sin in the mortal life, as a manifestation of Divine justice. Nonetheless, the extreme severity and/or infinite duration of the punishment might be seen as incompatible with justice. However, hell is not seen as strictly a matter of retributive justice even by the more traditionalist churches. For example, the **Eastern Orthodox** see it as a condition brought about by, and the natural consequence of, free rejection of God's love.

The **Roman Catholic Church** teaches that hell is a place of punishment brought about by a person's self-exclusion from communion with God, the free and continual rejection of God's forgiveness of sins. The church believes that this rejection is caused by committing and refusing to repent for a mortal sin. The church believes that those who die only in original sin are not predestined to hell, since God is not bound by baptism. The church believes that hell is eternal because the sinner refuses to turn away from his mortal sin to God's forgiveness of sins. The church believes that hell is its own chief punishment.

In some **ancient Eastern Christian traditions**, hell and heaven are distinguished not spatially, but by the relation of a person to God's love.
—Wikipedia

"Jews, atheists, agnostics and evangelical Protestants, as well as highly educated people and those who have religiously diverse social networks, show higher levels of religious knowledge, while young adults and racial and ethnic minorities tend to know somewhat less about religion than the average respondent does.

Jews are the top performers on questions about other world religions, getting 7.7 questions right, on average, out of 13 questions about Judaism, Islam, Buddhism, Hinduism, Sikhism and global religious demography. In terms of the survey overall, Jews get 18.7 questions right, on average. One possible explanation for why Jews, atheists and agnostics score among the highest on this survey is that all three of the groups are highly educated, on average. Jews, atheists and agnostics display greater religious knowledge than other groups even after controlling for education and other demographic characteristics associated with knowing more about religion."
—Pew Survey

Jennie. Groff, 42, grew up just outside Lancaster, Pennsylvania, in a Mennonite family that regularly helped to resettle refugees. "To love your neighbor is a really big, foundational part of what we believe," she said. "It is what people once did for us, so it's seeped into the cores of who we are as a community."
—*New York Times*

"Jesus, forgive me for ever being a Republican."
—Joe Scarborough (host of *Morning Joe* on MSNBC and former four-term Florida Republican congressman)

357

"When I was in 5th, 6th and 7th grade I attended a secular summer camp. One of the three owners was Jewish. We started each day by reciting *The Lord's Prayer*. I didn't know it was a Christian prayer until years later."
—The Author

"It is inconceivable that a rabbi would deliver a sermon on salvation through faith, a most common subject in Christian sermons."
—Rabbi Joseph Telushkin and Dennis Prager, *The Nine Questions People Ask about Judaism*

"My mother was a conservative Jew who eloped with a French Canadian Mohawk. My stepfather was a Scotch Irish convert. We were raised Reform, and I was Bat Mitzvah.

My husband is a very lapsed Catholic Arab. Our daughters celebrated the holidays with us but had no formal Jewish education because I could never afford to join a temple. They consider themselves Jewish, but secular. My oldest granddaughter also had virtually no religious education, but wears a *chai* [Jewish charm necklace] and considers herself a Jew.

I wrote earlier that Jews are not an ethnicity since we come from every country. Jews are not just followers of a religion since there are so many secular Jews. My educated conclusion is that we are members of a bronze-age tribe that survived to modern times. We are born into the tribe and encouraged to marry within the tribe.

But I was told that religion is all that matters, and you have to follow the Jewish religion to be a real Jew. So, am I Jewish since I no longer practice? Are my kids and grandkids? Is a JuBu Jewish? What is a Jew?"
—A Jewish group on Facebook

"Invoking God and calling for prayer should never seem obscene. But it is always obscene to use the Almighty to escape our own responsibility.

"God bless the people of El Paso Texas. God bless the people of Dayton, Ohio," President Trump said in a Sunday morning tweet from his New Jersey golf club.

Yes, may God bless them. But may God also judge Trump for a political strategy whose success depends on sowing racism, reaction and division. May God judge him

358

for stoking false and incendiary fears about an immigrant 'invasion,' the very word echoed by the manifesto that police suspect was the El Paso shooter's. May God judge the president for cutting programs to fight white extremism at the very moment when the FBI is telling us that we are more at risk from white-nationalist terrorists than Islamist terrorists."
—E. J. Dionne Jr., *Washington Post*

"When I say I don't believe in God, I don't mean that that is written on my pillow, and that's the first thing I say when I look in the mirror in the morning. I mean that you can't prove a negative like that. I never go around and do debates with people about the existence of God, because it's stupid! You can't prove that there is no God. I just say that for all of the evidence I've seen, my conclusion is that God does not exist."
—Susan Jacoby, *Religion News Service*

"How much history lies behind the story of Genesis? Because the action of the primeval story is not represented as taking place on the plane of ordinary human history and has so many affinities with ancient mythology, it is very far-fetched to speak of its narratives as historical at all."
—Jon Levenson (professor of Jewish Studies at Harvard)

"And they'll watch the game, and it'll be as if they've dipped themselves in magic waters. The memories will be so thick they'll have to brush them away from their faces."
—Terence Mann, played by James Earl Jones in *Field of Dreams*

"If the Jew did not exist, the antisemite would invent him."
—Jean-Paul Sartre (philosopher, playwright, novelist, screenwriter, political activist, biographer and literary critic)

"Christianity is the religious form of the formation, development, and advancement of Western Civilization; i.e.; the engine of bringing prosperity and equality to all of humanity.
   The Straight Pride Coalition recognizes that these foundational principles and values of life are under a massive coordinated attack. The 'enemies of the cross' (Phil. 3:18), for the purpose of estab-

lishing their own replacement belief system of Satanic Humanism as the dominant cultural and societal paradigm of an enslaved humanity, desire the total destruction of Christianity. Specifically, the destruction of the cultural and social institutions founded upon it including the natural nuclear family, the sovereign nation state; the inherent recognition of Christian value, wonder, and awesomeness of human life, and the most fundamental concepts of human identity including masculinity and femininity.

The Straight Pride Coalition hence declares our unequivocal and total allegiance to Christ ... and our equivalent opposition to Satanic Humanism and its anti-humanity principles.

With a firm recognition of our inadequacies we appeal to God, our Creator and Redeemer, to counsel, equip, and guide us to victory in the societal, cultural, and national War in which we are engaged.

May future generations celebrate our actions that protected these foundational pillars of culture, society, and nation as the standards upon which civilization is founded.

We hence seek God for all of our needs in this great endeavor, invite all people of good will to join us in the defense of our current and future generations in The War which is upon us."
—Straight Pride Coalition

"Religion is for the brain, not for the belly."
—The author's non-kosher mother

(Q) Why do nuns wear crosses?
(A) So nobody will think they're Jewish.
—The author's funny father

"A Jew is twenty-eight percent fear, two percent sugar, and seventy percent *chutzpah* (audacity)."
—Unknown

"We returned to Judaism recently and part of me struggles with the God thing. It's not that I deny the possibility. Rather I am mentally and spiritually exhausted trying to comprehend what I believe. I believe that it's up to me to make things in life better. No God snapped his fingers and fixed my problems. I disagree with my AA group because of magical thinking. It's almost mean-

ingless to debate theology because nobody can agree on what God is. I am currently a Reform Jew but wonder if we had them here that I would want to consider Reconstructionist or Humanistic."
—Facebook commenter

"Shut up and eat your *shiksa*."
—Woody Allen, *Sleeper*

"Over decades of polling, a majority of Americans have consistently indicated a negative opinion of atheists and nonbelievers. Even in this enlightened twenty-first century, where we've proved ourselves ready for a black president and welcomed elected officials representing every group, approximately half of all Americans say they would refuse to vote for a well-qualified atheist candidate for public office. In other words, one out of every two Americans admits to being prejudiced against fellow citizens who don't believe in God.

No other minority group in this country is rejected by such large numbers. This prejudice ought to concern us all. Because prejudice anywhere endangers not only its targets, but all who believe that we should be judged not by the color of our skin, or our gender, or sexuality, or by our religious preference or lack thereof, but by the content of our character. If we can convince ourselves today that one entire group comprising millions of people might be incapable of goodness, might be "no good," then we harbor inside us the ability to turn against and hate any other group as well, and no one should feel safe. It is not easy to live a good life or be a good person—with or without a god. The fact is that life is hard. Living well and being a good person are difficult to do. But that doesn't mean we should give ourselves permission to judge an entire group of people as incapable of goodness unless they're being good the majority's way."
—Greg Epstein, *Good Without God*

"Rabbis never agree. They're Jewish."
—Rabbi Alan Alpert

"Evangelical Christians have long supported Zionism not because they have affection for Judaism and its adherents but because of their powerful belief in biblical prophecy that

declares the Messiah's second coming will and must be preceded by God's gathering and resettling of the Jewish people in a homeland. For decades, support for Israel has been a key component of political platform of the evangelical right, as is evident in the words of prominent spokespeople such as Pat Robertson. The Christian narrative of the Messiah's return cannot be fulfilled without the existence of Israel."
—Tim Libretti, *PoliticusUSA*

"Mormon Church members who followed the [health] code had a life expectancy 8 to 11 years longer than the general white population of the United States."
—Mormon website

"People who may not have been that close to Jewishness, they feel suddenly like it's very important to express who they are as Jews in the context of their activism and in the context of their collective memory."
—Arielle Angel, *Jewish Currents*

"I would never dare challenge my grandfather. He believed that all of the answers to any of life's problems could be found in the Torah. He had his own synagogue and the family lived upstairs. I lived with my grandparents (in the synagogue) when I went to Yeshivah of Flatbush high school. It was very structured. That's probably why I rebelled. My grandfather never let me or my female cousins talk at the dinner table because he considered anything a girl said to be nonsense, so I became a trial lawyer and essentially get paid to talk."
—Joyce David, Facebook

"I'm either a Buddhist or a Catholic."
—Steven Colbert (comic genius)

"No, I am not a human being, I am a soul created by God indwelled in the flesh that is called a human being."
—Lee Gipson, Facebook

"A hot dog at the game beats roast beef at the Ritz."
—Humphrey Bogart ("the greatest male star of classic American cinema")

"A man once told me to walk with the Lord. I'd rather walk with the bases loaded."
—Ken Singleton (ball player)

"About 26 percent of Americans 65 and older identify as

white evangelical Protestants. Among those ages 18 to 29, the figure is 8 percent. Why this demographic abyss does not cause greater panic—panic concerning the existence of evangelicalism as a major force in the United States—is a mystery and a scandal. With their focus on repeal of the Johnson Amendment and the right to say "Merry Christmas," some evangelical leaders are tidying up the kitchen while the house burns down around them. ... Since 2000, according to Gallup, the percentage of Americans with no religious affiliation has more than doubled, from 8 percent to 19 percent. The percentage of millennials with no religion has averaged 33 percent in recent surveys."
—Michael Gerson, *Washington Post*

"The Hall of Fame is for baseball people. Heaven is for good people."
—Jim Dwyer (author, journalist)

Nearly four in 10 young adults ages 18 to 29 are religiously unaffiliated and are four times more likely as young adults a generation ago to identify this way, according to a study by the Public Religion Research Institute. Among college students surveyed by Trinity College, 32% identified their worldview as religious; 32% as spiritual; and 28% as secular.
—Religion News Service

"All religions change and develop. If they do not, they will become obsolete. "
—Karen Armstrong, *A History of God: The 4,000-Year Quest of Judaism, Christianity and Islam*

"The percentage of Americans who belong to a church, mosque or synagogue has declined in the past 20 years, forcing some congregations to sell their houses of worship. More than 6,800 religious buildings have sold in the past five years and more than 1,400 are currently for sale, according to a real estate database. While some will become home to new worshippers, others are being converted into bed-and-breakfasts, apartments, coffee shops and more."
—Shahla Farzan, NPR

"Given the growth of the [Catholic] faith in Africa, it seems reasonable to expect that an African may be in [Pope] Francis's seat before another two generations pass,

and perhaps much sooner. It is hard to see how European dominance of the College of Cardinals can persist indefinitely, given the demographics of the church. African leadership could take the church in a more progressive direction in some ways, but it might do quite the opposite in others. The only certainty is that while all roads still lead to Rome for now, the historic seat of the church is increasingly on the remote periphery of a new Catholic empire of the global south."
—Elizabeth A. Foster, *Washington Post*

"The source of love is God himself: the source of all of our lives."
— Episcopal Bishop Michael Curry

"The Jew may love God, or he may fight with God, but he may not ignore God."
—Elie Wiesel (writer, professor, political activist, Nobel Prize winner, Holocaust survivor)

"Greater acceptance of Jews into mainstream American society in recent decades means Jews are now welcome in all kinds of neighborhoods, universities, and workplaces,

and most Jews no longer live in tight-knit Jewish communities that enforce the norms and practices of traditional Jewish life. We also live at a time when many of us view religion as something we can choose from a marketplace of ideas rather than an inherited obligation we must unquestioningly fulfill. Today, we're all welcome to check out the offerings at the local Unitarian church or Buddhist sangha; or we can grab some crystals or hallucinogenic drugs; or we can do nothing religious or spiritual at all. The term "Jews by choice" is often used to refer to those who convert to Judaism. But these days, all American Jews are Jews by choice—and many of us are choosing to opt out."
—Sarah Hurwitz, *Here All Along*

"Observant Presbyterians are always part of gatherings at Rutgers Presbyterian Church. But much of the time, so are Roman Catholics and Jews, as well as a smattering of people who consider themselves vaguely spiritual.

Valerie Oltarsh-McCarthy, who sat among the congregation listening to a Sunday sermon on the perils of genet-

364

ically modified vegetables, is, in fact, an atheist.

'It's something I never thought would happen,' she said of the bond she has forged with the church's community, if not the tenets of its faith. She was drawn to the church, she said, by 'something in the spirit of Rutgers and something in the spirit of the outside world.'

Katharine Butler, an artist, was lured into Rutgers when she walked by a sandwich board on the street advertising its environmental activism. Soon, she was involved in more traditional aspects of the church, too.

'I can't believe I'm doing this, singing away and all the Jesus-y stuff,' she said. 'It was wonderful to find a place larger than me, that's involved in that and in the community and being of service. It's nice to find a real community like that.'"
—Rick Rojas, *New York Times*

"Secular Jews, like all people, are believers, as one cannot be a member of any human society or culture without espousing some form of creed. One that has pervaded secular Jewish culture since Spinoza is the belief in the veracity of our scientific knowledge of the universe, the processes of which are self-regulating, in accordance with fixed laws pertaining to the "natural" order of creation. In such a universe, there is no place for a God who governs the world according to his personal will and performs miracles contrary to the laws of nature, or imposes religious precepts that bind only members of the Jewish people. This approach to knowledge of the universe is reflected in the essential Judaic belief in the sovereignty of the human being—the responsibility we bear as individuals, free to choose our paths in life, limited only by physical, social, and cultural constraints."
—Yaakov Malkin, *Secular Jewish Culture*

"True Judaism is in the heart, not in a building."
—Rabbi Phillip Sher (after fire destroyed his synagogue)

"God is the force that transforms the acorn into the oak tree, a bad baseball player into a good one, and an immoral person into a moral one."
—Rabbi Elliot Dorff

Michael's Literary Gods

**I thank them for entertainment, stimulation
and setting very high standards for me to aspire to.**

Dave Barry is a Pulitzer Prize-winning humor columnist and author, and the funniest writer I know of. Dave is so funny that I had to stop reading his column because I got so jealous. No one packs more laughs into a paragraph than Dave does. He used a picture of my late dog, Hunter, in one of his books. It's called *Dave Barry's Money Secrets*. Here's his money secret: Dave didn't pay me any money for the picture, but I did get a free book. I'll let Dave read my books for free, too.

Jean Shepherd (1921-1999) was a radio and TV raconteur, and he probably ties with Mark Twain for storytelling ability. Shep's books include *In God We Trust—All Others Pay Cash*, *Wanda Hickey's Night of Golden Memories*, and *A Fistful of Fig Newtons*. Twain was a great writer, but Shep was much funnier.

Jack Douglas (1908-1989) was an Emmy Award-winning comedy writer on *The Jack Paar Show*, *The George Gobel Show*, *Laugh-In* and other programs. I remember him most for his book titles, including *My Brother Was an Only Child, Shut Up and Eat Your Snowshoes,* and *Never Trust a Naked Bus Driver.*

Michael Solomon and David Hirshey edited and provided the witty headlines for *Esquire* magazine's annual Dubious Achievement Awards in the 1990s. Why *is* this man laughing?

Don Martin (1931-2000) was an extraordinary cartoonist, best known for his work in *MAD* magazine. Don created such notable characters as Fester Bestertester and Freenbean Fonebone, and *printed* sound effects like "FAGROON klubble klubble." Don's books are available from Amazon.com. Buy them!

"Uncle" Tom McCahill (1907-1975) was an automotive journalist who wrote for *Mechanix Illustrated* magazine in the 1950s and 60s. He rated car trunks by the number of dogs they could hold, and described the ride of a 1957 Pontiac as "smooth as a prom queen's thighs." Tom was a Yale graduate, and knew classic literature as well as cars. When a reader asked how to pronounce "Porsche," Tom answered, "Portia." Some of us understood. Another reader asked, "How much is the parts cost and how much do the car?" Tom answered, "Sure."

Tom Lehrer claims he "went from adolescence to senility, trying to bypass maturity." Tom graduated from Harvard Magna Cum Laude at age 18 and made Phi Beta Kappa. He taught at MIT, Harvard, Wellesley and the University of California, but is best known for hilarious songwriting, much of it political satire in the 1950s and 60s. His musical career was powerful but brief. He said he performed a mere 109 shows and wrote only 37 songs over 20 years. Britain's Princess Margaret was a fan and so am I. I can still sing Tom Lehrer lyrics I first heard in seventh grade, back in 1958 and '59.

Matt Groening created *The Simpsons* and *Life in Hell. The Simpsons* has been the longest-running comedy show in American television history. Because it's a cartoon, some people make the mistake of assuming it's for kids. It's not, but kids love it.

Jay Ward created *Rocky & Bullwinkle, Dudley Do-Right, Peabody and Sherman* and *Crusader Rabbit*. The Rocky show was filled with literary allusions and magnificent puns (or horrible puns, depending on your outlook on such things). Unless you're an old fart who watched TV in the 1950s and know that Durward Kirby was the sidekick on *The Garry Moore Show,* you would not appreciate the pun in "Kerwood Derby." It was a hat that increased the intelligence of its wearer.

About The Author

Michael N. Marcus is a journalist, author, editor, blogger, maven, gourmand, advertising copywriter and founder and president of AbleComm ("the telecom department store").

He's provided words for about 50 websites and blogs, was an editor at *Rolling Stone* and has written for many other magazines and newspapers.

Born in 1946, Michael's a proud member of the first cohort of the Baby Boom, along with Dolly Parton, Candy Bergen, Donny Trump, Billy Clinton and Georgie Bush.

At the urging of a misguided guidance counselor, he went to Lehigh University to become an engineer, and was quickly disappointed to learn that engineering was mostly math—and slide rules were not as much fun as soldering irons.

Michael was one of a few literate people in his engineer-filled freshman dormitory and made money editing term pa-pers. While in college he co-owned a band management company. One of its groups turned down the chance to re-cord *Yummy Yummy Yummy, I've Got Love in My Tummy*, which became a hit for Ohio Express.

Later, his college apartment had an elaborate and illegal multi-line phone system, a phone booth with a toilet in it and an invisible phone activated by two hand claps.

Michael lives in Connecticut with his wife, Marilyn, the ghost of Hunter, their Golden Retriever, and a lot of stuff—including a telephone booth, a "Lily Tomlin" switchboard, lots of books, CDs and DVDs, and many black boxes with flashing lights. Marilyn is very tolerant.

Despite his religious skepticism, Michael is an or-dained minister for the Universal Life Church, just like Conan O'Brien and Stephen Colbert. Can Michael perform weddings? Sure. Will the weddings be legal? Maybe.

Text For Michael's Gravestone:

When I was in my 20s, I had delusions of immortality. I honestly thought that if I was on a plane with 393 other people and the plane crashed, I would be the *sole survivor*. It was probably a combination of innocence, ignorance, egomania and utter lack of confidence in others.

I also felt that if I went into a jungle alone and had to face hostile tigers, alligators or Viet Cong I would survive; but if I was part of a huge army, someone else would mess up and we would all get killed. I didn't like teamwork.

Now, decades later, I have a more realistic assessment of my future. I know I won't live forever. And since I don't want someone else to mess up my epitaph, here it is.

Michael N. Marcus
1946 – 2XXX
"OK, what's next?"

I like "Rockwell Bold" for the typeface. Someone just has to fill in the final date and pick a nice piece of rock.

As for the words, yes, I'm an incurable optimist. I've always been resilient. I recover quickly from setbacks and disappointments and I'm always looking ahead. On freezing days in January I know that the Earth gets more sunlight each day and is warming up. Spring is coming. I used to say that "soon my dog and I will be in the pool and my ancient Fiat Spider will be out of the garage." Sadly, both the dog and the car are gone.

Someone, *please* make sure my stone is done right. My words are important to me. If you screw up my stone, I'm gonna come back and bite your neck. Thanks very much.

MNM

Photo & Illustration Credits

Archangel Michael: Guido Reni (public domain)
Ark: Edward Hicks (public domain)
Baseball: Rawlings
Billy Graham: public domain
Bob Dylan: Columbia Records
Buddha statue: Michel Wal
Burka: Amazon.com
Calendar: GoGraph
Caroline Kennedy: public domain
Casper: Amazon.com
Cathedral of St. John the Divine: William Porto
Chinese food container: GoGraph
Cholent: Gilabrand
Christian Sci. church: Sarah Nichols
Creation: Michelangelo
God: Cima da Conegliano
Crucifixion: Diego Velázquez (public domain)
Dog's bark mitzvah: author
Dome of the Rock: Paolo Massa
Dreidel: Amazon.com
Eastern Orthodox Metropolitan: Arungeothomas
Edward Levi: public domain
Cat: Elvjec
Episcopal Church: St. Peters in Milford CT
Front cover: Adam Kazmierski
Gorbachev: Ronald Reagan Library
Guru: Creatista
Hebrew alphabet: Jewish Virtual Library
Helen Prejean: herself
Hijab: Amazon.com
Higgins/Hillerman: public domain
Ice cream: Amazon.com
Kingdom Life: itself

K of C HQ: Seth Tisue
Kyra Sedgewick: Angela George
Laban & Jacob: public domain
Library: Ralf Roletschek
Liz Taylor: public domain
Marilyn Monroe: public domain
Mezuzah: Amazon.com
Mormon temple garments: Mr. Packham
Neptune: Antoine Coysevox
Nun & priest: couplescostumes.com
Old man praying: Eliel Schafler
Passover table: Gilabrand
Peace Cross: Ben Jacobson
Peace Park: Jim Henderson
Red Skelton: public domain
Roger Williams statue: public domain
Sammy Davis, Jr.: public domain
Sheitel: Freeda.com
Snake handling: Russell Lee (public domain)
Star Charm: Amazon.com
Sun god: Käyttäjä:Kompak
Synagogue interior: Congregation Kneses Tifereth Israel
Templar pendant: Amazon.com
Theodore Roosevelt: public domain
Torah: Willy Horsch
Triumph: public domain
Wash. National Cathedral: Carol M. Highsmith (public domain)
White House: public domain
Whore of Babylon: Hans Burgkmair, (public domain)
Woman wearing hijab: David Dennis
Yahrzeit candle: Rokeach
Yankee Stadium: Matt Boulton
Yogi Berra: Major League Baseball

"Public domain" means that a photo is not protected by a copyright, usually because the copyright has expired or the copyright owner deliberately put it in the public domain. Anyone can use work in the public domain without permission, but no one can ever own it.

Recommended Books By Others

(in no particular order, with a few I have not read yet)

The Year of Living Biblically: One Man's Humble Quest to Follow the Bible as Literally as Possible, by A. J. Jacobs

Back to Basics: God's Word vs. Religion, by Steven R. Bruck

River of Fire: My Spiritual Journey, by Helen Prejean

Good Without God: What a Billion Nonreligious People Do Believe, by Greg Epstein

The Founding Myth: Why Christian Nationalism Is Un-American, by Andrew L. Seidel, Susan Jacoby, Dan Barker

When Bad Things Happen to Good People, by Harold S. Kushner

Holy Sh*t: A Brief History of Swearing, by Melissa Mohr

Humanimal: How Homo sapiens Became Nature's Most Paradoxical Creature-A New Evolutionary History, by Adam Rutherford

(((Semitism))): Being Jewish in America in the Age of Trump, by Jonathan Weisman

Meyer Lansky: The Thinking Man's Gangster, by Robert Lacey

Which of the 613 Laws Apply to Me?: Which to Keep and Which to Ignore, by Prof. (Dr.) W.A. Liebenberg

Judaism Without God? Judaism as Culture and Bible as Literature, by Yaakov Malkin

A History of God: The 4,000-Year Quest of Judaism, Christianity and Islam, by Karen Armstrong

Why Be Jewish?, by David J. Wolpe

Jewish Traces in Unexpected Places: (and Unexpected Traces in Jewish Places), by Al Kustanowitz

A Plain Language Guide to Reading and Understanding the Bible, by Bill Monks

Leaving Home, Going Home, Returning Home: A Hebrew American's Sojourn in the Land of Israel, by Jason Alster

Stolen History: How the Palestinians and Their Allies Attack Israel's Right to Exist by Erasing Its Past, by David Meir Levi

Jewish Theology, by Kaufmann Kohler

God Revealed: Revisit Your Past to Enrich Your Future, by Fred Sievert

The Improbability Principle: Why Coincidences, Miracles, and Rare Events Happen Every Day, by David J. Hand

Unorthodox: The Scandalous Rejection of my Hasidic Roots, by Deborah Feldman

An Empire of Their Own: How the Jews Invented Hollywood, by Neal Gabler

Jewish Literacy: The Most Important Things to Know About the Jewish Religion, Its People, and Its History, by Joseph Telushkin

Opening the Gates: How Proactive Conversion Can Revitalize the Jewish Community, by Gary A. Tobin

Star Crossed, by Bette Isacoff

Leaving Jesus: A Book Every Christian Should have Read Before They Believed in Jesus, by James Wood, Jr.

Here All Along: Finding Meaning, Spirituality, and a Deeper Connection to Life—in Judaism (After Finally Choosing to Look There), by Sarah Hurwitz

The Nine Questions People Ask About Judaism, by Dennis Prager and Rabbi Joseph Telushkin

All That's Wrong with the Bible: Contradictions, Absurdities, and More, by Jonah David Conner

The Baseball Gods are Real: A True Story about Baseball and Spirituality, by Jonathan Fink

More Books By Michael
(There may be others by the time you read this.)

- *Love For and From My Four-Legged Son*
- *What's Wrong With Trump?*
- *Anthology of Third-World Email Scams: Learn from the best and worst!*
- *Stories I'd Tell My Children (but maybe not until they're adults*
- *Do As I Say, Not As I Did*
- *Internet Hell*
- *What I Most Wanted to Get Out of School Was Me*
- *Do You Really Want to Know the Secret Ingredient In the World's Greatest Coleslaw? Unappetizing Encounters with scary foods*
- *What Do You Call That Funny-Looking Thing? Terminology for Self-Publishers*
- *Self-editing for Self-Publishers*
- *YOU Can Have Your Own Book Publishing Company*
- *Writers Can Get Away With Apparently Absurd Tax Deductions That Ordinary People Can't*
- *No More Ugly Books!*
- *Publish Your Book Without Losing Your House*
- *Typography for Independent Publishers*
- *the One-Buck Book Marketing Book*
- *the One-Buck Author's Website Book*
- *the One-Buck Indie Author's ISBN Book*
- *the One-Buck Author's Press Release Book*
- *the One-Buck Indie Author's Type Book*
- *the One-Buck Indie Author's Book Cover Book*
- *How To Not get Screwed by a Self-Publishing Company*
- *The Look of a Book*

- *Independent Self-Publishing: The Complete Guide*
- *STINKERS! America's Worst Self-Published Books*
- *Brainy Beginner's Guide to Self-Publishing*
- *499 Essential Publishing Tips for a Penny Apiece*
- *1001 Powerful Pieces of Publishing Advice*
- *Get the Most out of a Self-Publishing Company*
- *The 100 Worst Self-Publishing Misteaks (co-author)*
- *Become a Real Self-Publisher*
- *Stupid, Sloppy, Sleazy*
- *Phone Systems & Phones for Small Business & Home*
- *The AbleComm Guide to Phone Systems*
- *Telecom Reference E-Book*
- *I Only Flunk My Brightest Students*
- *Which Phone System Should I Buy?*
- *CB Bible* (co-author)

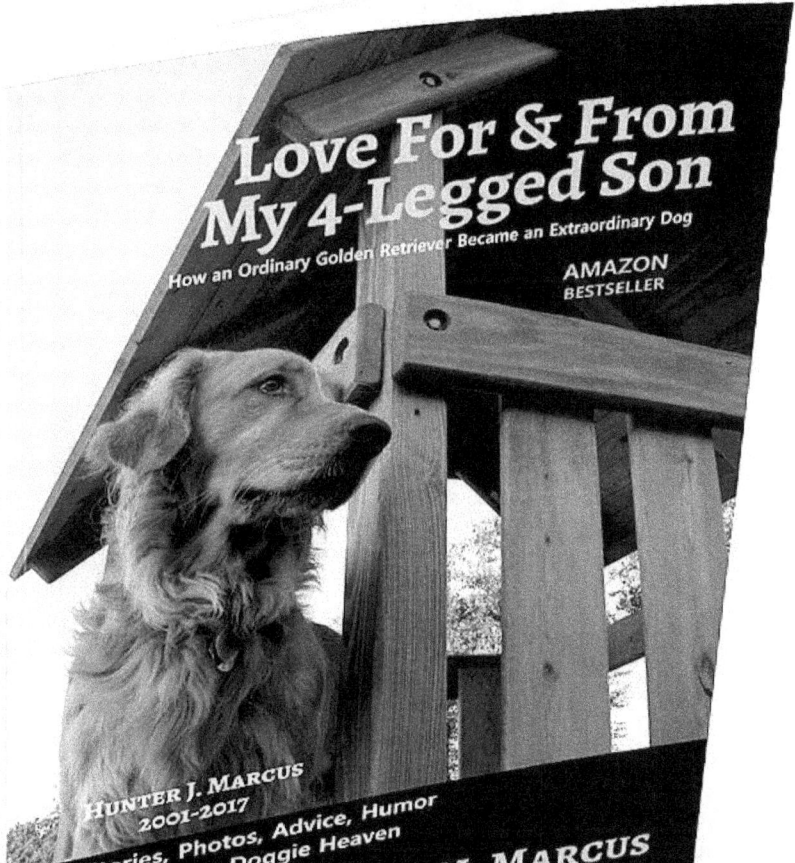

Love For & From My 4-Legged Son

How an Ordinary Golden Retriever Became an Extraordinary Dog

AMAZON
BESTSELLER

HUNTER J. MARCUS
2001-2017
Stories, Photos, Advice, Humor
Emails from Doggie Heaven

MICHAEL N. MARCUS
Bestselling author of more than 40 books

Love For & From My 4-Legged Son   Michael N. Marcus

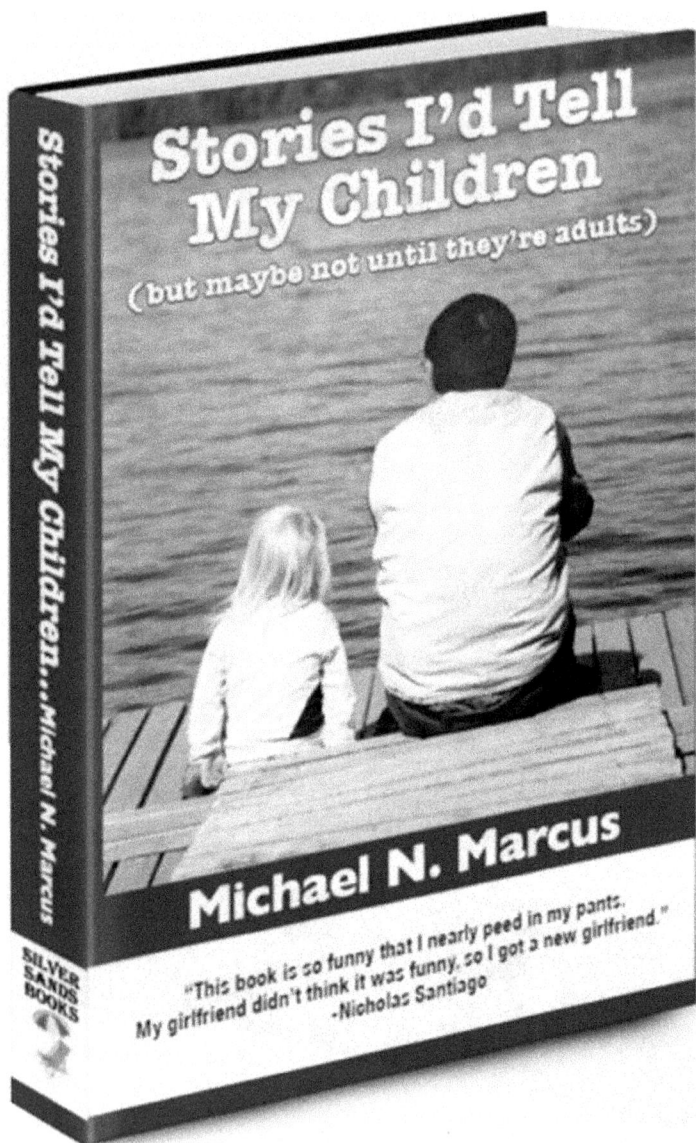

Stories I'd Tell My Children
(but maybe not until they're adults)

Michael N. Marcus

"This book is so funny that I nearly peed in my pants. My girlfriend didn't think it was funny, so I got a new girlfriend."
-Nicholas Santiago

SILVER SANDS BOOKS

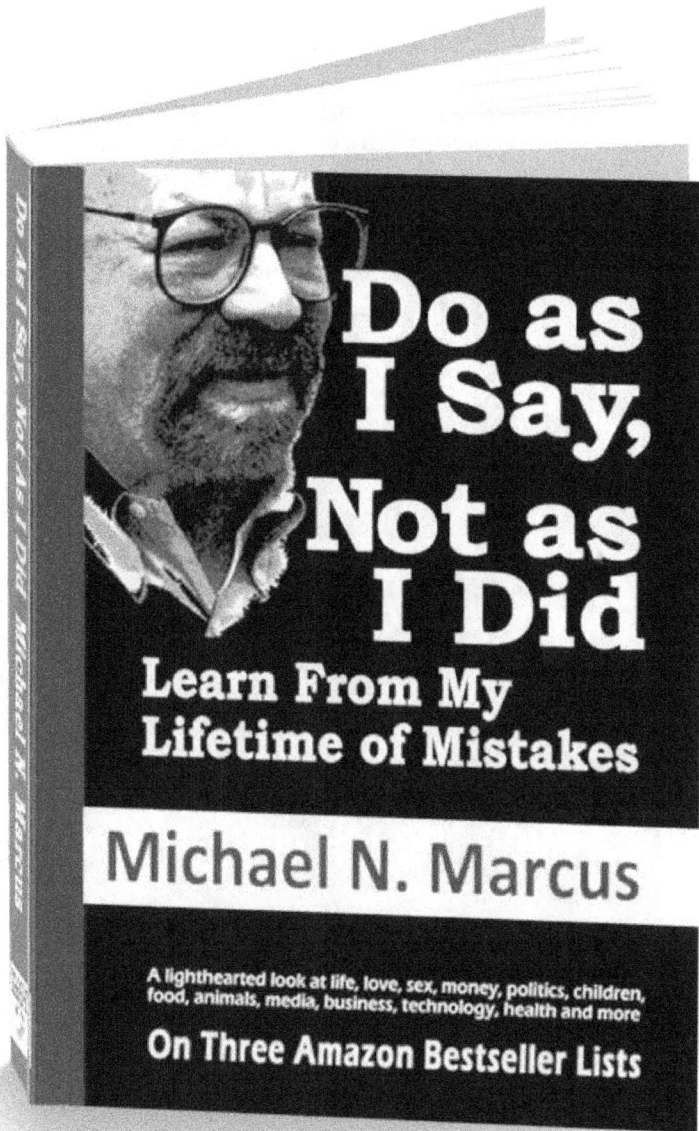

Do as I Say, Not as I Did

Learn From My Lifetime of Mistakes

Michael N. Marcus

A lighthearted look at life, love, sex, money, politics, children, food, animals, media, business, technology, health and more

On Three Amazon Bestseller Lists

Based on a True Story

internet HELL

A lying psychopath used the Internet to make false accusations about me. People wanted me maimed or murdered.

Even the FBI couldn't help.

Michael N. Marcus

LEARN FROM THE BEST AND WORST!

Anthology of Third-World Email Scams

"A treat for connoisseurs of awful English and dubious deals"

edited by

Michael N. Marcus

What's Wrong With Trump?

A Catalog of Crookedness, Incoherence, Incompetence, Crudeness, Craziness, Contempt, Collusion, Chaos & Craving

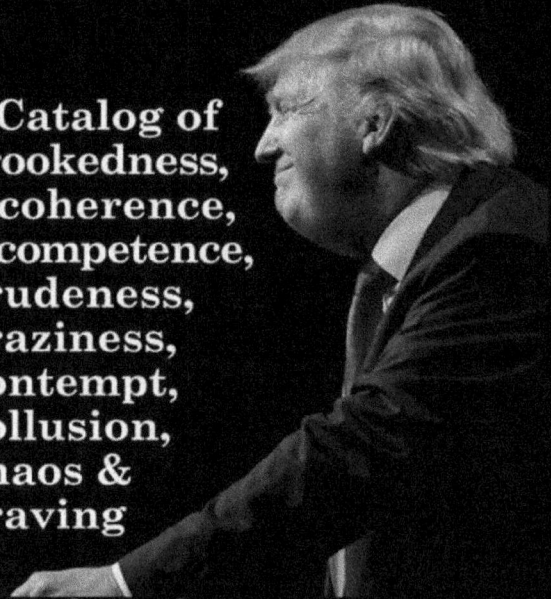

Michael N. Marcus

Bestselling Author of More Than 40 Books

"#1 New Release in Political Leadership" —Amazon.com

"It ain't over till it's over."
—Yogi Berra
"This book is over."
—Michael

www.ingramcontent.com/pod-product-compliance
Lightning Source LLC
Chambersburg PA
CBHW051938090426
42741CB00008B/1190